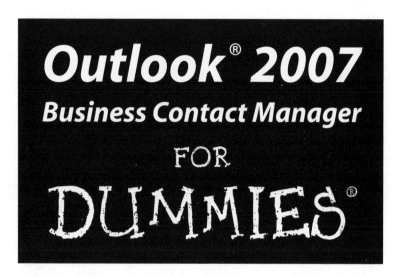

by Karen Fredricks and Lon Orenstein

BICENTENNIAL
1807
WILEY
2007
BICENTENNIAL

Wiley Publishing, Inc.

Outlook® 2007 Business Contact Manager For Dummies®

Published by
Wiley Publishing, Inc.
111 River Street
Hoboken, NJ 07030-5774
www.wiley.com

Copyright © 2007 by Wiley Publishing, Inc., Indianapolis, Indiana

Published by Wiley Publishing, Inc., Indianapolis, Indiana

Published simultaneously in Canada

For general information on our other products and services, please contact our Customer Care Department within the U.S. at 800-762-2974, outside the U.S. at 317-572-3993, or fax 317-572-4002.

For technical support, please visit www.wiley.com/techsupport.

Wiley also publishes its books in a variety of electronic formats. Some content that appears in print may not be available in electronic books.

Library of Congress Control Number: 2006939498

ISBN: 978-0-470-10789-8

Manufactured in the United States of America

10 9 8 7 6 5 4 3 2 1

WILEY

About the Authors

Karen S. Fredricks began her life rather non-technically growing up in Kenya. She attended high school in Beirut, Lebanon, where she developed her sense of humor while dodging bombs. After traveling all over the world, Karen ended up at the University of Florida and has been an ardent Gator fan ever since. In addition to undergraduate studies in English and Accounting, Karen has a master's degree in Psycholinguistics. Beginning her career teaching high school English and theatre, Karen switched to working with the PC during its inception in the early '80s and has worked as a full-time computer consultant and trainer ever since.

Karen is an ACT! Certified Consultant, an ACT! Premier Trainer, a Microsoft Office User Specialist, and a QuickBooks Pro Certified Advisor. She is the author of four *For Dummies* books on *ACT!* In addition, she has co-authored *Outlook 2007 All-in-One Desk Reference For Dummies* and is completing work on *Microsoft Office Live For Dummies*. A true fan of the *For Dummies* series, she helped organize *The Authors Unconference,* the first ever gathering of *For Dummies* authors.

Karen resides in Boca Raton, Florida. Her company, Tech Benders, specializes in contact management software and provides computer consulting, support, and training services. She is also a regular guest on several syndicated computer radio talk shows. In her spare time, Karen loves to spend time with family and friends, play tennis, work out, road bike, and write schlocky poetry.

Karen loves to hear from her readers. Feel free to send her your comments about the book to dummies@techbenders.com or visit her Web site www.techbenders.com to learn more about the products listed in this book.

Lon Orenstein has been in the computer business since 1981, the birth date of the PC. Certified by Microsoft as both an Independent Software Solutions and Mobility Partner, Lon has been working with Microsoft since 1990. Having been a beta user of ACT! in 1986 and its first Certified Consultant, Lon is a dynamic and experienced consultant of sales force automation and customer relationship management strategies. He combines a businessperson's understanding of how to re-engineer your sales processes with a highly technical knowledge of the computer as the tool with which to do it. Creating elegant software solutions for business problems is what gets Lon energized every day. His company, pinpointtools (www.pinpointtools.com), produces software that enhances Business Contact Manager.

Dedications

Karen Fredericks: This book is dedicated to all of you who take the time out of your busy schedules to learn new things by buying a *For Dummies* book!

Lon Orenstein: If they needed a model for a great human being, Bonnie Miller would be the choice. I'm lucky enough to be her husband and dedicate this book to her. Patient, kind, supportive, loving, integrity, fun, wonderful, Nonnie — she's been the best partner for 25+ years! I love you and thank you for your support.

Authors' Acknowledgments

Karen Fredricks: This is my fifth book for Wiley Publishing and as usual they have made writing this book a pleasure! My acquisitions editor, Greg Croy, is a joy to work with. This is the second book I've done with my project editor, Rebecca Senninger; I know when to stick with a good thing! Heidi Unger, my copy editor, had the unenviable task of making me look good; Heidi, your edits were always right on! Technical editor Damir Bersinic's sharp eye helped to spot all the changes between the beta and final versions of BCM.

Andy Cummings, Kathy Nebenhaus, and Diane Steele are no Dummies — but they are the brains behind the *For Dummies* series. They have truly helped to put a *For Dummies* book in a heck of a lot of households!

Rich Tennant is the coolest cartoonist ever. I am astounded by the thought, research, and time that he devotes to each one of his cartoons. I'm not sure which is funnier — his cartoons — or his stories about creating his cartoons!

My various tennis buddies (Kalle, Nancy, Susan, Sue, Joanne, Jo, Jennifer, Denise, and Linda) keep me sane; they make me focus on a round yellow ball instead of a square yellow book! An ace goes out to John Steinmann, my fabulous coach, who is an unofficial Dummy because he is able to teach with a great sense of humor.

I love my daughters, Andrea and Alyssa. Andi is a great tour guide and travel partner; of course, she gets extra points for being a Gator. Even though Alyssa is a Seminole she's still a lot of fun to "go on a date with"; I am definitely looking at margaritas in a whole new light! My mom, Frances Conn, brought me into this world (which is a good thing), exposed me to unique cultures, and has hopefully passed along her longevity gene to me.

And quickly, — to Gary, you give me love, support, humor and red licorice. See ya later, bye!

Lon Orenstein: As I approach 60, it's amazing to look back and see all the twists and turns I made to get to where I am now. While trying to acknowledge the people who helped me make those turns and passages, I am afraid I'll leave out some — so here's a collective "thank you" to all my relatives, friends, teachers, mentors, bosses, co-workers, customers, employees, and enemies who helped make me into what I am today.

Special thanks go to my parents, Babette and Jacques, my brother Jon, my grandparents Nan & Pops Millstone, my wife Bonnie, my children Janine and Tad, Barry Frank, Chuck Massie, Hallie Mae Shaw, Andy McCollum, Phyllis Hager, Paul & Nannette Holland, Gary Richman, David Ives, Delores Bentley, Joel Presser, and Tiff Hawks for their love, friendship, and support throughout my life.

Pat Sullivan and Mike Muhney founded ACT! software and I found them to be good friends and role models for how to build software with a soul. Thank you for doing it right!

My business contacts at Microsoft were invaluable in the writing: Jeff Keyes, Guy Gilbert, Samir Manjure, Bret Dangelmaier, Balaji Balasubramanyan, and Tom Abshire. Thanks very much, gentlemen!

A great thanks to all the *For Dummies* folks at Wiley Publishing who helped get my book produced, especially Greg Croy, Mary Bednarek, Leah Cameron, and Rebecca Senninger. I'm now a *For Dummies* author, thanks to your guidance!

An extra special thanks goes to my grandson, Max Werner, for reminding me every day that my purpose in life is to be a great old man and for being so understanding when I couldn't play because I was writing this book.

Publisher's Acknowledgments

We're proud of this book; please send us your comments through our online registration form located at www.dummies.com/register/.

Some of the people who helped bring this book to market include the following:

Acquisitions, Editorial, and Media Development

Project Editor: Rebecca Senninger

Acquisitions Editor: Greg Croy

Copy Editor: Heidi Unger

Technical Editor: Damir Bersinic

Editorial Manager: Leah Cameron

Media Development Manager: Laura VanWinkle

Editorial Assistant: Amanda Foxworth

Sr. Editorial Assistant: Cherie Case

Cartoons: Rich Tennant
(www.the5thwave.com)

Composition Services

Project Coordinator: Heather Kolter

Layout and Graphics: Claudia Bell, Jonelle Burns, Heather Ryan

Proofreaders: Aptara, Jessica Kramer

Indexer: Aptara

Anniversary Logo Design: Richard J. Pacifico

Publishing and Editorial for Technology Dummies

    Richard Swadley, Vice President and Executive Group Publisher

    Andy Cummings, Vice President and Publisher

    Mary Bednarek, Executive Acquisitions Director

    Mary C. Corder, Editorial Director

Publishing for Consumer Dummies

    Diane Graves Steele, Vice President and Publisher

    Joyce Pepple, Acquisitions Director

Composition Services

    Gerry Fahey, Vice President of Production Services

    Debbie Stailey, Director of Composition Services

Contents at a Glance

Table of Contents

Introduction

*O*utlook is the bestselling personal information manager that's included as part of the Microsoft Office suite of products. There are 400 million users of Office worldwide and a high percentage of those folks also use Outlook. In 2003, Microsoft added the Business Contact Manager (BCM) piece to Outlook. For many users, BCM represents their first foray into the area of contact relationship management (CRM). CRM software is a little more complex to understand than other types of software in this respect: With a word processor, each document that you create is totally separate; if you make a mistake, you need only to delete your current document and start fresh. CRM, however, builds its way into a final product; if you don't give a bit of thought as to what goal you wish to achieve, you can end up with a muddled mess.

We are huge proponents of CRM, and not ashamed to admit it. We use CRM software at work. We use it on the road. We use it at home. We've even inspired our friends to use CRM — or at least those that are looking to make more money in less time. We're excited about the product and know that by the time you figure out how to unleash the full power of BCM, you'll be excited, too.

So what are we so excited about? We've seen firsthand how CRM software can save you time and help make you more efficient in the bargain. To us, accomplishing more in less time is an exciting thought — it allows you to quit work earlier. Best of all, BCM is a program that's easy to get up and running in a very short time. You'll be amazed not only at how quickly you can set up a database but also at how easily you can put that database to work.

About This Book

Outlook 2007 Business Contact Manager For Dummies is a reference book. As such, you can read each chapter independently and in the order you want. Each chapter focuses on a specific topic, so you can dive right in, heading straight for the chapter that interests you most. Having said that, however, we must say that we've tried to put the chapters into a logical sequence so that those of you who are new to BCM can just follow the bouncing ball from chapter to chapter. More experienced users can use the Table of Contents and the index to simply navigate from topic to topic as needed.

Essentially, this book is a nuts-and-bolts how-to guide for accomplishing various tasks. In addition, drawing on many of our own experiences as full-time CRM consultants, trainers, and software developers, we include specific situations that should give you a feeling for the full power of BCM.

Conventions Used in This Book

Like most Windows-based software programs, you often have several different ways to accomplish a task in BCM.

For the most part, we show you ways to perform a function by using the BCM menus. When an instruction reads Choose File⇨Open, you must access the File menu (located at the top of the Outlook screen) by clicking it with the left mouse button and then choosing the Open option from the subsequent menu that appears. In most cases, you can access these commands from anywhere within BCM, although we generally advise new BCM users to always start a task from the Business Contact Manager dashboard view, which is the first window you see when BCM opens. If you must be in a particular area to complete a task otherwise, we tell you where.

We also present you with keyboard shortcuts here and there. Generally, BCM shortcuts are triggered by simultaneously pressing the Alt key and another key on the keyboard. For instance, the shortcut for seeing your Business Contacts is Alt+U.

When you need to access one of BCM's hidden menus, click an appropriate area of the screen with the right mouse button and then choose from the contextual menu that appears. In these instances, we simply say *right-click* when you need to right-click.

What You Should Read

Of course, we hope that you're going to sit down and read this entire book from cover to cover. But then again, this book isn't The Great American Novel. And, come to think of it, the whole reason you bought this book in the first place is that you want to organize your business as quickly as possible because you're probably finding yourself with too much to do and too little time in which to do it.

For the time being, we're going to let you get away with reading just the parts that interest you most. You can read the last chapter first and the first chapter last if you like because this book is designed to allow you to read each chapter independently. However, when you find yourself floating in a swimming pool, soaking up the sun, and wondering what to do with all your spare time, you might want to go back and read some of those chapters you skipped. You just might discover something!

What You Don't Have to Read

This book is intended for both new and existing Outlook and/or BCM users. Most of the instructions apply to both groups of readers. Once in a while, we include some information that might be of special interest to more advanced readers. Also, any information tagged with a Technical Stuff icon is there for the truly technically inclined. Everyone else can just skip this information.

Foolish Assumptions

One of our least favorite words in the English language is the word *assume,* but we have to admit that we've made a few foolish — albeit necessary — assumptions when writing this book. First of all, we assume that you own a Windows-based computer and that the Office 2007 Professional, Small Business, or Ultimate Edition is installed on it. Secondly, we assume that you have a basic knowledge of how to use your computer, keyboard, and mouse, and that BCM isn't the very first application that you're trying to master.

We also assume that you have a genuine desire to organize your business and have determined that BCM is the way to go.

Finally (and we feel quite comfortable with this assumption), we assume that you'll grow to love the whole concept of contact relationship management as much as we do.

How This Book Is Organized

We organized this book into seven parts. Each part contains chapters covering related topics. The following is a brief description of each part, with chapter references directing you where to go for particular information.

Part I: Getting to Know Your Business Contact Manager

In Part I, you get an introduction to the concept CRM and why BCM has become such a popular choice of database users (Chapter 1). In this part, you read about what to expect the first time you fire up BCM (Chapter 2) and how to create a database and set the main preferences in BCM (Chapter 3).

Part II: Putting BCM to Work

Part II focuses on putting your contacts (Chapter 4) and business accounts (Chapter 5) into BCM. We even show you how to use those same accounts with your accounting software.

We're all different and often like to do things in our own unique ways. BCM understands that concept, and Part II helps you to customize BCM to your heart's content. BCM makes it easy to create categories (Chapter 6) so that you start focusing on the key elements of your business. You can even hone your organizational skills a bit better by customizing BCM to include additional form fields and drop-down lists (Chapter 7). You'll even find out how to customize the way you view the various BCM components.

Part III: Organizing Your Day

There are only 24 hours in a day, and, if you're like us, you like to make the most of the ones you spend at work so that you can have a few more hours to spend on play. In this part, you'll discover how to manage your calendar (Chapter 8) and use a task list (Chapter 9). After you finish your business chores, you can record the important events through the use of a business history (Chapter 10).

Part IV: Show Me the Money

The goal of every business is to make money, and this part focuses on exactly that. First, you'll find out how to share your data with other people in your organization (Chapter 11) so that they can help you increase your bottom line. You can even integrate BCM with Office Accounting 2007 so that you can devote your time to sales rather than to data entry.

This part shows you how to manage your sales opportunities (Chapter 12) and how to generate a quote should the need arise. Finally, you'll put on your green eye shades and take over the role of accountant (Chapter 13) as you create quotes, sales orders, invoices — and money!

Part V: Communicating with the Outside World

One of the best features of BCM is the ability to communicate easily with the outside world. In Part V, you'll discover how to create templates in Publisher or Word (Chapter 14) that you can use for mass mail merges — whether by snail mail or e-mail. You'll even be able to track the results of your marketing campaigns using E-Mail Marketing Service (Chapter 15).

If you need to go somewhere at the drop of a hat — and take your data with you — you can synchronize your data to a mobile device, laptop, or Microsoft Office Live (Chapter 16).

Part VI: Digging in a Bit Deeper

Part VI shows you some of the most advanced — nonetheless important — BCM features. Entering your contact and account information into BCM is half the fun — the other half is finding it again through the use of queries, sorts, and views (Chapter 17). Corporate America lives for reports, and BCM is up to the challenge. Whether you want to present your boss with a pipeline report or customize an existing report, Chapter 18 shows you how.

As your business continues to grow, you'll find that BCM is willing to grow right along with you. BCM can help you to create projects and teams, and track their progress (Chapter 19). Finally, it's always a good idea to expect the unexpected and be able to troubleshoot your database should something go wrong (Chapter 20). And, should something bad happen, your job security might depend on your ability to back up your database — and restore it.

Part VII: The Part of Tens

With apologies to David Letterman, Part VII gives you two of our Top Ten BCM lists. First, we discuss a few of our favorite tips and tricks (Chapter 21). Finally, we give you ten of our favorite ways to help move data in and out of BCM (Chapter 22).

Icons Used in This Book

 A Tip icon indicates a special timesaving tip or a related thought that might help you use BCM to its full advantage. Try it; you might like it!

 A Warning icon alerts you to the danger of proceeding without caution. *Do not* attempt to try doing anything that you are warned not to do!

 Remember icons alert you to important pieces of information that you don't want to forget.

 A Technical Stuff icon indicates tidbits of advanced knowledge that might be of interest to IT specialists but might just bore the heck out of the average reader. Skip these at will.

Where to Go from Here

For those of you who are BCM old-timers, you might want to at least skim the entire contents of this book before hunkering down to read the sections that seem the most relevant to you. The average BCM user probably uses only a portion of the program and might not even be aware of some of the really cool features of BCM. You might be surprised to discover all that BCM has to offer!

For the BCM newbie, we recommend heading straight for Part I, where you can acquaint yourself with BCM before moving on to other parts of the book and the BCM program.

Part I

Getting to Know Your Business Contact Manager

"It's contact management software. It analyzes my sales history and makes suggestions. Right now, it's suggesting I try selling my old Atari games to a 40-year-old who still lives at home with his parents."

In this part . . .

We know that you're excited about all the possibilities that BCM has to offer and want to dive into the
program as soon as possible. Here's where you find an
overview of some of the cool features that you find in
BCM. You also become familiar with the many faces
of BCM; after all, you wouldn't want to get lost along
the way. But first, you have to do a bit of homework and
whip BCM into shape by fiddling with a few preference
settings to ensure that BCM produces the type of results
that you're looking for.

Chapter 1

What Is Outlook Business Contact Manager?

In This Chapter

▶ What is BCM?

▶ Who uses BCM?

▶ Basic BCM concepts

*W*e know you're probably anxious to dive into Business Contact Manager (BCM). Chances are that someone you know uses BCM or that you've already purchased BCM and read at least the outside of the box. Some of you might have even thumbed through this book already. Before we set you off and running, we would like to tell you a little bit about BCM's history and what you can expect from the BCM program.

And Then There Was BCM

Once upon a time, before the advent of the personal computer, busy people everywhere were forced to rely on such archaic tools as Day Timers and yellow sticky notes to keep themselves organized. You could easily spot busy people — various bits of paper trailed after them as they rushed frantically from appointment to appointment. These busy people were also generally late to their appointments. You would often see busy people crying or mumbling to themselves. Busy people, you see, often scheduled conflicting appointments because they had failed to compare the schedules hanging on their refrigerators at home to the schedules they carried in their somewhat disorganized briefcases. Divorce rates were high as busy people missed anniversaries and soccer games!

As Bill Gates and his minions were creating the world of personal computing, they realized that disorganization could be prevented through the use of cool software, so they created Outlook. Computer users everywhere rejoiced and used Outlook because it helped them organize their contacts and calendars. As an extra bonus, Microsoft threw in a robust e-mail client, which meant that the disorganized people in the world could send e-mail to the contacts they stored in Outlook — hopefully about the appointments they had created. Life was good.

But hark! Microsoft soon heard rumblings about a new type of software: customer relationship management (CRM) software. The newly organized wanted to become even more organized. Business people wanted to manage their relationships with their customers (or prospects or leads or vendors) so that all their employees could see who's done what to whom, what's been promised and delivered, what money is owed, and what receivables are coming in. Even nonprofit organizations and soccer moms felt a need to share contact and calendar information with other members of their organizations.

Enter Business Contact Manager (BCM). BCM is the entry-level CRM program that Microsoft has integrated with Outlook. Chances are pretty good that you're already using Outlook to communicate with your business associates and friends. BCM is built right into Outlook as another address book. Because it's part of Outlook, you can schedule tasks and appointments with these BCM contacts and see them in the business history — and have a complete, chronological record of all your interactions with your people.

Finding Out Exactly What BCM Does

Probably the hardest thing you have to do with BCM is explain exactly what it is. By the time you've read this book from cover to cover and marked it up a few times with your trusty highlighter pen, you, too, will probably be a true fan of BCM. Many of your friends will start to notice a difference in you; you'll no longer rush into meetings five minutes late with a sticky note stuck to your shoe. Your colleagues will marvel at the change and wonder about the secret of your success. Now comes the hard part — explaining what BCM can do for you.

Here's what you can do with Business Contact Manager:

✔ **Store the basic information about the contacts in your life — names, addresses, e-mail addresses, and phone numbers.** If you deal with companies or accounts, BCM can keep track of the companies' information and link all their contacts to one centralized account. If you need more data tracked than what BCM comes with out of the box, you can add more fields from which to store, sort, and report.

✔ **Set up marketing campaigns and track their effectiveness.** BCM links to Microsoft's E-mail Marketing Service to send e-mail blasts. When someone responds to your e-mail, you can create a sales opportunity to start tracking that person's voyage through the sales process. BCM even has reports showing your return on investment (ROI) for a campaign.

✔ **Enter contacts only once.** BCM integrates with Microsoft Office Accounting 2007. The customers in Office Accounting are the same contacts as in BCM, which means that you don't have to resort to double entry of your contacts. You can start sales opportunities in BCM and then turn them into invoices or sales orders in Accounting with just a few clicks and no reentry of data.

✔ **Keep track of your client-based projects.** BCM even integrates with Office Accounting in such a way that you can bill the time from a project without having to reenter any data.

✔ **Share information across a network so everyone in the office can see the same data.** You can even let co-workers take a subset of your BCM database with them when they leave the office and synchronize their changes to yours when they return.

✔ **Hold lots of data safely and integrate it with other programs.** If you're using BCM, you own a suite that contains Word and Excel; all these products speak the same language, so you can create a BCM template using Word or import data from Excel without a hitch.

What's the difference between BCM and Outlook?

If you're a current Outlook user, you're probably already getting a feel for the exact differences between Outlook and BCM. Just in case, we provide you with the differences in a nutshell — or at least in a bulleted list:

✔ Outlook is basically an e-mail program, address book, and calendar. Although you can link these three elements together, this feature is generally not visible to the naked eye.

✔ Because BCM stores its information in SQL Server 2005 Express Edition and uses many of its features, BCM can hold more contacts than Outlook.

✔ You can add many new fields to track more data in BCM.

✔ Outlook has a simple task list of things to do. You can link tasks in BCM to specific projects.

✔ You can link BCM to your accounting software.

So, think of Outlook as the foundation for your daily computing needs, or the bowl. Inside the bowl is your e-mail, your BCM contacts and account database, your list of tasks, your calendar of appointments, your BCM marketing campaigns, and your BCM project tracking. So, even though BCM is a part of Outlook, think of BCM as "Outlook on steroids."

Taking a Sneak Peek at BCM

One of the basic tenets of customer relationship management is that you can interact with your customers much better when all their information is readily accessible so that you can have a 360-degree view of your contacts. Having some data in your address book, some in your e-mail program, and some in your accounting system is just the electronic version of big stacks of paper on your desk. Fortunately, Outlook Business Contact Manager solves that problem by keeping it all together, and keeping you together, too!

Figure 1-1 shows one of our BCM contacts. You can find areas for everything from the contact's name and account name to his phone number and address. A Show area is on the Ribbon near the top of the screen. BCM is able to hold so much data for each contact or account that it takes multiple screens to hold it all. Each button in the Show area represents another screen of information about that one contact. We cover the various BCM views in more detail in Chapter 2.

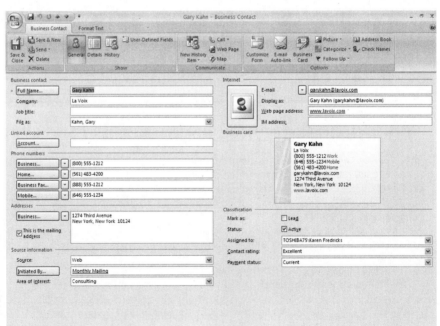

Figure 1-1:
The
Business
Contact
window.

Who Should Be Using BCM

While Microsoft hasn't imposed any restrictions on who should use BCM, you might find that certain kinds of organizations and certain individuals are better suited to BCM than others. Even though it says "business" contact manager, nonprofits, churches, soccer moms, and more can use BCM's functions.

So just who should be using BCM? Here are some suggestions:

- ✔ A CEO who needs to know what his salespeople are doing and how his customers are being treated
- ✔ An administrative assistant who wants to automate routine tasks and keep a schedule of various tasks and activities
- ✔ A salesperson to make sure that she's following up on all her prospects
- ✔ A disorganized person to become more organized
- ✔ A smart person because she knows she'll have more time to play by working more efficiently
- ✔ Anyone who wants to separate personal contacts from business contacts or keep track of multiple sets of contacts.
- ✔ Anyone who needs to track some money through a process — whether it's a pledge or a donation to a charity
- ✔ A lazy person because he knows it's more fun to play than to work

So what kinds of businesses are ideal BCM candidates? All kinds.

- ✔ Large businesses that want to improve communication among employees
- ✔ Small businesses that have to rely on a small staff to complete a multitude of tasks
- ✔ Businesses of all sizes looking for software that can automate their processes and make them more productive in less time
- ✔ Businesses looking to grow by marketing to their prospects
- ✔ Businesses looking to retain their current customers by providing an excellent level of customer service and developing lasting relationships

So who shouldn't be using BCM? Okay, a few stubborn folks remain out there who aren't looking to organize their lives, such as these:

✔ Workaholics who live to spend every waking moment at work

✔ Hermits who don't need to schedule any appointments or remember to make follow-up phone calls

✔ Individuals with photographic memories who retain all information and never need to take a note

✔ Companies that require no paperwork

✔ Businesses that do no marketing or that have no interest in expanding their customer base

Getting Started with a Few Concepts

Nobody likes technical jargon, but in the course of showing you how to use BCM, we might end up lapsing into Geek Speak and use a handful of somewhat technical terms; we just can't avoid it. Becoming familiar with them now is less painful in the long run.

First things first. BCM is a database program. A *database* is a collection of information organized in such a way that the user of the database can quickly find desired pieces of information. Think of a database as an electronic filing system. Although most BCM users create a database of contacts, some users develop BCM databases to collect information about things other than contacts. For example, you might create a BCM database to catalog all the CDs and DVDs in your collection.

Traditional databases are organized by *fields, records,* and *files:*

✔ **Field:** A *field* is a single piece of information. In databases, fields are the smallest units of information. A tax form, for example, contains a number of fields: one for your name, one for your Social Security number, one for your income, and so on. In BCM, you start with 50 separate fields for each individual contact. You find out how to add information to these fields in Chapter 4, and in Chapter 7, we show you how to change the attributes of existing fields and how to add new ones to your database if you're the database administrator.

✔ **Record:** A *record* is one complete set of fields. In BCM, all the information you collect that pertains to one individual contact is a *contact record.*

✔ **File:** A *file* is the entire collection of data or information. You can create more than one file or database in BCM — head to Chapter 3 to find out how.

Chapter 2

Finding Your Way Around
Business Contact Manager

. . . .

. . . .

*I*n this chapter, we give you a bit of a Business Contact Manager (BCM) tour. We start with the basic, vanilla, out-of-the-box BCM components. Then, we show you the various ways that you can view BCM. Because BCM's middle name is "Contact," we discuss contacts and then show you how they're different from accounts.

Taking a Look at BCM

You use BCM only in conjunction with Outlook. Therefore, it stands to reason that the two products are pretty well enmeshed with one another. Although you find some features only in BCM, with a little customization, it might be impossible to tell where Outlook stops and BCM begins.

Figure 2-1 shows the basic Outlook with Business Contact Manager window. *Remember:* Your window might look different than Figure 2-1 if you've customized it already.

Activating BCM

BCM is included with the Ultimate, Professional, and Small Business versions of Microsoft Office. And who said there was no such thing as a free lunch!

If you have one of those versions of Microsoft Office and don't see the BCM toolbar (third from the top), you don't have BCM installed or activated yet. To activate it, follow these steps:

1. **From any Outlook window, choose File⇨ Data File Management.**

The Account Settings dialog box appears.

2. **Click the Data Files tab if it isn't already selected.**

3. **Click the Add button and select Business Contact Manager Database from the New Outlook Data File dialog box.**

After a minute or so of whirring and hissing, you're the proud owner of BCM.

Figure 2-1: The initial BCM window.

Title bar　　BCM toolbar　　Outlook menu bar　　Outlook toolbar　　To-Do bar

Outlook Navigation pane

Folder Contents pane

Preview pane

Although BCM's opening screen might seem very confusing at first, it becomes a bit easier if you break it down into a few basic elements:

- ✔ The **title bar** runs along the very top edge of Outlook and indicates which of the Outlook elements you have currently selected.

- ✔ The **Outlook Navigation pane** runs along the left side of Outlook. You find the folders housing all the items that Outlook has to offer — such as your e-mail Inbox, Calendar, Contacts, and so on. You also find buttons on the bottom portion of the Navigation pane that let you focus on any one of those items.

- ✔ The **Outlook menu bar** (starts with File, Edit, View, and so on, as the menu bar for most Microsoft products do) is directly beneath the title bar. It contains virtually every option that Outlook has to offer.

- ✔ The **Outlook toolbar** sits directly beneath the Outlook menu bar. These icons change as you select different items in the Navigation pane.

- ✔ The **BCM toolbar** is below the Outlook toolbar. You use this toolbar to access features that are found only in the Business Contact Manager application.

- ✔ The **Folder Contents pane** is the big area smack in the middle of the Outlook window. This is where you see the contents of the item that you select from the Navigation pane.

- ✔ The **Preview pane** (optional) shows up if you select the Inbox item in the Navigation bar. It shows you the content of the currently selected e-mail message.

- ✔ The **To-Do bar** is kind of like your nagging mother. Click it to see the mountains of upcoming tasks that you have to complete; click it again, and it disappears from sight.

Knowing the Toolbars and Menus

You can get to your BCM data in multiple ways. As you work with BCM and customize it, you can find new ways of arranging data so that it jumps out at you. The goal is to make BCM feel comfortable to you so you don't have to wonder where to click to find your data or make a function work. Think of BCM as a new set of golf clubs — you might take a while to decide which clubs you'll rely on the most. You might even stop using some of your clubs altogether. And so it is with BCM.

BCM choices on the Outlook menu bar

You can access almost all the Contact Manager features from the Business Contact Manager menu on the Outlook menu bar. Clicking the options on this menu, shown in Figure 2-2, is a great way to familiarize yourself with the BCM functionality.

Figure 2-2:
The Business Contact Manager menu.

Some of the choices, such as Reports, Accounting Tools, and Database Tools, have little arrowheads to the right of their names. These signify that there are *cascading menus* — another menu appears when you click an option with an arrow to the right of it.

Most of these options also appear on the Navigation pane and BCM toolbar, which we discuss later in this section. Here are a few of the features that you find on the BCM menu:

- ✔ **Reports:** Access the reports that come with BCM and the modified reports you've saved. We talk a lot more about reports in Chapter 18.

- ✔ **Accounting Tools:** If you're using Microsoft Office Accounting, here's where you can set up your connection to Small Business Accounting and customize the link. Check out Chapters 4, 5, and 13 for more detailed information about using Office Accounting with Business Contact Manager.

- ✔ **Database Tools:** Manage multiple BCM databases plus import and export BCM data. Chapter 3 includes all the information on how these tools work.

✔ **Offline:** You can take your data with you when you leave the office. See Chapter 16 to find out how this works.

✔ **Import Skins and Customizations:** You can customize fields, menus, drop-down values, screen layouts, reports, and more. You can even distribute these customizations to other people in your organization. Sound intriguing? We discuss this more in Chapter 7.

✔ **Customize Business Contact Manager Forms:** You can add fields to the BCM database and customize the values that go into drop-down lists. For example, the Contact Rating field has drop-down values of Excellent, Good, Average, Fair, and Poor. Maybe you want those to say Big Spender, Average Customer, Tightwad, and Deadbeat. This is where you'd change those values. Chapter 7 has more information about this.

✔ **Product and Service Items List:** Enter the items that you sell, such as Blue Widgets, Green Widgets, Consulting Services, or Training Services. Chapter 12 covers this function.

Using the BCM toolbar

The BCM toolbar (refer to Figure 2-1) includes four buttons:

✔ **Business Contact Manager Home:** Clicking the Business Contact Manager Home button takes you to the *dashboard* (or Home window) of BCM, shown in Figure 2-3. This area of BCM gives you the 20,000-foot view of what's happening with your business. You can view a snapshot of just about any area of BCM from here. You can see an opportunity funnel showing a chart of your expected revenues, run a report, and even find out more about BCM. If that's not enough information for you, you can click the Sales, Marketing, or Projects tab, where you can create a new account or contact, start a new marketing campaign, or view the progress of your current projects. You can customize this view to your liking — Chapter 7 shows you how.

✔ **Display:** View your accounts, contacts, opportunities, projects, project tasks, and marketing campaigns. You see these very same options displayed in the Business Contact Manager section of the Navigation pane.

✔ **E-Mail Auto-Link:** Link incoming and outgoing e-mail messages to specified accounts or business contacts.

✔ **Link to Record:** Click this button when you want to link an item on a *one off* basis — in other words, link an item this one time but don't link subsequent items automatically in the future. You can link an e-mail or task to an account, contact, opportunity, or project.

Figure 2-3:
The BCM
Home
window.

Customizing BCM's Look to Suit Your Needs

By customizing your BCM views, you can improve your efficiency by putting the features you use most often in the places you find most handy. You might want to change what you see when you first open BCM. You might want to change the options on the Navigation pane. You might even prefer to sort your contacts in your own unique style. Whatever the option, you can accomplish it — at no additional cost.

Changing the default startup option

One of the first areas you might want to customize is the view you see when BCM first opens. For example, the project manager of a construction company might set tasks for the different steps in a construction job; he'll probably want to see those tasks first thing when he opens BCM. Perhaps an inside salesperson has a rather large quota that she needs to meet; she'll want to see which deals are going to close, should be closing, and were supposed to close, as soon as she opens BCM.

You can customize BCM to open in the task list, the Opportunity list (customized the way you want it to look), or the BCM Home screen so that you can see charts showing your progress. Follow these steps to designate the startup page:

1. **From the Outlook, choose Tools⊏⟩Options.**

   The Options dialog box opens.

2. **Click the Other tab and click the Advanced Options button.**

   The Advanced Options dialog box opens. (See Figure 2-4.)

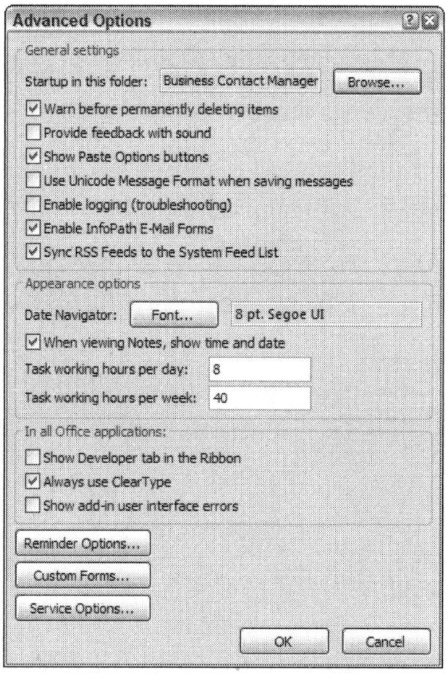

Figure 2-4: The Advanced Options dialog box.

3. **Click the Browse button.**

   The Select Folder dialog box opens. (See Figure 2-5.)

4. **Choose the item that you want to open when you start Outlook and click OK.**

   We've chosen Business Contact Manager, but you can choose any option you want.

5. **Click OK to close the Advanced Options dialog box and click OK to close the Options dialog box.**

   The next time you open BCM, it opens to the window you've specified.

Figure 2-5:
Choosing
the default
BCM
startup
option.

Navigating the Navigation pane options

Although you can navigate to just about any portion of BCM by using the
menu bar, you might prefer to find your way around BCM using the Navigation
pane on the left side of the main BCM window. Follow these steps to change
your BCM view:

1. **Click one of the buttons on the bottom of the Navigation pane.**

   The buttons along the bottom edge of the Navigation pane (see Figure 2-6)
   are a quick way to zoom in on one particular aspect of BCM.

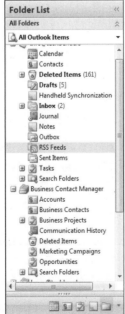

Figure 2-6:
BCM's
Navigation
pane.

For example, we clicked the Contacts button and got the view shown in Figure 2-7. The Folder List that is normally present on the Navigation pane disappears and is replaced by contact-specific choices.

2. **Choose one of the Current View options on the Navigation pane.**

We selected the Address Cards option (see Figure 2-7). The option you choose remains in effect even if you navigate to another area, such as the calendars; when you view any of your contacts or accounts, you see them in the view that you selected.

3. **Click the Folder List button on the bottom of the Navigation pane to return to the main BCM folders.**

Near the bottom of the Navigation pane is a horizontal slider bar with five dots on it. Underneath the slider bar are the icons that represent the various Outlook functions. Drag the slider bar up and down; as you drag it up, buttons with the actual folder names replace the icons, as shown in Figure 2-8.

The purpose of the buttons is to help you customize the way your information shows up. For example, if you click the Contacts button, BCM shows different ways in which you can view your contacts. (See Figure 2-9.)

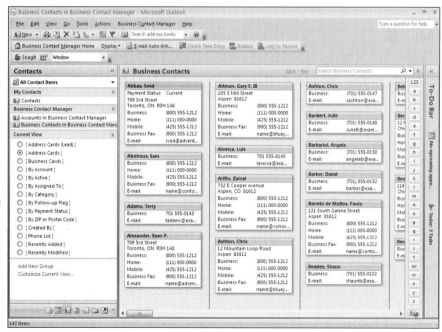

Figure 2-7:
The Navigation pane showing the Contacts options.

Figure 2-8:
Moving the
slider bar
on the
Navigation
pane.

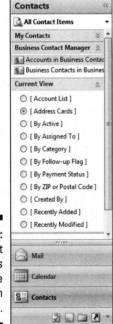

Figure 2-9:
Contact
options
in the
Navigation
pane.

Click the Folder List button conveniently located near the bottom of the Navigation pane to get back to the Folder List!

Viewing via the View menu

Logically enough, if you want to change how you view things in BCM, you might want to start in the View menu. (See Figure 2-10.)

Figure 2-10:
The View
menu.

Two of the choices — Navigation Pane and To-Do Bar — determine if the Navigation pane shows up on the left side of your screen and the To-Do bar shows up on the right side. If you don't see the Navigation pane or the To-Do bar, check them here.

The View menu can also help you to sort your projects, communication history, marketing campaigns, and opportunities. Follow these steps to sort these items:

1. **Click a BCM folder.**

   You can't sort your contacts and accounts from the View menu so you want to choose the Business Projects, Communication History, Marketing Campaigns, or Opportunities folder.

2. **From the Outlook menu bar, choose View⇨Arrange By.**

   You'll see the choices shown in Figure 2-11.

3. **Click the sort option of your choice.**

   If you had chosen the Business Projects folder in Step 1, you might want to see your projects sorted by due date. If you had chosen the Opportunities folder, you might want to have them sorted by importance.

Your changes remain in effect even if you close and reopen Outlook.

Opening and switching between multiple windows

Because you can do so much in BCM, you might want different windows to display different types of data at the same time — for example, you might want to see your contacts, task list, and projects at the same time. You can even drag these windows to different monitors if you use more than one — Bill Gates uses three at a time!

Here's how this works:

1. **Right-click one of the buttons at the bottom of the Navigation pane and select Open in New Window.**

For example, if you right-click the Contacts button, your contacts appear in their very own window. Drag or resize the window to a free spot on your monitor.

2. **Right-click a second button and select Open in New Window.**

You can continue opening as many windows as you desire. By dragging each window to a new location you can view as many windows at the same time as you'd like.

You have to repeat this exercise each time you start Outlook — you can't save those settings.

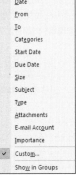

Figure 2-11: Customization choices for a BCM folder.

Finding Your Contacts and Accounts

No tour of BCM can be complete without locating your contacts and accounts; after all, BCM does stand for Business Contact Manager. You can find your BCM contacts and accounts in a number of places:

✔ **Navigation pane:** Click the plus sign to the left of Business Contact Manager and click either Accounts or Business Contacts.

✔ **BCM toolbar:** Click the Display button and choose either Accounts or Business Contacts from the drop-down menu.

✔ **Outlook menu bar:** Choose Business Contact Manager⇨Accounts or Business Contacts.

Getting to know your contacts

Contacts are the heart and soul of the Business Contact Manager. A *contact* is the record for one person, and BCM comes with many fields of information so that you can store information about that person. You can add more than a dozen phone numbers, three addresses, and even show the person and/or process that was responsible for finding the contact in the first place. (If that's not enough, Chapter 7 shows you how to add more fields.)

Most people immediately think about grouping or separating contacts into logical categories — business contacts and friends, or good guys and bad guys. Sometimes, it's hard to separate people into hard and fast groups; some of your best friends might also be business acquaintances. Fear not; BCM has two great ways to handle this conundrum — categories (which we discuss in Chapter 6) and multiple contact lists (which we discuss in Chapter 4).

Organizing contacts with accounts

Accounts organize contacts into their company affiliations. You have another entire record of data that you can customize separately from a contact. It can contain fields that are specific to the company instead of the people working at the company. For example, you might include a sales rep's address on the Business Contact record but have the company's headquarters showing on the account record. This is quite handy if your style of business is to work with multiple people at the same company — the purchasing manager, the production manager, the accounting department. You can add notes for each individual contact that is linked to an account — and then see all of those notes together on the account record. This allows you — or anyone else in your organization — to see what's going on with an account at a higher level.

You might find yourself relying on accounts even if you're not using BCM to manage a business. You can use accounts to group all sorts of people together. Perhaps you want to keep track of a soccer team or a PTA or your kid's home-room class. These might translate into your business accounts.

Chapter 3

Getting Down to Business Contact Manager

● ●

In This Chapter

▶ Creating a new database

▶ Adding contacts to a database

▶ Exporting information to other products

● ●

*A*fter you start learning the ins and outs of BCM, you're probably ready to go prime time — or at least to create a database. If you've been using another software program, you might prefer to simply import those contacts directly into your new BCM database, which is certainly quicker than typing hundreds of contact records. At that point, you might be satisfied to rest on your laurels — or you might consider creating another database to house another segment of your life. Finally, you might have a need to export all of that information to another source. You can find out how to do all of those things in this chapter.

Creating a New BCM Database

There are two reasons to create a new BCM database:

✔ You've installed BCM but you're not seeing the BCM toolbar, folders, or menu items.

✔ You want separate databases for totally separate aspects of your life.

One database is probably more than enough to run your business or organization. However, you might want to have multiple databases if you

✔ Run two or more totally separate companies.

✔ Keep track of the records for an organization that you're associated with, such as a soccer team or networking group.

✔ Purchase a rather large list of prospects that you don't want to mix with your existing clients.

To create a new database, follow these steps:

1. **From the Outlook menu bar, choose Business Contact Manager➪ Database Tools➪Create or Select a Database.**

    The Microsoft Office Outlook 2007 with Business Contact Manager Wizard opens with the Create or Select a Business Contact Manager Database screen showing, as shown in Figure 3-1.

2. **Select the Create a New Database radio button.**

3. **Enter the name of the new database in the Database Name text field and click the Connect button.**

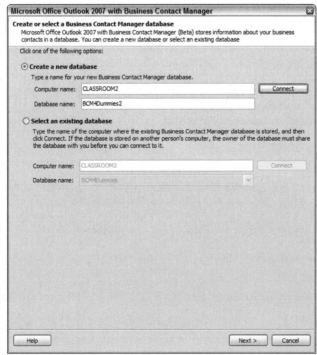

Figure 3-1:
Creating a
new
Business
Contact
Manager
database.

You want to name your database something that you can pick out of a crowd, such as CoolBeans or LetsMakeMoney. You'll also need to avoid spaces in the name and characters such as @, #, $, %, ^, &, and *, especially if you don't want your computer to think you're swearing at it. If you don't suggest a name, Business Contact Manager suggests one for you: MSSmallBusiness.

4. **Click Next to create your database.**

   As quick as a bunny, your database is created. You might want to stand back because your computer might make some noise. If smoke starts to appear — run!

Your database opens automatically. If you had a database open when you started creating a new one, don't freak out when your old one disappears. We show you how to switch between databases in the next section.

BCM uses SQL Server 2005 Express Edition as its database engine. When you create a new database, two data files are actually created: one with the .mdf extension and the other with the .ldf extension. These files are buried somewhat deep in the bowels of your computer — or in Documents and Settings\User Name\Local Settings\Application Data\ Microsoft\Business Contact Manager. If you'd like to rename those files, you can stop the SQL service, navigate to that folder, and rename the two files in question.

Opening a Database

If you created a database in the previous section, you might actually want to use it. Here's how you can open your database if it isn't already open:

1. **From the Outlook menu bar, choose Business Contact Manager⟹ Database Tools⟹Create or Select a Database.**

   The wizard opens with the Create or Select a Business Contact Manager Database screen showing. (Refer to Figure 3-1.)

2. **Select the Select an Existing Database radio button.**

3. **Select the name of your database from the Database Name drop-down list and click Next.**

   You might have to wait a minute or two while BCM whirrs and hisses and opens your database.

Viewing Your Current Database

Nothing is worse than getting lost in an endless maze of databases. Okay, there are worse things, but not knowing which database you're using can be extremely frustrating — especially if you've spent the day entering tons of contact information, only to learn that you entered it into the wrong database. Unfortunately, BCM doesn't provide you with a sign that tells you the name of the currently opened database. However, with a bit of detective work you'll be able to uncover the name of your database as well as a few other tidbits of information.

Here's a simple way to get the MO on a database that might be MIA:

1. **From the Outlook menu bar, choose Business Contact Manager⇨ Database Tools⇨Manage Database.**

   The Manage Database dialog box opens.

2. **Click the Backup/Restore tab if it isn't selected.**

   The Backup/Restore tab appears, as shown in Figure 3-2. This tab displays the name of your current database, the name of your computer, the date and time you created the database, the owner of the database, and the size of the database.

3. **Click Close when you're done.**

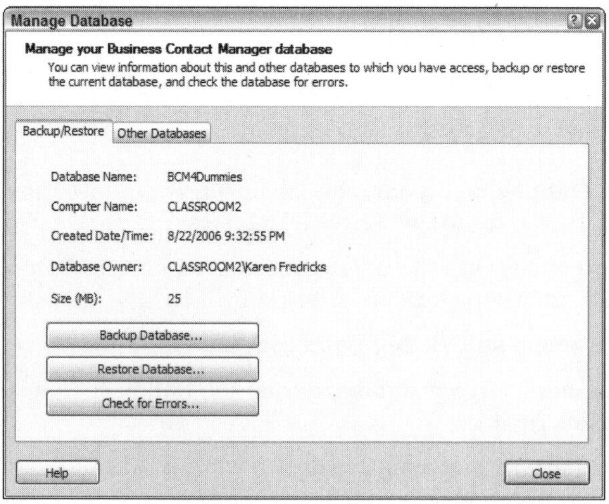

Figure 3-2:
Finding out
what
database
you're in.

Manage Database

Manage your Business Contact Manager database
You can view information about this and other databases to which you have access, backup or restore the current database, and check the database for errors.

Backup/Restore | Other Databases

Database Name:	BCM4Dummies
Computer Name:	CLASSROOM2
Created Date/Time:	8/22/2006 9:32:55 PM
Database Owner:	CLASSROOM2\Karen Fredricks
Size (MB):	25

Backup Database...
Restore Database...
Check for Errors...

Help   Close

Deleting a Database

Life changes, things happen, and your cheese gets moved. Maybe you created a database for the leads that you purchased and you now find that you no longer need them. Or maybe you created a database in error and want to get rid of the evidence before the boss sees it. Whatever the reason, it's just as easy to delete a database as it is to create it in the first place. Here's all you have to do:

1. **If you're in the database you want to delete, close it by opening a different database.**

   As a safety precaution, the database you're currently using is excluded from the list. This allows you to delete a BCM database that isn't active.

2. **From the Outlook menu bar, choose Business Contact Manager⇨ Database Tools⇨Manage Database.**

   The Manage Database dialog box opens.

3. **Click the Other Databases tab.**

   The Other Databases tab displays a list of your databases. (See Figure 3-3.)

   As a safety precaution, the database you're currently in isn't included on the Other Databases tab.

Manage Database

Manage your Business Contact Manager database
You can view information about this and other databases to which you have access, backup or restore the current database, and check the database for errors.

Backup/Restore	Other Databases			
Database Name	Size(MB)	Type	Owner	Created
MSSmallBusiness	35	Private	CLASSROOM2\Karen F...	8/3/2006 12:45:43 PM
MSSmallBusiness3	35	Private	CLASSROOM2\Karen F...	8/6/2006 6:30:00 PM
MSSmallBusiness4	35	Private	CLASSROOM2\Karen F...	8/22/2006 6:58:34 PM
ACT_Import	25	Private	CLASSROOM2\Karen F...	8/23/2006 11:49:40 AM
BCM4Dummies2	35	Private	CLASSROOM2\Karen F...	8/23/2006 1:14:42 PM
BCM4Dummies3	35	Private	CLASSROOM2\Karen F...	8/23/2006 1:17:07 PM

Delete Database

Help   Close

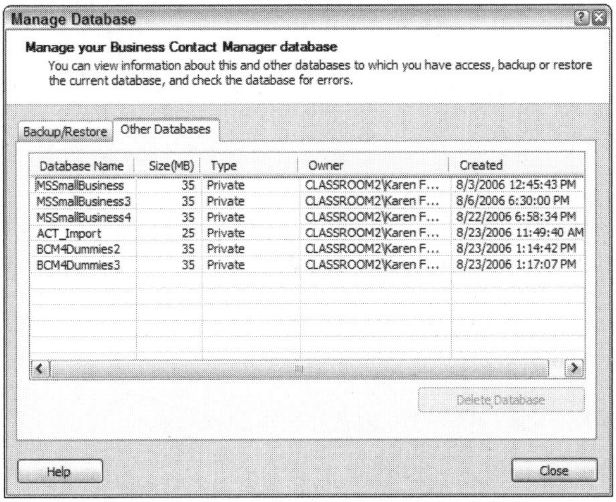

Figure 3-3:
Deleting
a BCM
database.

4. **Click the database you want to delete; then click the Delete Database button.**

5. **A warning asks if you're sure you want to delete the database.**

6. **Click Yes if you really want to get rid of the database in question.**

   Unfortunately, BCM doesn't believe in lengthy goodbyes. Wham! Your database is gone, permanently (as in forever), so think carefully before clicking that Yes button.

7. **(Optional) Click another database and follow the preceding steps to delete another database.**

8. **Click Close to close the Manage Database dialog box.**

Importing Contacts into BCM

The only thing worse than doing a bunch of work is having to do that bunch of work over again. With that thought in mind, BCM has thoughtfully included an import wizard that magically transforms your old database information into a shiny, new BCM database. That means if you're using a program like ACT! or Access and decide to switch to BCM, you can do so without losing — or having to retype — your data. If you're currently using QuickBooks, you can import your various lists of customers and vendors into BCM. Many of you might even be using an Excel spreadsheet to keep track of your contacts. Not to worry; BCM helps you move those contacts easily and painlessly.

If you have multiple users — salespeople, for example — that keep their own lists of contact data, you can import all these into your new BCM master database for your company. You can even import another BCM database into your current BCM database, if that's what will float your boat.

Determining your data type

So what specific data types can you bring into BCM? When you import data, that's the first piece of information you're asked for in the Business Data Import and Export Wizard. (We tell you how to get to that wizard in the section that follows this one.)

Four of your options involve bringing existing BCM data into your database:

✓ **Business Contact Manager Data (.bcm):** Import all the good stuff, including business contacts, accounts, opportunities, and communication history. Use this option if you accidentally created two separate databases and would like to merge them together, or if someone else in your organization is already using an existing BCM database. This is also a good way to collect data from remote guys; you can import their data into the company database at regular intervals.

✔ **Business Contact Manager Customizations (.bcmx):** Import your business contacts, as well as any user-defined fields that you might have created for your database.

✔ **Microsoft E-Mail Marketing Service Contacts (.bcm):** If you're using E-Mail Marketing Service for your e-mail campaigns, you can bring that list of contact information into BCM.

✔ **Microsoft Sales Leads (.bcm):** If you're using a previous version of BCM, you don't have to worry about losing any data.

The rest of the import choices actually involve a two-pronged attack: Your data is converted to a BCM database, and then you need to import that BCM database into your existing database. Whew! Sound confusing? After BCM converts your data, BCM automatically prompts you to import it into your existing database. You can convert and import the following types of data files:

✔ **Comma Separated Values (.csv):** This is the one-size-fits-all option for importing data. All you have to do is ask someone, "Can you send me those names in a CSV format?" and you're good to go. BCM's import function allows you to *map* (link the field in one database to the corresponding field in another database) incoming fields from the CSV file into the fields that BCM stores in its database. This allows you to get the right data in the right place.

This is the format of choice for organizations that run trade shows or that sell prospect lists.

Basically, if you can get your information *out* of a program, you can get it *into* BCM. Most software programs allow for an export to a text file. Even if you're using a (gasp!) DOS-based program, you'll probably find a Print to File option that, in essence, creates an ASCII, or *text,* file. You can then open that text file in Excel and save it as a .csv file.

✔ **Access Database (.mdb or .accdb):** You can import business contact or account information from Access.

✔ **Excel Workbook (.xls or .slsx):** You can import either your business contacts or accounts from Excel.

✔ **Outlook Contacts Folder:** This option brings your Outlook contacts and plunks them into your business contacts.

If you plan on building your database with information that another user is keeping in Outlook, you need to wrestle a copy of his .pst file from him and open it on your machine. Only then can you import all of his contacts.

✔ **ACT! (.pad or .dbf):** This is actually one of the coolest of the import options. BCM can capture your existing contacts, companies, groups, opportunities, notes, and histories from an ACT! database.

✔ **QuickBooks:** This option is helpful if you're using QuickBooks. You can export various lists out of QuickBooks including your Customer, Vendor, and Employee lists and import them into BCM. Figure 3-4 shows the QuickBook options.

When exporting from QuickBooks, you might find that your import into BCM works better — albeit much slower — if you export your files from QuickBooks one at a time.

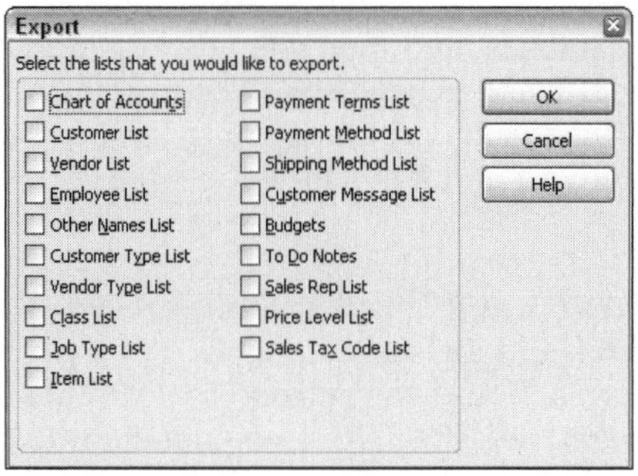

Figure 3-4:
You can export these types of lists from QuickBooks.

Export		
Select the lists that you would like to export.		
☐ Chart of Accounts	☐ Payment Terms List	OK
☐ Customer List	☐ Payment Method List	Cancel
☐ Vendor List	☐ Shipping Method List	Help
☐ Employee List	☐ Customer Message List	
☐ Other Names List	☐ Budgets	
☐ Customer Type List	☐ To Do Notes	
☐ Vendor Type List	☐ Sales Rep List	
☐ Class List	☐ Price Level List	
☐ Job Type List	☐ Sales Tax Code List	
☐ Item List		

Performing the data import

When you know what kind of data you can bring into BCM, it's time to start working. You have to follow quite a few steps along the way, but the effort is worth it when you think of all the time you save by not having to spend hours on data entry! Of course, BCM comes equipped with an import wizard that steps you through the process and guarantees that you don't get lost along the way.

Follow these steps to import your data into Business Contact Manager:

1. **From the Outlook menu bar, choose Business Contact Manager⇨ Database Tools⇨Import and Export.**

   Or choose File⇨Import and Export⇨Business Contact Manager for Outlook.

   The Business Data Import and Export Wizard opens.

2. **Select Import and click Next.**

3. **Select the type of data file you want to import and click Next.**

   If you're not sure what type of data you have, see the "Determining your data type" section earlier in this chapter.

   The next screen of the wizard opens, as shown in Figure 3-5.

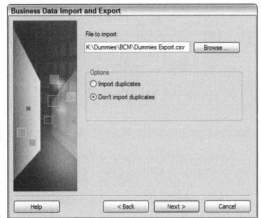

Figure 3-5:
Choose a file to import.

4. **Click the Browse button, navigate to the location of your data file, and then click Open.**

   For many of you, this is one of the hardest parts. You need to know where your data file is lurking before you can import it into BCM.

5. **Indicate your duplicate option, and click Next.**

   Here's where you can decide if you want to import duplicates into your database. We're not quite sure why you would want to add duplicate contacts to your database, but if you feel the urge — go for it.

   The next screen of the wizard appears. (See Figure 3-6.)

6. **Choose which files you want to import and whether you want to import your data into your contacts or accounts.**

   We know choosing the files to import again seems kind of silly because you just did that in Step 4, but go ahead and do it again.

   If you don't know the difference between a contact and an account, see Chapter 2.

7. **Click the Map button.**

   Holy guacamole! The Map Fields dialog box (see Figure 3-7) springs to life. The import fields (in the From area) are on the left side of this window, and the BCM fields (in the To area) are on the right side of the window.

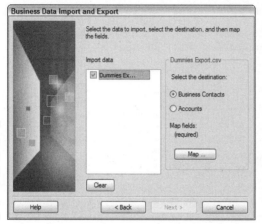

Figure 3-6:
Choose
where to
import your
data.

Mapping is a way of translating field names between programs. For example, BCM includes the Mobile Phone field and your other software may use the Cellular Phone field. If you don't map the fields of your two databases correctly, you might end up with your data in the incorrect place.

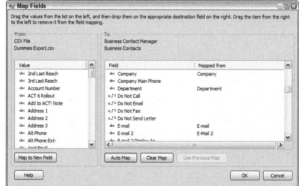

Figure 3-7:
Mapping
the import
file fields to
the BCM
contact
fields.

You can map your data in three different ways:

- *Automatically mapping fields:* Click the Auto Map button. Any fields from your import file that are an identical match to a BCM field appear in the Mapped From column.

- *Manually mapping fields:* Drag a field from the From area (left side of the dialog box) to the To area (right side of the dialog box).

Figure 3-8 shows the Birthday field mapped manually to the Birth Date field.

- *Creating new fields:* If you want to import information that BCM doesn't have a field for, click that import field and then click the Map to New Field button. Fill in the field name, data type, and format in the Add a Field dialog box and click OK.

Figure 3-8:
Manually mapping a field.

8. **Click OK when you're done mapping your fields and then click Next.**

At this point, you see a rather reassuring message that tells you that your information is going to be imported.

9. **Click Next to continue.**

This part is pretty easy — you get to sit back and watch a moving graphic that illustrates how your data information is flying from your import file into the arms, er, fields of BCM. When your data finishes flying through cyberspace, you're treated to a congratulatory message. Too bad it doesn't include champagne and bonbons.

10. **Click the Close button to close the wizard.**

11. **Give yourself a really big pat on the back — you deserve it!**

Moving contacts from Outlook

Entering new contact data into BCM can be a drag — but not if you're able to drag them into your database from Outlook. Just drag yourself through the following steps to transform Outlook contacts into BCM contacts or accounts:

1. **Click the Contacts folder on Outlook's Folder List.**

   You'll now be able to see all of your contacts. What? You can't find the Folder List? Refresh your memory in Chapter 2.

2. **Select the contacts that you want to transform into business contacts or accounts:**

   • *To select all your contacts:* Press Ctrl+A.

   • *To select multiple (but not all) contacts:* Press Ctrl and click the contacts you want.

3. **Hold down your right mouse button on the selected contacts and drag them to either the Accounts or Business Contacts folder.**

4. **Let go of your mouse button.**

   The contextual menu dialog box appears.

5. **Indicate whether you want to move or copy the Outlook contacts to their new destination.**

Exporting Data from Business Contact Manager

There might come a time when you need to export your information out of BCM. Perhaps your printer needs a list of your contacts to print out all those brochures you just ordered. Maybe you want to get a copy of your database onto another computer. Or you just might want to share the neat customizations that you created in BCM with an associate.

BCM can export your data to one of the following data formats:

✔ Business Contact Manager data (.bcm)

✔ Business Contact Manager customizations (.bcmx)

✔ Comma Separated Values (.csv)

Here's all you need to get rolling on your export project:

1. **From the Outlook menu bar, choose Business Contact Manager⇨ Database Tools⇨Import and Export.**

   Or choose File⇨Import and Export⇨Business Contact Manager for Outlook.

The Business Data Import and Export Wizard opens.

2. **Select Export and click Next.**

   The screen asks you to select the type of file to export to. (See Figure 3-9.)

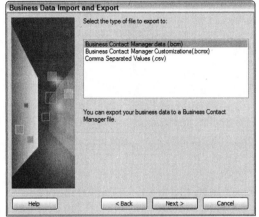

Figure 3-9:
Decide
what type
of file to
export to.

3. **Choose the file type of your choice and click Next.**

   The next screen of the wizard appears. (See Figure 3-10.)

4. **Choose the contacts export options you want and then click Next.**

   - *Export Everything:* Exports both your business contacts and your accounts.

   - *Select Specific Records:* Allows you to export either all of your business contacts or all of your accounts — or select the Select Specific Records of the Type Specified Above check box to specify the business contact or account records that you want to export.

   If you select the Select Specific Records of the Type Specified Above check box, you'll want to click the Select button. At this juncture, the Filter dialog box opens, and you can give the parameters of the type of business contacts or accounts you want to export. Chapter 17 provides you with more information on filtering.

Not sure of the difference between business contacts and accounts? Head over to Chapter 4 for more information on business contacts and Chapter 5 for the 411 on accounts.

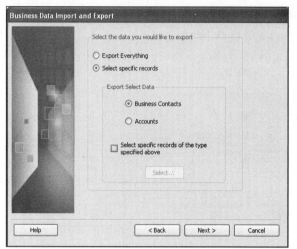

Figure 3-10:
Decide
what data
to export.

5. **Click the Browse button in the Business Data Import and Export dialog box to specify the name of your export file and its location.**

6. **Click Save to save the export file and return to the Business Data Import and Export dialog box.**

7. **Select the radio buttons to indicate if you'd like to export history information and/or your products list and click Next to continue your way through the export wizard.**

   BCM leaves nothing to chance; this screen of the wizard confirms that you're going to be exporting data — and that you might have to twiddle your thumbs for a moment or two while the export takes place.

8. **Click Next to finish the export wizard.**

   As expected, BCM whirs and hisses a bit as it strives to get you that export file ASAP. You'll soon realize that whirring and hissing is a good thing because you're rewarded with a congratulatory message extending best wishes on an export job well done.

9. **Click Close to close the export wizard.**

Part II
Putting BCM to Work

The 5th Wave   By Rich Tennant

"Okay people, remember – use your Business Contact Manager. It's customizable, so those of you collecting 'juice' will use a slightly different entry from those of you doing shakedowns or fencing stolen goods."

In this part . . .

*O*kay, after you whip BCM into shape (see the preceding part of this book), it's time to start adding some data. BCM is a *contact manager,* which (as the name implies) makes it a great place to manage your contacts. First, you add new contacts into your database. Then, if your business needs to track company data, you can add accounts and link those contacts to their respective accounts. As you create more contacts and accounts, you'll want to categorize them. Finally, you may want to try your hand at customizing BCM to include any and all data about your contacts and accounts.

Chapter 4

Getting to Know Your Business Contacts

*C*reating business contacts is the *raison d' etre* for BCM. As its name implies, a business contact is someone that you do business with. This chapter deals with entering business contacts one by one instead of importing them in bulk — flip to Chapter 3 for that information. We also discuss how to create a new contact with just a few clicks from an e-mail you receive.

After you create a business contact, you might need to modify or even delete it; don't worry, you find out how to do all of that in this chapter. But how about those duplicate records? Not a problem; we show you how to deal with those pesky critters. And for the smart members of the audience, we even show you how to link your BCM data to your Office Accounting 2007 data.

Working with Business Contacts

There are all types of people you need to stay in touch with — prospects, customers, friends, enemies, vendors. And each one has information that is specific to just that particular person. You enter each piece of information about a contact — name, business phone, fax, mobile phone, e-mail address — into a *field*. All the fields for one contact are stored together as a *record;* so if you have 500 people in your BCM database, you have 500 records, each record holding many fields of data.

BCM comes configured, out of the box, with over 50 fields for data that you can store for each person. You can add more fields, if you like, to further customize BCM to fit the needs of your business. Check out Chapter 7 for instructions on adding more fields and customizing them.

Entering a Business Contact from Scratch

You probably have a lot of people that you come into contact with. Some of you might even be storing information on some of those people, or contacts, in Outlook already. Although you can store lots of information about a contact in Outlook, BCM provides even more powerful methods of keeping track of all those contacts. For example, you might have several contacts that you want to bundle together in a master account record. You might want to keep track of all the products that you sold to a contact, or have a log of all the times you've visited with him.

Enter the BCM business contact record. A business contact can be associated with various other parts of BCM: accounts, marketing campaigns, opportunities, or even business projects. Contacts allow you to view traditional information such as a person's name, address, and phone numbers, as well as more advanced information such as notes or histories.

Don't let the name *business contact* fool you. You might want to set up some of your personal contacts as business contacts. For example, you might want to keep track of all the practices that each of your team members has attended, or make notes about their progress.

Here's how to add a business contact to BCM:

1. **Select the Business Contacts folder in the Folder List.**

2. **From the Outlook menu bar, choose File⇨New⇨Business Contact.**

   The Business Contact window appears, as shown in Figure 4-1. You enter all the pertinent information for your new contact in this window.

3. **Fill in your tidbits of information in the following fields:**

   • *Business Contact:* Click the Full Name button, and the Check Full Name dialog box appears. Enter a contact's title (Mr., Mrs., and so on), first, middle, and last names, and suffix in the appropriate text boxes. (See Figure 4-2.) Click OK to save the contact name. BCM fills in the File As field automatically; you can change how the name appears in an alphabetical sort by filling in this field.

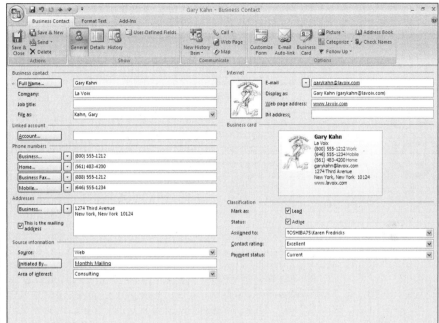

Figure 4-1:
Business
Contact
window.

The only field in the Business Contact window that you must enter is the Full Name field. However, this is just the proverbial tip of the BCM contact iceberg. The more information you enter about a business contact, the more useful BCM is to you.

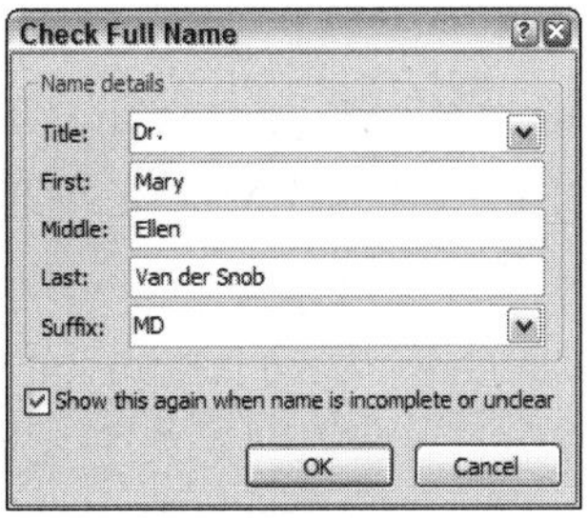

Figure 4-2:
The Check
Full Name
dialog box.

• *Company Name or Linked Account:* Click the Account button if you want to link the Business Contact record to a master Account record.

- *Phone Numbers:* BCM comes with more phone numbers than you can shake a stick at including two business, two home, two mobile, and even an *other* phone number. Although you can store 19 phone numbers, only 4 phone numbers display at a time. If you click the down-arrow button to the left of one of the text fields, you can choose which phone number field you want to display. Clicking the phone labels themselves allows you to change the country code for that number.

Don't worry about messing with dashes and parentheses when entering a phone number — BCM thoughtfully adds them when you leave a phone field.

- *Addresses:* Click the down-arrow button to choose a set of address fields: Business, Home, or Other. Choose which one you want as the mailing address and select the This Is the Mailing Address check box.

- *Source Information:* Enter the generic referral source (advertisement, trade show, telemarketing) of the contact in the Source drop-down list. Click the Initiated By button to link this contact to another contact, marketing campaign, opportunity, or business project. This is a great way of keeping track of how this contact came into your world. The Area of Interest field houses the product that the contact is particularly interested in.

- *Internet:* BCM stores three e-mail addresses per contact; just choose the one you want to use from the E-Mail drop-down list. The Display As field fills in automatically with the contact's name and e-mail address. This information shows up in the To field when you e-mail the contact. Enter the contact's URL in the Web page Address field. If your contact has an Internet message address, enter it into the IM Address field.

The fields found in the Internet area are hyperlinks; after you add the data to any of those fields, you can click them to launch your browser or IM window.

- *Business Card*: As you're entering information into a Business Contact record, an electronic business card is built automatically. You can use this business card when you show a list of your business contacts. You can also send the business card to your friends and enemies via e-mail if you want them to have either your contact information or that of one of your contacts.

- *Classification:* Several areas of BCM use a Mark As field to help you find your prospects. Deselect the Status check box if a business contact is no longer someone you are actively working with. Associate the business contact with a specific member of your organization in the Assigned To field. If you categorize your contacts as A, B, or C level contacts, fill in the Contact Rating field. Use the Payment field to help you find those contacts that are current in their payments — or those that aren't.

4. **Click the Save & Close button when you finish entering your contact information.**

   Or you can click the Save & New button if you had so much fun adding one contact that you just can't wait to do it again. You save the record you were entering and a new, blank, Business Contact window opens so that you can start working on your next victim.

Adding a Business Contact from an E-Mail

Unfortunately, Microsoft forgot to include the ability to create a business contact from an incoming e-mail; however, you can create a new contact record with a work-around. Basically, you create the Outlook contact and then move it to BCM.

If you regularly receive e-mails from people that aren't in your business contact database, this is a good habit to get into to make sure you start tracking your activities with the e-mail senders immediately.

Follow these steps to add a business contact from an e-mail:

1. **Open the new e-mail message.**

2. **Right-click the name of the person who sent the e-mail to you and choose Add to Outlook Contacts from the menu.**

   Outlook's Contact dialog box opens. It's already filled in with the contact's name and e-mail address.

3. **Fill in any other information you might have for that person.**

4. **Click Save & Close to save the record.**

5. **Click the Contacts folder from the Folder List and find the record you just saved.**

6. **Drag the contact record from the Contacts folder to the Business Contacts folder.**

   Your newly created contact is now one of the contacts in your Business Contacts folder. You might want to open that business contact and tweak it slightly to include some of the BCM fields that aren't available when setting up a plain, vanilla Outlook contact.

Adding a Business Contact from an Account Record

You might want to picture a BCM account as a super-sized business contact. Here's where you can enter information about an organization or company. (You can find out a lot more about accounts in Chapter 5.) In general, you create a business contact for a single individual and an account for a bunch of individuals.

In many cases if you're dealing with an account, you're probably dealing with a group of individuals who share several things in common: the same address, main phone number, and signature at the bottoms of their paychecks. You can enter each person's name, phone number, and so on individually in a contact record, get a migraine, and storm into your boss's office complaining that you're overworked or underpaid. Or you can use this method to enter a bunch of business contacts, sneak out to the driving range for an hour, and then storm into your boss's office complaining that you're overworked or underpaid.

Follow these steps to set up several business contacts from an account:

1. **Click the Accounts folder in the Folder List.**

2. **Find the account to which you want to add a business contact.**

   If you need to start a new account, see Chapter 5.

3. **Double-click the account to open it.**

   The Account window opens.

4. **In the Business Contacts section, click the Add button.**

   The Business Contacts section is near the bottom of the Account window.

   A list of all of your existing business contacts opens.

5. **Click the New button.**

   A new Business Contact window opens, just like magic. And just like magic, the address and phone information are already filled in. The Account name appears in the Account field and the Web site address is in the Web Page field. Talk about automation!

6. **Fill in the business contact's name, phone extension, and any other information that's pertinent just to him.**

   Okay, BCM is pretty good, but it's not psychic. You have to add a few tidbits of information on your own.

7. **Click Save & Close to save your entries.**

Making Changes to a Business Contact

You've worked really hard at adding all sorts of new contacts to your database. Life is good. The birds are singing. Time to try out that new putter. However, even the best laid plans of mice, men, and golf carts can get messed up. Perhaps one of your clients has the audacity to change his e-mail address, and another one changes his phone number. You might even have a low-down, nasty, former client decide to take his business elsewhere — and you can't wait to remove all remnants of him from your database. Fear not — stuff happens and BCM makes it really easy to deal with change.

Changing data in a business contact

Changing business contact data is as simple as one, two, three: Open the business contact, make your changes, and save them.

Here's all you have to do:

1. **Click the Business Contacts folder in the Folder List.**

   A list of your business contacts appears. (See Figure 4-3.)

2. **Double-click the record of the business contact that you want to edit.**

   If you don't see the contact you're looking for, try one of these search methods:

   • Navigate to the last name of your contact by clicking one of the lettered buttons running down the right side of the screen.

   • Fill in the name (first, last, or even a part of the name does the trick) in the search field at the top of the Business Contacts window and click the magnifying glass.

3. **Type your new information.**

   The Backspace and Delete keys come in handy for this task.

4. **Click Save & Close when you finish changing your information.**

   Okay, we know we promised that this would be as easy as one, two, three, but you have to admit it was pretty darn easy!

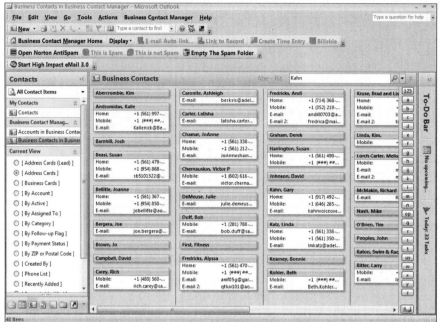

Figure 4-3:
Finding a
business
contact
to edit.

Deleting a business contact

Every so often, it's time to say bye-bye to one of your contacts. They don't make the grade, or you didn't make the sale and you don't need them cluttering up your life or database. So, *adios, muchacho!*

The procedure for deleting a business contact is ridiculously easy. And you can get the job done a number of ways — feel free to use the method that you like best.

Click the Business Contacts folder in the Folder List and do one of the following:

- ✔ Right-click the business contact in question and choose Delete. So long!

- ✔ Double-click the business contact to open the record and click the Delete button in the Actions group of the Ribbon (located at the top of the Business Contact window).

- ✔ Highlight a business contact and press Ctrl+D.

- ✔ Highlight a business contact and choose Edit⇨Delete from the Outlook menu bar.

When you click Delete, the business contact is gone but not forgotten. Deleted records are placed in the Deleted Items folder conveniently located in the Business Contact Manager folder in the Folder List. Click the Deleted Items folder; you'll see your deleted business contact sitting forlornly on the right side of your screen. Think of his joy as you drag him back to the Business Contacts folder!

Resolving Duplicates

Duplicates are the natural enemy of a contact database! BCM uses the Name and E-mail Address fields to determine whether a new record is a duplicate. If you save a business contact with the same name or e-mail address as a business contact that's already a part of your database, BCM displays the A Duplicate Item Has Been Detected dialog box, as shown in Figure 4-4.

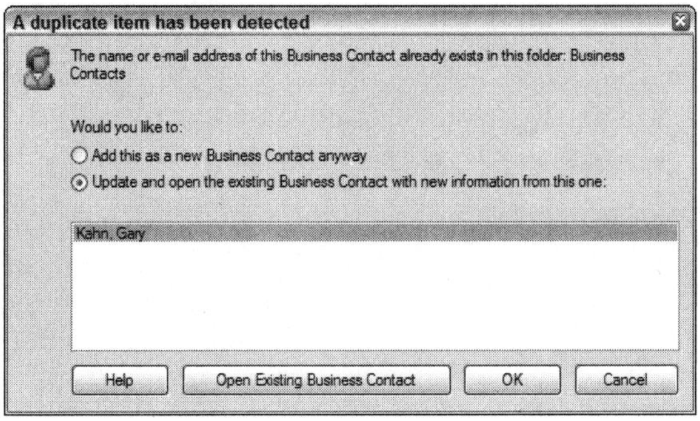

Figure 4-4:
BCM warns
you that
you're
adding a
duplicate
business
contact.

A duplicate item has been detected
The name or e-mail address of this Business Contact already exists in this folder: Business Contacts
Would you like to:
○ Add this as a new Business Contact anyway
⊙ Update and open the existing Business Contact with new information from this one:
Kahn, Gary
Help	Open Existing Business Contact	OK	Cancel

You have a couple of options to help manage those duplicate records:

- ✔ **If the new contact isn't a duplicate:** Select the Add This as a New Business Contact Anyway radio button. After all, as scary as the thought might be, there could be more than one John Smith running around.

- ✔ **Merge your newly inputted information with the existing business contact record:** Click the Update and Open the Existing Business Contact with New Information from This One radio button.

- ✔ **Compare your new contact to the original contact:** Click the Open Existing Business Contact button if you'd like to open the original Business Contact record and investigate a bit further.

Unfortunately, the duplicate warning doesn't spring into play until you save the new business contact record. Although it still saves you from adding a duplicate business contact to your database, you might feel a bit used and abused that you wasted your time re-entering all that data. It's always best to look before you leap — look to make sure a business contact isn't already in your database before leaping in to enter a new business contact record!

Exploring the Business Contact Window

Just when you think it can't get any better, something hits you — hopefully, it's not a golf ball. You have a flashback of sorts. Wait, you wonder. Isn't there something else up at the top of the Business Contact window? Right you are — like most Microsoft products, a Ribbon is sitting up there for all the world to see. You might even notice a tab or two at the top of that window.

You might have heard that Rome wasn't built in a day. You're also not going to memorize all of BCM's functionality in a day — or two, or three, or four!

Tying a ribbon around your business contacts

A BCM contact is a lot more than just a simple Rolodex card. After you enter the basic contact information — and know how to get back to it — you can explore a few of the features that you might have missed when you started the contact.

You can see the Ribbon inside the Business Contact window when you add or edit a contact. It's divided into four groups: Actions, Show, Communicate, and Options.

Getting into the middle of the action

You find these options in the Actions and Show groups of the Ribbon:

- **Save & Close:** Click this button to get out of a business contact and save your choices. It saves the record in the database and closes this window. If you make some edits and don't want to save them, press Esc and click No to saving changes.

- **Save & New:** Click this button to save the current business contact information, and BCM provides you with a new, blank window to enter the next contact.

- **Delete:** Click this button to delete the business contact you're looking at.

✔ **General:** This is the default window that opens when you open one of your business contact records. You enter all your contact's information in this screen. (See the earlier section, "Entering a Business Contact from Scratch.")

✔ **Details:** The Details window (shown in Figure 4-5) houses additional job and personal information. In your records, you can define how this person likes to be contacted. You can even add a time-stamped comment — or two or three — if you're so inclined.

There is an extra-cool thing that happens if you add a birthday or anniversary date to the Details window. When you close the business contact record, BCM asks you whether you want a reminder set on your calendar. Isn't automation wonderful?

✔ **History:** The Communication History Items window (shown in Figure 4-6) is the storage area of everything you've communicated (or done) with this contact. You find all the e-mails sent or received, tasks, appointments, opportunities, business notes, phone logs, and attached files stored here. Double-click an item to open it in its appropriate window so you can see more details. You can add new items by clicking the New button or remove an item by clicking the Remove button. Click the View drop-down menu and you can sort your history items in a number of other ways.

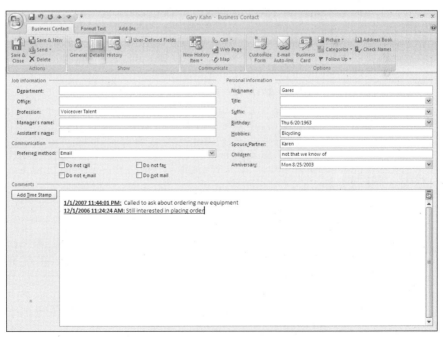

Figure 4-5:
The Details window.

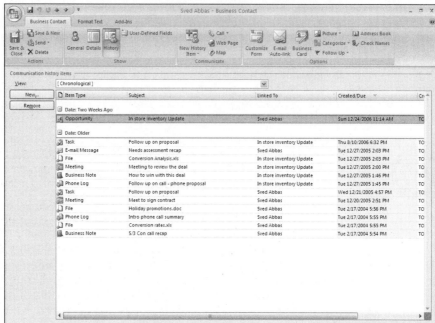

Figure 4-6:
Business
Contact
Communi-
cation
History
window.

✔ **User-Defined Fields:** The User-Defined Fields window is where you can get really creative with BCM — we tell you how to do that in endless detail in Chapter 7. You can add your own fields, and then customize the tab that houses them.

Communicating with the outside world

The next group on the Ribbon is the Communicate group. This is a particularly fun place to camp out. Here's what you find there:

✔ **New History Item:** You can attach a note, phone log, opportunity, project, task, e-mail, appointment, or file to the current business contact.

✔ **Call:** If your phone system is hooked up to your PC, you can dial the contact by clicking the Call button. The drop-down menu displays all the phone numbers you've entered for that contact. Choosing the number initiates the call.

✔ **Web Page:** Your Internet browser launches and goes to the contact's Web page. It does exactly the same function as clicking the Web Page Address field in the General window.

✔ **Map:** Your browser opens to Microsoft's Sympatico Web site to see that contact's address on a map.

With this model you get plenty of options

You can find these features in the Options group of the Ribbon:

- ✔ **Customize Form:** Add fields and place them on a new tab. Flip to Chapter 7 to find out exactly how to do it.

- ✔ **E-mail Auto Link:** Automatically links all the incoming and outgoing e-mail messages to/from this contact so that you have a record of all the incoming and outgoing e-mail messages to the business contact.

- ✔ **Business Card:** Customize the data displayed in the electronic business card in the General window.

- ✔ **Picture:** Links the contact's picture to his business contact record and to the electronic business card.

- ✔ **Categorize:** Assigns the contact to one or more categories so you can keep track of groups of contacts. Chapter 6 tells you everything you need to know — and more — about categories.

- ✔ **Follow Up:** Set a follow-up for a contact so that your contact doesn't become buried in a mountain of other contacts. Chapter 9 tells you more about scheduling follow-ups.

- ✔ **Address Book:** Allows you to navigate to one of the other address books contained in Outlook. You can check to see if a person's contact information already exists in another address book, or you can open a second contact record, copy information from a specific field, and paste it into the new business contact record.

- ✔ **Check Names:** Checks the entry of the business contact's e-mail addresses to make sure that you've used correct e-mail formatting.

Tabbing your way to more features

Besides the tabs on the Business Contact part of the Ribbon, two more tabs are at the top of the Business Contact window:

- ✔ **Format Text:** Transforms the Ribbon into a formatting toolbar that allows you to change the attributes (font type, font size, bold) for selected text. You can also copy and paste information from one field to another.

  If the formatting options are grayed out, you can't make any changes to the formatting.

✔ **Add-Ins:** This tab is populated with add-in software that links to BCM and Outlook. Don't be worried if your bar is blank — you won't have any add-ins unless you have purchased and installed them.

Clicking a few more options

If you're one of those people who is mesmerized by gadgets, then, by golly, you're going to absolutely love BCM. It comes equipped with a whole lot of bells and whistles. You'll find another batch of buttons on the Quick Access toolbar located at the very top of the Business Contact window:

✔ **Office Button:** This button, cleverly attired in the Office logo, allows you to do all kinds of fun things, including moving a Contact to another folder. You'll find that most of the other fun tasks are also found in other places on the Business Contact window.

✔ **Save:** Saves any changes you've made to the business contact without closing the record.

✔ **Undo:** Undoes the very last change you made to the business contact.

If you make lots of changes and want to undo them all, you need to close the record by clicking the X in the top-right corner of the screen and clicking No when asked if you want to save your changes.

✔ **Repeat:** Repeats the last thing you typed — which is useful if you want to use the same information in a number of fields.

✔ **Print:** Sends the 411 — as the kids say — of the Business Contact record to your printer.

✔ **Previous:** Takes you to the previous business contact, as listed alphabetically by last name.

✔ **Next:** Takes you to the next business contact, as listed alphabetically by last name.

Chapter 5

Setting Up Your Business Accounts

· ·

In This Chapter

▶ Adding an account record

▶ Making changes to an account record

▶ Knowing what you can do with an account record

· ·

*A*n account is, quite simply, a group of business contacts that all hang out together at the same water cooler. In this chapter, you find out how to create an account record, as well as how to modify or delete it should the need arise. You also find out about some of the cool things you can do with an account.

This chapter deals with entering account records manually instead of importing them in bulk — flip to Chapter 3 for more information about importing account records en masse.

Getting the 411 on Accounts

Face it: Bureaucracy is alive and well and living in most civilized countries. Actually, it probably lives in uncivilized ones as well. Your important-work-stuff database might contain the names of the head guy (also know as The Decision Maker), the lady you get in touch with the most, the guy who signs the checks, and the person who actually does all the work (the Administrative Assistant). Seems easy at first until the head guy gets fired, the check signer takes off for Brazil — and new people replace both of them.

You might think of an account as a company or a "super" business contact. Most companies do business with other companies or *accounts,* as opposed to with individuals or, in the case of BCM, business contacts. If you deal with really large companies (generally those that have their own cafeteria and a lot of cubicles), you probably deal with numerous business contacts as well. All of these business contacts can be linked to an account.

In Business Contact Manager you can

- ✔ Create an account and add new contacts to it.
- ✔ Create a business contact and add a new account to it.
- ✔ Link an account to existing business contact records.
- ✔ Link a business contact to an existing account record.

BCM comes configured, out of the box, with more than 50 fields for data for every account record. You can add more fields if you'd like to; check out Chapter 7 to find out how.

Another huge benefit of using accounts is that you can link them to Microsoft's Office Accounting software.

You might be tempted to create either a business contact or an account record for every new person you meet. If you're using accounts, you're much better off entering both the account and first business contact record at the same time. Creating them on the fly is easier than having to hunt each contact down and link it to an account later.

Entering the Account

You can get the account creation process going in a variety of ways:

- ✔ Choose File⇨New⇨Account from the Outlook menu bar.
- ✔ Choose Business Contact Manager⇨Accounts⇨New from the Outlook menu bar.
- ✔ Click the Accounts folder in the Folder List and then click the New button on the Outlook toolbar.

Any of these methods lead to Rome, and the Account window opens, as shown in Figure 5-1.

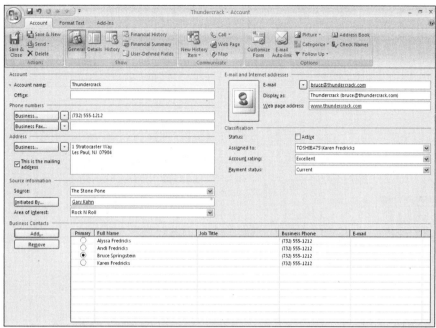

Figure 5-1:
Account
window.

These fields make up the Account window:

- ✔ **Account:** Enter the name of the organization in the Account Name field. This field is the only one you must fill in. You can designate different locations or divisions within the company in the Office field.

- ✔ **Phone Numbers and Address:** Enter a phone number and address in the corresponding fields. To add a second (or third) phone number or address, click the drop-down arrow.

- ✔ **Source Information:** Click the Initiated By button and you get the Select a Campaign, Business Contact, Opportunity, or Project dialog box. (See Figure 5-2.) Select an item from the list, click Link To, and then click OK so that you can track where all your business comes from. You can also create a new account, business contact, or marketing campaign by clicking the New button.

- ✔ **Business Contacts:** Link to a new or existing business contact. Simply click the Add button and the Select the Business Contacts to Link to the Account dialog box opens. Select the name of the business contact that you want to associate with this account and click OK. If you hold down the Ctrl key while selecting those critters, you can associate multiple business contacts to the account at the same time.

Figure 5-2:
Selecting an
Initiated By
source.

Can't find the business contact that you're trying to associate with the account? Click the New button in the Select the Business Contacts to Link to the Account dialog box. BCM presents you with a brand-new Business Contact window and the keys to the city. See Chapter 4 to find out how to fill in the Business Contact window.

✔ **E-Mail and Internet Addresses:** Enter an e-mail address. You can add a second or third one by clicking the drop-down arrow. (You can see only one at a time, though.) Enter a Web address for the company in the Web Page Address field.

✔ **Categories:** Assign a category (or two or three) to an account and it appears at the top of the Account window. Chapter 6 shows you everything you've ever wanted to know about categories — and then some!

Creating an Account from an Existing Business Contact

We ponder the age-old question: What comes first, the account or the business contact? Okay, maybe that's not an age-old question, but it's one that we can attempt to answer. In the previous section, we show you how to create an account first. In this section, we show you how to create a new account from an existing business contact. After that, you're going to pull a rabbit out of a hat — but we're jumping ahead of ourselves.

To create a new account from an existing business contact, follow these steps:

1. **Open a business contact record.**

   Not sure how to do it? Turn to Chapter 4.

2. **Click the Account button in the Company Name or Linked Account area.**

   A list of all your existing accounts appears in the Select an Account to Link to This Business Contact dialog box.

3. **Click the New button.**

   The Account window opens (refer to Figure 5-1). The window is already partially filled with information from the Business Contact window.

4. **Continue filling in additional account information.**

   See the previous section if you need help filling in the fields.

5. **Click Save & Close in the Actions group on the Ribbon when you finish.**

Doing Your Account Housekeeping

When you have a few accounts under your BCM belt, they need a bit of care and feeding — or maybe some editing and deleting. That might seem painfully easy to you, but we want to make sure you know what to do if a company moves to Podunk Junction or decides to permanently shut its doors. You might even be up late worrying that you might have entered an account twice into your database by accident. Go back to sleep — BCM has your back (or another piece of your anatomy) covered!

Editing an existing account

Changing data in an account record is simple. Follow these steps:

1. **Choose Accounts from the Folder List.**

2. **Double-click the account record that you want to change.**

The Account window opens. (Refer to Figure 5-1.)

3. **Make any necessary changes.**

   You can delete information by pressing the Delete or Backspace key, or fill in new information for fields that you had originally left empty.

4. **Click Save & Close in the Actions group on the Ribbon to save your changes.**

   If you decide you don't want to save the changes, press the Esc key or click the Close button in the upper-right corner; when asked if you want to save changes, click the No button.

Deleting an account record

Every so often, you need to say bye-bye to some of your accounts. They don't make the grade, or you didn't make the sale, and you don't need them cluttering up your life or database. So, *adios muchacho!*

The procedure for deleting an account is really easy. From any account view, you can do one of the following procedures:

- ✔ Right-click the record and choose Delete. So long!
- ✔ Double-click the record to open the Account window and click the Delete button in the Actions area on the Ribbon. *Au revoir!*
- ✔ Highlight the account record and press Ctrl+D. Farewell!
- ✔ Highlight the account record and choose Edit➪Delete from the Outlook menu bar. See ya!

BCM doesn't believe in long good-byes, so don't expect a reminder that asks if you really, truly, want to get rid of your account. Deleted accounts are placed immediately in the Deleted Items folder. You can undelete any account by dragging it from the Deleted Items folder back to the Accounts folder. Whew!

Resolving duplicates

Duplicates are a very confusing — and annoying — part of a database. BCM considers two accounts to be duplicates if they have the same account name or e-mail address. Any new, duplicate account you try to add triggers a warning message that tells you the new account you're trying to add is a duplicate.

You have a choice of either adding the account anyway or opening the existing account and updating the old information with the new information.

Adding More Details in the Account Window

A BCM account record has more than just a pretty face. The Ribbon, which runs along the top of every account record, provides lots of additional accounting power. On the Account tab, three of the Ribbon groups — Actions, Communicate, and Options — are identical to what you find on a business contact record; check out Chapter 4 to find out what these areas are about. In this section, we focus on the Ribbon groups that are specific to an account record.

The Show group of the Ribbon (on the Account tab) hides a lot of database treasures. Four buttons are specific to an account record:

- **Details:** This button, shown in Figure 5-3, opens a window that contains fields of data that are more corporate in nature:

    - The *Company Profile* section includes fields for an account number, ticker symbol, and number of employees.

    - The *Communication* section allows you to specify the best way to keep in contact with this account.

    - The *Comments* section is a place where you can keep notes about your calls, negotiations, and interactions with the account. It's really one field of data, but you can make it look like multiple notes by clicking the Add Time Stamp button to enter the exact date and time of each new comment.

- **Financial History:** This button, shown in Figure 5-4, opens a window that shows you all the financial transactions related to the account contained in Microsoft Office Accounting — if you have BCM linked to it. You see invoices, payments, orders, quotes, checks, and other transactions that belong to this account. You can sort the columns in this table by clicking their corresponding column headers. You can double-click an item, and it opens in its appropriate Office Accounting window.

- **Financial Summary:** This button, shown in Figure 5-5, opens a window that gives you a live snapshot of the account's financial picture, including details about current balances, terms, month-to-date and year-to-date sales, and credit rating.

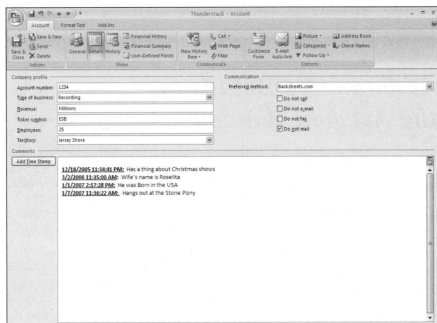

Figure 5-3:
The
Account
Details
window.

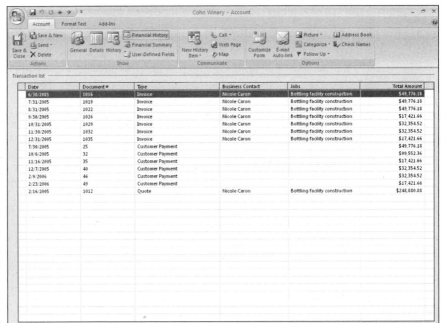

Figure 5-4:
Account
Financial
History
window.

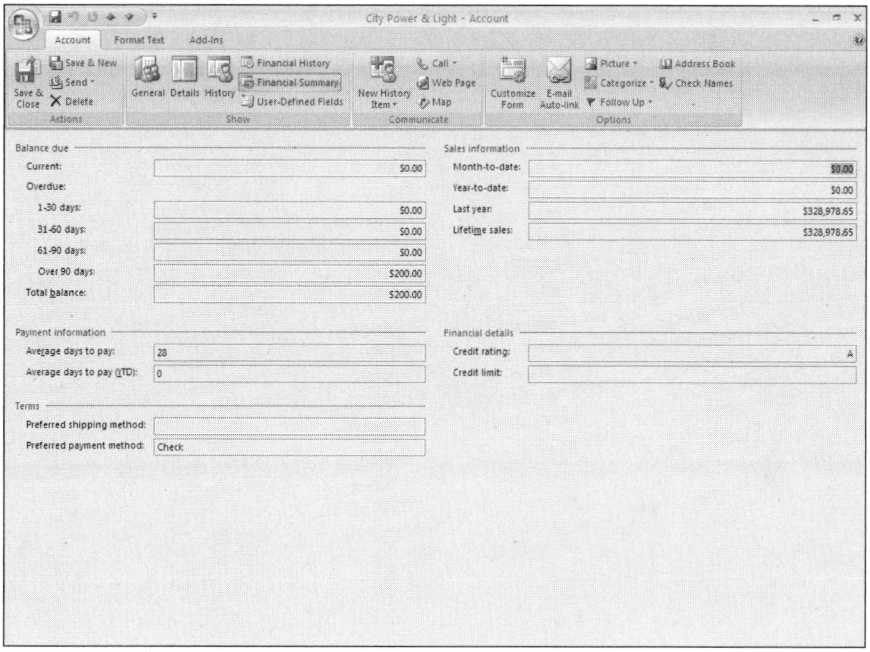

Figure 5-5:
The
Account
Financial
Summary
window.

You can't modify the data in either the Financial History or Financial Summary window because the information comes directly from Microsoft Office Accounting. And, as of this writing, BCM can link only to Office Accounting. However, don't be surprised if add-on products soon appear that will link BCM to other accounting software, such as QuickBooks and Peachtree.

✓ **User-Defined Fields:** This button opens a window where you can add a few more fields specific to your accounts. You can find out more about these custom fields in Chapter 7.

Chapter 6

Color Your World with Categories

In This Chapter
▶ Discovering the power of categories
▶ Creating and editing categories
▶ Working with categories

Categories are a pervasive part of BCM. Categories span the different data types (contacts, accounts, opportunities, projects, tasks, and appointments) and are easily assignable from the Ribbon. Items can belong to multiple categories and show up in your lists and views in multiple places. In this chapter, we explain why categories are so powerful and show you how to create new categories (or edit existing ones) and assign them to your BCM records.

Understanding the Power of Categories

Most of you rely on paper folders to keep yourself organized. And you probably create catchy labels such as Taxes and Insurance to help sort all of your stuff. Occasionally, however, you run into an overlap. For example, you might wonder if your car insurance paperwork belongs in the Car folder or Insurance folder.

In Outlook and BCM, unlike in the paper folder example, items can belong to multiple categories and show up in your lists and views in multiple places. If you diligently assign categories to your data, you can find, sort, and filter your information quickly and easily. This, in turn, means that you work more efficiently, which means you'll have more time for the fun stuff in life.

You might want to start by separating your contacts into designations such as Friend, Enemy, Customer, Vendor, and Really Important Guy. You might then start to organize the rest of your BCM records along the same line so that you can easily find all your vendor accounts, projects, and histories.

Categories are also a great way to see all the elements that make up a project. For instance, maybe you're in charge of your company's spring golf outing. You can create a Spring Outing category and assign to that category all the contacts you're inviting, all the tasks you create on your task list, and all the associated appointments. In one place, you can see everything that pertains to your Spring Outing just by using a category.

Officially, categories are named *color categories* because each category has a color associated with it. There are many colors to choose from when you create the category, so you can coordinate your categories to your office décor, if you so desire. You can also define a quick-click color/name so that when you click the category icon in a task list or contact list column, it automatically assigns that category to that item.

Figure 6-1 shows how accounts look when they're sorted by category. Because this is a black-and-white book, you'll just have to imagine the colors.

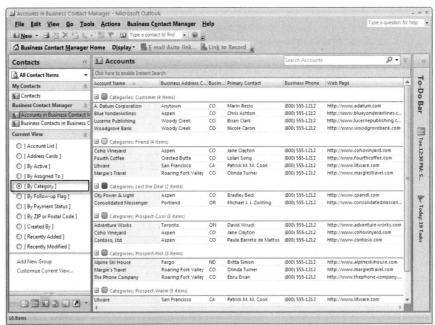

Figure 6-1:
Accounts
displayed by
category.

Creating and Defining Categories

Defining categories isn't as complicated as naming stars or chromosomes, but you probably want to give it a bit of thought before blindly jumping in to create your categories. If you're trying to track prospects through the sales process, it might be best at first to have categories such as Lead, Prospect, Customer, and Lost the Deal. You can use a Source field (see Chapter 4) in the contact record to track where the lead came from, instead of naming the categories Lead-Trade Show, Lead-Website, and Lead-ColdCall.

Don't try to get terribly detailed on the first try. Start with fewer categories, use them with all your data (contacts, accounts, tasks, appointments, and so on), and see how they work for you. You can always get more detailed later, but it's important not to feel overwhelmed initially.

Adding a new category

As you begin to set up BCM for your specific needs, you want to create your very own master category list. Here's all you need to do:

1. **From any BCM item, choose Edit⇨Categorize⇨All Categories from the Outlook menu bar.**

   If you're so inclined, you have two alternative ways of getting there:

   • From any Ribbon, choose Categorize⇨All Categories.

   • Right-click any category icon/color in any list where they're displayed and then choose Categorize⇨All Categories.

   The Color Categories dialog box opens, as shown in Figure 6-2.

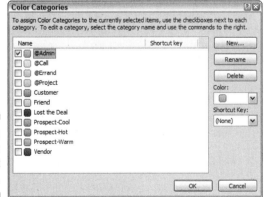

Figure 6-2: Assign or edit categories.

2. Click the New button.

The Add New Category dialog box opens. (See Figure 6-3.)

Figure 6-3:
The Add
New
Category
dialog box.

3. Type the name for your new category.

4. Choose the color and a shortcut key for your new category from the appropriate drop-down lists.

5. Click OK to close the Add New Category dialog box.

You can have as many categories as you like, but you can't have subcategories. However, you can create the same effect by naming them something like this:

- Customer-Platinum
- Customer-Gold
- Customer-Silver

This allows you to see all the customers in one view and break them out into subsets in another view.

You can use your categories to categorize all aspects of your BCM life, from contacts and accounts to projects and activities. But be careful your category list doesn't veer out of control if you mix Errands and Projects with Employees and Prospects. David Allen, renowned time management expert, solves this problem through the use of a few well-placed symbols. He advocates using category names like @Call, @Errand, or @Project for time-related categories so that those items appear together at the top of your category list. The @ sign makes these items rise to the top of the category list. We can also recommend that you use similar symbols, such as *, >, #, &, but then you might think we're swearing at you.

Renaming an existing category

Changes are an inevitable part of life, and eventually you'll want to change your categories. Perhaps the name of that air conditioning part has changed, or maybe you inadvertently misspelled one of your categories. Whatever the reason, you can edit your categories in these four easy steps:

1. **Choose Edit⇨Categorize⇨All Categories from the Outlook menu bar.**

   The Color Categories dialog box opens. (Refer to Figure 6-2.)

2. **Select the category you want to edit and then click the Rename button.**

   Your cursor jumps over to the existing category name. If you look really closely, you'll notice that the name is now highlighted.

3. **Type the new category name.**

   While you have the category highlighted, you can also change its color or shortcut key by changing those options on the right side of the dialog box. Use the Color and the Shortcut Key drop-down lists to do that.

4. **Click OK to save your changes.**

Deleting a category

Easy come, easy go. You might want to perform a bit of spring cleaning by deleting a few unused categories. Maybe you no longer need to track air conditioning parts, or maybe you no longer want to keep the names of your friends in BCM. Rest assured that deleting a category doesn't delete the items associated with that category; those items remain.

Follow these steps to delete an unwanted category:

1. **Choose Edit⇨Categorize⇨All Categories from the Outlook menu bar.**

   The Color Categories dialog box opens. (Refer to Figure 6-2.)

2. **Click the category you wish to delete in the Color Categories dialog box.**

3. **Click the Delete button.**

   You're asked to confirm that it's what you really want to do. Feel free to click the Cancel button if you change your mind.

4. **Click OK, and the category is deleted from your list.**

Don't worry about accidentally deleting a category; all the items retain the category assignment. You just won't be able to add any new items to that deleted category. Sound confusing? Categories that have been deleted but are still being used by the item are shown with a (Not in Master Category List) marker. (See Figure 6-4.)

Figure 6-4:
Viewing
an item's
categories
when the
categories
were
removed
from the
master list.

Assigning and Unassigning Items to Categories

After you've created a category, you can put it to use. You can virtually categorize every aspect of your BCM life, including tasks, accounts, opportunities, appointments, and projects. Best of all, you'll find that you use the same method in all cases.

Assigning a category to an item

Here's how to assign a category to a contact:

1. **Right-click the item you wish to categorize.**

   We racked our brains trying to come up with a harder set of instructions, but we just couldn't do it. If you see an account card, right-click it. Looking at a list of contacts? Go ahead; give it a right-click. Wondering how to categorize your tasks? A right-click of any task does the trick quite nicely.

2. **Choose Categorize from the menu.**

   A list of your categories appears.

3. **Select your category.**

   If you're the type of person who requires a lot of reinforcement from your software, you might be a bit disappointed because the item is assigned to that category instantly. If you want to add another category to the same item, simply right-click the item again and choose another category. You can repeat these steps to assign as many categories as you want to the item.

If you want to assign a whole lot of categories to an item, you might want to choose the All Categories item that appears on the bottom of the category list.

Select the various categories you want and then click OK to save your choices.

Unassigning a category from an item

Don't you just hate it when you click the wrong thing? Fortunately, BCM is very forgiving. And very easy, because you follow nearly the same steps to unassign a category as you use to assign the category in the first place. Follow these steps to unassign a category:

1. **Right-click the item for which you'd like to change the categories.**

2. **Choose Categorize from the menu.**

3. **Select any categories that you no longer want to associate with the item.**

   The good news is that the process you use to remove a category is nearly identical to the process for adding a category. The bad news is that you might have trouble determining which categories were selected in the first place. If you look very carefully — and we mean *very carefully* — you'll see a faint orange outline around the color box of each selected category. Clicking the category deselects it.

   If you're having trouble deciphering which categories are selected — or not selected — select All Categories at the bottom of the Category list. The Color Categories dialog box (refer to Figure 6-4) opens, allowing you deselect categories.

Assigning a category to a new item

The techniques we've discussed so far all make the assumption that you're assigning a category to a previously created item. However, you can add a category to an item as you're creating it — provided, of course, that you've already created the category. Follow these steps:

1. Create a new item.

In Figure 6-5, we're creating a task.

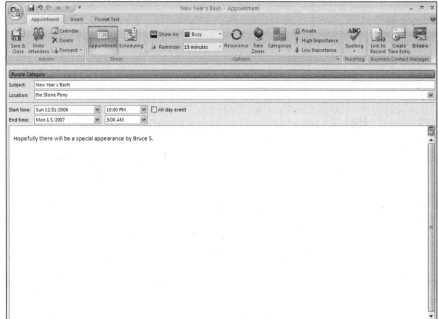

Figure 6-5:
Adding a
category to
a new item.

2. Click Categorize in the Options group on the Ribbon.

3. Click the category you wish to associate with the item.

You can also apply this method when editing existing items. While in any view, double-click an item to open it. Not only do you have all the editing choices available for that item, you can also assign and unassign categories.

Chapter 7

Creating Customized BCM Fields

● ●

● ●

*Y*ou might find yourself humming a few bars from an old hamburger commercial throughout this chapter because here's where you can determine exactly what you want to see and how you want to see it. Not happy
with the fields that come right out of the BCM box? Want to reorganize which
tab holds a field? You've come to the right chapter. You also find out how to
attach drop-down lists to your fields. And if that's not enough to keep you
busy, you find out how to change your view on life — or at least the various
views you use to see your data.

Planning Your Custom Fields

In BCM, you can create new fields for business contacts, accounts, opportunities, or business projects and add them to a tab. You can also choose the
column location where the groups and fields are displayed on the User-
Defined Fields tab. After you create them, you can edit, move, or remove your
custom fields.

A little knowledge is a dangerous thing. Although adding a field to your BCM
database is not a hard thing to do, it is something that you should think
about and plan. This is particularly true if you intend to share your database
with other users. Planning is important because it will help you achieve your
goals. If your goal is to create a customized report with three columns — one
for the contact name, one for the birthday, and one for the Social Security

number — you need to make sure that all those fields exist in your database. Planning also prevents you from adding thousands of contacts to your database, only to find you have to modify each record to include information that was omitted the first time around!

These three steps are involved with adding fields to a database:

1. **Understand why you want to add fields and what purpose these fields will serve.**

2. **Determine what fields you need to add and what drop-down lists, if any, you want available in each.**

   We can't stress enough the importance of this step. Plan ahead! Or you might end up with a big mess. . . .

3. **Add the fields.**

   And, *voilà!* You're done. (Okay, this one has a whole bunch of steps, but you get what we mean.)

For most of you, adding a field to your database will be easy. After all, you're good at following directions. However, for some of you, knowing *why* to add a field can prove to be more challenging.

To explore the question of why, we first want to reiterate the basic concept of fields. What the heck is a field? A *field* is a single piece of information. In general, a field contains just one piece of information. For example, you have only one business zip code; therefore, you have one Business Zip/Postal Code field. Alternatively, you probably have at least six phone numbers: home, business, toll-free, cellular, fax, beeper, and the list goes on. Each of these phone numbers requires a separate field.

A good field holds one fairly specific piece of information. A bad field contains too much information. For example, having separate fields for your street address, city, state, and zip code is a good thing. These separate fields allow you to perform a query based on any of the criteria: You can find clients by zip code, city, or state. An example of a bad field is one that lumps all the address information into a single field; you then lose your ability to perform a query by zip code, city, or state. (Not sure about how a query works? Head to Chapter 17.)

You might want to consider the following basic rules when determining the criteria for adding a field to your database:

- ✔ A field contains an important tidbit of information.

- ✔ You can perform a query or sort on a field. For example, you might want to send a mailing to all your customers in New York and sort your mailing by zip code. To do this sort, you need separate fields for category, state, *and* zip code.

✔ You can insert information from a field into a report or template. For example, if you want to create thank-you letters to customers, you can thank one person for buying a purple polka-dotted vase and another for buying a leopard-print vase. To do that, you add a Vase Type field.

✔ BCM allows you to use a field name only one time, no matter where that field is located in your database. You can, however, use the same user-defined field for account, business contact, opportunity, or business project records.

Before jumping in and adding new fields to your database, follow these steps to determine which fields your database needs:

1. **Jot down all the fields that you want to see in your database.**

   Most of the fields you want to see, such as Company, Name, Phone Number, and Address, are already included in BCM. What you need to decide here is what fields, if any, are specific to your business.

2. **Scurry around the office and collect any documents that you want BCM to create for you. Highlight any information in each document that is contact specific.**

   For example, each contact has its own unique address. Maybe you're thanking particular contacts for meeting to discuss purchasing widgets (as opposed to gadgets, which you also sell). This means that you need a Product field.

   Collect both forms and form letters for this step.

3. **Think of how to populate the fields with drop-down lists. Then on the list that you started in Step 1, jot down your proposed drop-down choices to the side of each of the fields.**

   For example, if you run a modeling agency, you might need a field for hair color. The drop-down choices could contain Red, Blonde, Black, and Punk Pink.

4. **Sketch out any reports that you want to create from BCM, and add the column headings to the now rather-long list that you created in Step 1.**

   The idea here is to get your thoughts down on paper so that you can visualize what you want your BCM report to look like. If you already have a sample of your report in Excel, you can use that. If not, get out your trusty pencil and outline what you'd like your report to actually look like on a piece of paper.

5. **Get out a red pen, and at the top of your paper, write 100%, Well Done, and draw a smiley face. Hang your list on your refrigerator.**

   Okay, that last step isn't really necessary, but now you're well on your way to having the database of your dreams!

Dust off your thinking cap as you create your list. Sometimes, one field does the job, and other times you might need multiple fields. For example, say you sell red, white, and blue widgets. In one scenario, a customer would need to buy only one of the widgets; in this case you'd create a Product field with three choices in the drop-down list — Red, White, and Blue. Perhaps you manufacture three different kinds of widgets; in this case, a customer would (hopefully) buy one of each color. This time, your purposes would be better served by creating three separate fields — one for each type of widget.

Adding a New Field to Your Database

Believe it or not, after planning your fields (see the preceding section), you're done with the hard part of the task. The actual addition of fields is relatively easy, although quite a few steps are involved. Take a deep breath, relax your shoulders, and just follow these steps:

1. **From the Outlook menu bar, choose Business Contact Manager⇨ Customize Forms⇨Manage User-Defined Fields.**

   Wow. Although that's a rather simple step, it sure contains a mouthful of words. Take a breather before going on to the next step.

   Alternatively, you can open an account, business contact, opportunity, or business project record and click Customize Form in the Options group of the Ribbon.

2. **Choose Account, Business Contact, Opportunity, or Business Project.**

   You create new fields for all four options in exactly the same way. As you create the new field it will be added to the corresponding form.

   The appropriate dialog box — whether for account, business contact, opportunity, or business project — opens. We chose to add a new field for an account; Figure 7-1 shows the Account – Manage User-Defined Fields dialog box.

   You'll notice that the Manage User-Defined Fields dialog box is divided into Left and Right Columns. That's because the User Defined tab of your business contact, contact, opportunity, or business project record contains two columns. New fields and groups that you add appear in the Left Column. However, you can move any of those items to the Right Column so that your tab is more balanced.

3. **Choose the page to which you'd like to add the new fields from the Page drop-down list.**

   You have four to choose from: User-Defined Fields, General, Details, and Communication History. These pages correspond to the tabs that you see in an account, business contact, opportunity, or business project record. Interestingly enough, those same choices appear whether you're adding Account, Business Contact, Opportunity, or Business Project fields.

Figure 7-1:
Adding
custom
Account
fields.

4. **Click the Add Group button.**

   Fields are grouped into areas of interest. That's what you're creating here. If you refer to Figure 7-1, you can see an example of two groups of fields.

   The Add a Group dialog box opens. (See Figure 7-2.)

Figure 7-2:
Adding a
new group
of custom
fields.

5. **Fill in the Group Name field and click OK.**

   Your newly created group will appear in the Left Column, which is located on the left side of the Manage User-Defined Fields dialog box.

   If you skip this step and add a field without first adding a new group, BCM automatically creates a new group for you and gives it a name of New Group 1. Don't worry — if you come up with a better name later, you can always rename it.

6. **(Optional) Add more groups.**

Go for it. Here's your golden opportunity to keep yourself organized. Decide how to organize your fields and create a group for each category of fields.

7. **Select the group that you want to house your new fields.**

8. **Click the Add Field button.**

   The Add a Field dialog box opens. (See Figure 7-3.)

9. **Enter the name of the new field in the Field Name box.**

   If you happen to give the field a name that's already in use, BCM gently reminds you that the field name is already being used and that you need to come up with a better handle.

10. **Choose a data type from the Data Type drop-down list.**

    You have a choice of eight options, including Number, Currency, Date/Time, and Drop-Down List. If you pick some of the selections, you're prompted for a bit more information. For example, if you select Drop-Down List, BCM asks you to supply the drop-down list items. You can find out how to add new items to the drop-down list in the "Working with Drop-Down Lists" section, later in this chapter.

11. **Choose a format from the Format drop-down list.**

    You have a variety of options here that depend on the data type that you selected. If you chose Date/Time in Step 10, you can now select the date format that you'd like to use. If you chose Number in Step 10, you can decide how you want to deal with everything from commas and decimal points to negative numbers.

12. **Click OK when you finish adding the new field.**

13. **(Optional) Reorganize the fields.**

    One of the things you'll grow to love about BCM is the fact that very few things are set in stone. Here's a great example of that. Select a field and use the buttons provided to modify any of the fields that you just created:

    • *Edit:* Don't like the name you chose? Here's your chance to change it.

    • *Delete:* Easy come, even easier go.

• *Move To:* In case you change your mind — after all, this is *your* database — you can move your new fields to one of the other tabs in the Move to Tab dialog box, as shown in Figure 7-4.

Figure 7-4:
Moving the
new fields
to a
different
tab.

• *Move Up/Move Down:* You might want to play around with these buttons even if you really don't have an overwhelming desire to place a field higher or lower on the tab.

• *Double left-pointing/Double right-pointing arrows:* If you see a group of fields in the Left Column that looks enticing, click the double-pointing right arrows to move your fields to the right column. If you want to move a field to the left side of the tab, select the field from the Right Column and select the double left-pointing arrows to move it.

14. (Optional) Reorganize the groups.

As you add more and more fields and groups, you might become a bit unhappy with the way your tab is shaping up. You might have too many fields on one side or the other. There are a number of ways to redecorate a tab. Luckily, none of them require heavy lifting of any kind. You edit or delete a group using the same method you use for editing or deleting fields. The fun part comes when you move a group up or down because all the fields contained within that group move right along with it. Is the tab looking a bit lopsided? No *problemo* — simply move a group to the left or right; again, all the associated fields move right along with it.

15. Click OK when you finish adding new fields and groups.

Your computer whirrs and hisses for a moment, and you're treated to the progress indicator and then a message telling you that you won't see your changes until you open up one of your records. Duh!

Recycling Your New Fields

Suppose that sometimes you deal with business contacts rather than accounts and want to have some of those same fields showing on the records of your business contacts. You can't create those field names, but you can *recycle* them. Here's all you need to do:

1. **Choose Business Contact Manager⇨Customize Forms⇨Manage User-Defined Fields from the Outlook menu bar.**

2. **Choose the type of record you want to customize.**

   If you had previously added fields to the accounts record, you can choose Business Contact.

   The appropriate Manage User-Defined Fields dialog box opens. (Refer to Figure 7-1.)

3. **Click the Add Field button.**

   The Add a Field dialog box opens.

4. **Select the Add Field from a Different Entity Type radio button.**

   Holy guacamole! You see all those fields that you worked so hard to create sitting right there in front of you. (See Figure 7-5.)

Figure 7-5:
Reusing
newly
created
fields.

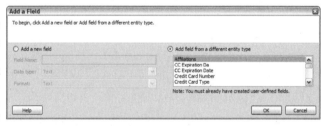

5. **Select the field of your choice and then click OK.**

   The recycled field now appears in the Manage User-Defined Fields dialog box. Click the Add Field or Add Group button to start adding a few more of the fields.

   You can't *recycle* groups so you have to create the group areas over again from scratch.

6. **Click OK when you finish.**

   Wait for the smoke to stop rising from the back of your computer, open a business contact record, and *voila!* — you're the proud owner of a lot of new fields. You might want to make sure that your boss hears a bunch of grunts and groans emanating from your office — just make sure that you hide your magazine and look like you're working if he stops to check in on you.

Working with Drop-Down Lists

The sure-fire way to destroy a database is by adding information in an inconsistent manner. Drop-down lists help ensure that users input data in a uniform way. As an extra bonus, drop-down lists also save you time; when you type the first several letters of an item in your drop-down list, BCM responds by completing the word for you.

BCM has several list types. Chapter 6 tells you everything you need to know — and then some — about the importance of BCM categories. Chapter 12 shows you how to build a bigger and better Product and Service Items list. The other list type — the drop-down list — is associated with your account, business contact, opportunity, and business project fields. Although you can add new items to a list as you're using it, managing your lists in one central location is easier.

BCM contains several fields that consist of drop-down lists. In addition, you can create new, user-defined fields and designate them as drop-down fields. For example, you might want to add the Affiliation field to include a list of the organizations with which your contacts might be associated.

So sharpen your typing fingers and follow these steps:

1. **Choose Business Contact Manager➪Customize Forms➪Edit Lists.**

   The Edit Lists dialog box opens.

2. **Click the Selected List drop-down list to select the field to which you want to add new drop-down items.**

   The drop-down fields that you can select from indicate which record type (account, business contact, opportunity, or business project) they're associated with. (See Figure 7-6.) The word *(shared)* after an item indicates that the item is used by more than one record type.

3. **Click the Add button.**

   The Add a Value dialog box, shown in Figure 7-7, careens open.

4. **Add a new value to the drop-down list and click OK.**

   You once again land in the Edit Lists dialog box.

Figure 7-6:
Selecting a
drop-down
list field.

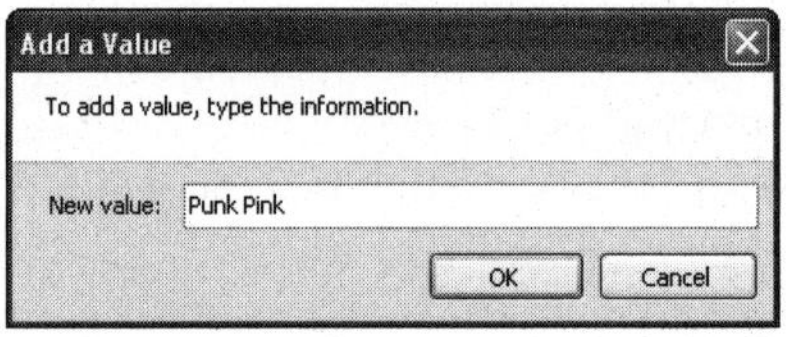

Figure 7-7:
Adding
values to
the drop-
down lists.

5. **(Optional) Select a drop-down value and choose from the following options:**

   • *Rename:* Make a change to an existing value.

   • *Delete or Replace:* Delete an entry or replace it with another existing drop-down item in the Delete or Replace a Value dialog box.

   • *Move Up/Down:* Unlike some programs, your drop-down list doesn't have to be in alphabetical order. Feel free to move the drop-down list items up or down to put them in order of importance.

   • *Make Default:* Set an item as the default value if you use that specific drop-down value the majority of the time.

6. **Click OK to save your options and close the Edit Lists dialog box.**

Customizing Your Dashboards

One of the coolest new features of BCM is the addition of the dashboard. Quite simply, a *dashboard* is a graphic that gives you a visual snapshot of a part of your business. Some of the dashboards come in the form of a neat chart; others come in the form of a list.

The dashboards are on the Business Contact Manager Home page. You can divide your dashboards across four tabs: Home, Sales, Marketing, and Projects. The fun part is that you can decide which dashboard you want to stick on any given tab.

Here's how you add a dashboard to the Home tab:

1. **Click Business Contact Manager Home on the BCM toolbar.**

2. **Click the Home tab.**

3. **Click Add or Remove Content.**

   The Add or Remove Content dialog box, shown in Figure 7-8, opens.

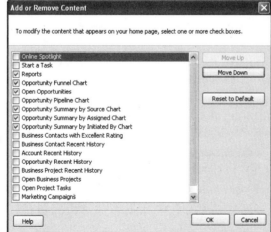

Figure 7-8:
Adding
dashboards
to the BCM
home page.

Dashboards come in a variety of flavors — 17 to be exact. The object of the game is to place the dashboards on the appropriate tab. It's perfectly legal to place a dashboard on more than one tab. Here's a run-down of the dashboards that might help you with your BCM decorating attempts:

- *Online Spotlight:* Features direct links to some sites on the Internet that might help you expand your business.

- *Start a Task:* Provides an alternative way to access your accounts, business contacts, opportunities, business projects, project tasks, and marketing campaigns rather than using the Folder List.

- *Reports:* Allows you to quickly display or print a report.

- *Business Contacts with Excellent Rating:* Shows the contacts that you rated as Excellent.

- *Business Leads:* Shows the contacts you marked as leads.

- *Business Contact Recent History* and *Account Recent History:* Show a list of the business contacts or accounts for whom you've recently created a note, phone log, task, or appointment.

- *Marketing Campaigns:* Lists all your current and planned marketing campaigns.

- *Open Business Projects:* Lists all your open projects.

- *Open Project Tasks:* Shows your project-related tasks that you still need to complete.

- *Business Project Recent History:* Shows all the recent project activities.

There are also a number of opportunity charts and lists, which we discuss in Chapter 12.

4. **Select the dashboards that you want to include on the Home tab of the Business Contact Manager Home page.**

   Although you can place any and all of the dashboards here, we recommend including basic information by including the Spotlight, Reports, Contact, and History dashboards.

5. **(Optional) Click the Move Up or Move Down button to change the order in which the dashboards will appear.**

6. **Click OK to save your changes.**

7. **Repeat Steps 2–6 for the Sales, Marketing, and Project tabs.**

   The dashboards that you select are purely a matter of personal taste. You might decide that some of the dashboards aren't important to you and not include them on any of the tabs. Alternatively, you might find the Reports and Start a Task dashboards to be so important that you include them at the top of every tab.

Figure 7-9 shows the Start a Task, Reports, and Opportunity Pipeline Chart dashboards on the Sales tab.

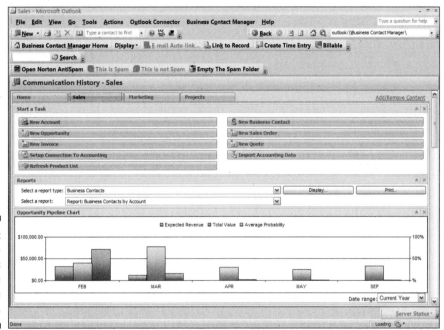

Figure 7-9:
A customized Sales tab on the BCM home page.

Part III
Organizing Your Day

The 5th Wave   By Rich Tennant

"The funny thing is he's spent 9 hours organizing his contacts in BCM."

In this part . . .

It's time to get your life in order. You can schedule an appointment and link it to one of your contacts or accounts. You'll find that a task list is a great way to keep track of all those pesky items that you have to get "around to." Although you can't change history, you can create some with one of the BCM history items. You might add some notes for good measure. (Sure beats the heck out of a yellow sticky note!)

Chapter 8

Managing Your Calendar

· ·

· ·

*I*n this chapter, we show you how to schedule activities with your contacts and how to view those activities and modify them. You find out how to link — and unlink — your activities to other important parts of BCM, including your accounts and business contacts. We also show you how to transform an existing Outlook activity into a more functional BCM appointment.

Scheduling an Appointment with Existing Records

One of the most useful features of BCM is its ability to tie an appointment to a record. More basic calendaring programs allow you to view your appointments on your calendar, but they don't offer a way of cross-referencing an appointment to a contact. For example, if you schedule an appointment with a contact and forget when that appointment is, you have to flip through your calendar until you see your contact's name. Plus, you can't easily see a list of all appointments that you've ever scheduled with that contact. But BCM offers these helpful features.

In BCM, every activity is scheduled with a specific record. You can schedule activities with the following record types:

✔ Account

✔ Business contact

✔ Business project

    ✔ Opportunity

You might wonder how to schedule an appointment with someone that doesn't exist in your database. For example, maybe you have a doctor's appointment or want to track your vacation days. You can still schedule appointments that are nonrecord related using the Outlook calendar. BCM and Outlook share the same calendar. When you view your calendar, both Outlook and BCM activities appear on it.

Here's what you do to add an activity related to a specific record to your busy schedule:

1. **Go to the record with which you're scheduling an activity.**

   You know the drill. Choose Accounts, Business Contacts, Business Project, or Opportunity from the Folder List. Once there, double-click the record you want to schedule a little time with.

2. **Click New History Item in the Communicate group of the Ribbon and choose Appointment.**

   The Appointment tab of the Appointment window opens, as shown in Figure 8-1.

Figure 8-1:
Scheduling an appointment.

3. **Fill in all the juicy details of your appointment.**

   BCM leaves nothing to chance and supplies you with several fields in which you can enter the appointment details, as follows:

   - **Subject:** Provide a brief synopsis of the appointment.

   - **Location:** List where the big event takes place.

     After you add a location, BCM automatically adds it to the Location drop-down list. The next time you have an appointment at the same location, you can choose it from the drop-down list.

   - **Start Time/End Time:** Enter start and end dates and times for the event. If you're dealing with people in other time zones, select a time zone as well.

   - **All Day Event:** Select this check box if the appointment is an all-day affair.

   - **Details:** Feel free to write a book about your event — or at least include a few details to jog your memory. You might want to include items that you need to bring to your appointment — brochures, price lists, aspirin.

4. **(Optional) Fill in the Ribbon options.**

   Just when you think that BCM has thought of everything you might find, BCM has a few more activity tricks up its sleeve — or at least up its Ribbon. Here's a description of the features you'll find there:

   - **Invite Attendees:** Sends e-mail invitations to notify others of the big event.

     Don't assume that the business contact with whom you're scheduling the appointment will automatically receive an e-mail notification — you'll have to include him as one of the attendees as well.

   - **Calendar:** Flips over to your calendar so that you can double-check your busy social schedule.

   - **Forward:** Sends a copy of your appointment to another one of your contacts.

   - **Scheduling:** Checks the calendars of the other users who're sharing your BCM database if you included them in your e-mail announcement.

   - **Show As:** Gives you the choices of Free, Tentative, Busy, and Out of Office so that other users of your database can check your schedule and know what you're up to.

   - **Alarm:** Sounds an alarm at the given interval prior to the big event; fire truck helmet is optional.

• **Recurrence:** Repeats the activity that you're scheduling on a regular basis. You can designate an appointment as repeating in the Appointment Recurrence dialog box, as shown in Figure 8-2.

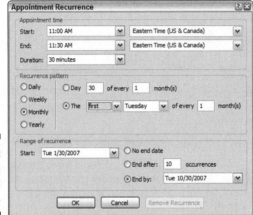

Figure 8-2:
Scheduling
a recurring
activity.

• **Time Zone:** Opens the Time Zone option if you're scheduling an appointment with someone in another time zone.

• **Categorize:** Assigns the appointment to one of your categories.

• **Link to Record:** Links the appointment to multiple accounts, business contacts, opportunities, and business projects.

• **Create Time Entry:** Creates a time entry in Office Accounting 2007 if you want to track an employee's time.

• **Billable:** Designates the activity as something that is going to cost one of your contacts some money.

If you haven't linked BCM to Office Accounting 2007, you won't see the Create Time Entry or Billable options on the Ribbon. Flip over to Chapter 13 to get the lowdown on how to connect the two products so that you can keep track of all that billable time.

5. **(Optional) Fill in additional details on the Insert and Format Text tabs.**

From the Insert tab, you can insert just about anything under the sun in the Details section of the appointment: a picture, document file, table, or hyperlink.

The Format Text tab lets you choose formatting options so that you can apply bold and underline, and use all sorts of font tricks to make the appointment stand out.

6. **Click Save & Close when you finish creating the appointment.**

Linking an Outlook Appointment to a Record

If you've been using Outlook's calendars prior to using BCM, you know Outlook appointments are not automatically linked to a Business Contact Manager account, business contact, opportunity, or business project record. But you can associate an Outlook appointment with a BCM record. The linking adds an entire new dimension to the appointment because you can now cross-reference it with the account, business contact, opportunity, or business project record.

To link an existing Outlook appointment to a BCM record, follow these steps:

1. **From the Outlook menu bar, choose Go⇨Calendar.**

2. **Double-click the appointment that you want to link to a record.**

   Outlook's Appointment window opens. If you feel like you've been here before, it's because it looks exactly like the Appointment window you used when scheduling an appointment directly from a BCM contact record.

3. **Click Link to Record in the Business Contact Manager group on the Ribbon.**

   The Link to Business Contact Manager Record dialog box opens, as shown in Figure 8-3.

4. **Select Accounts, Business Contacts, Opportunities, or Business Projects from the Folder drop-down list.**

5. **Type the name of the record you're looking for in the Search box or select the name from the record list.**

6. **Click the Link To button to add the account, business contact, opportunity, or business project record to the Linked Records box.**

   The name of all your linked contacts appears in the Linked Records dialog box.

   You can link multiple records to an appointment. This ensures that you can view the appointment from a variety of places.

7. **Click OK to close the Link to Business Contact Manager Record dialog box and then click Save & Close on the Ribbon to save the appointment.**

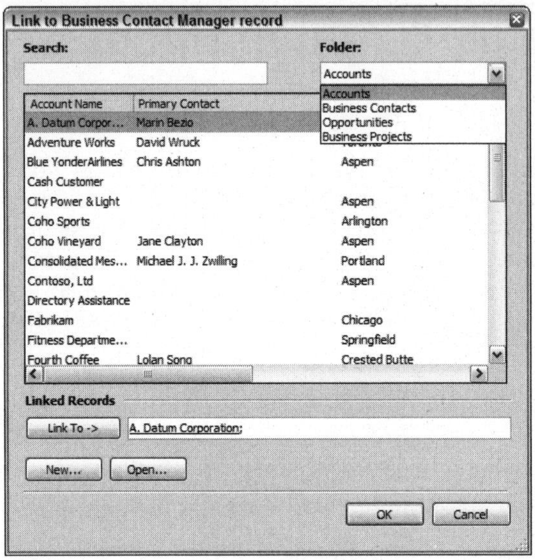

Figure 8-3:
Link an
Outlook
appointment
to BCM.

Making Changes to Your Appointments

After you create activities, BCM is a worse nag than your mother! You can see
your activities — and BCM reminds you about them — in a number of ways,
including the following:

- An **alarm**, if you ask BCM to ring the alarm when scheduling an activity

- The **communication history** portion of an account, business contact,
opportunity, and business project record

- The **communication history folder** in the Folder List

- All **Outlook calendars,** including the daily, weekly, and monthly views

- The **To-Do bar**, shown in Figure 8-4, which is located to the right of the
BCM Home window

Editing your activities

Like all the best-laid plans of mice and men, your activities change, and you
need a way to make note of these changes in BCM. If you can see an activity,
you can edit it. That means you can edit your activities from the Communication History folder, the Communication History tab, or from any of the
Outlook calendars. To edit an activity, all you have to do is double-click it or
right-click it and select Open.

Figure 8-4:
The BCM
To-Do bar.

Your appointment opens, and you can change or add to any of the information. (See the "Scheduling an Appointment with Existing Records" section
earlier in the chapter for details on the information your appointment can
contain.)

Resist the urge to simply change the date for rescheduled appointments.
Although you can easily change anything in an appointment, you might end up
losing some key information. Say, for instance, a particularly high-maintenance
customer stands you up four times — and then complains to your boss about
your lack of service. If you simply change the date of the original appointments,
you can't document the dates on which they were originally scheduled. Instead,
you consider changing some of the appointment details to reflect the no-show.
You might like to think of this as CYA technology!

Clearing an alarm

If you decide to set an alarm for an activity, eventually the alarm goes off.
Figure 8-5 shows the Reminder dialog box that pops up when the alarm
sounds.

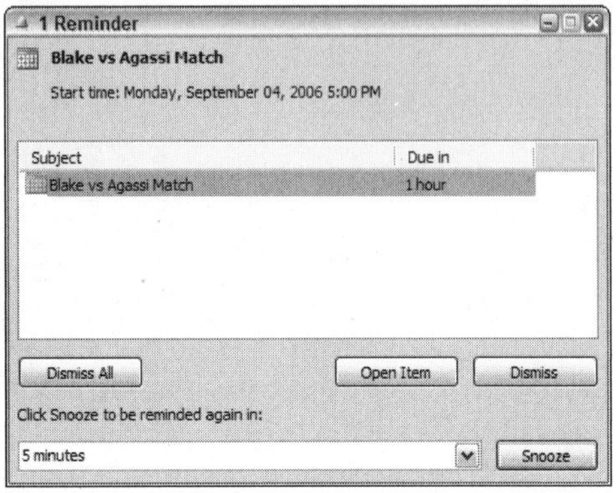

Figure 8-5:
The
Reminder
dialog box.

If you have your speakers turned on, you hear some sound effects. If you've set reminders for several activities, they show up in the same Reminder dialog box. Depending on your mood, you have a couple of alarm options:

- **Dismiss All:** You have everything under control and no longer need a reminder of this upcoming event.

- **Open Item:** Open the activity to edit it.

- **Dismiss:** Turns off the alarm for only the selected activity.

- **Snooze:** Postpones the alarm for the time period that you select.

Unlinking an appointment

You can unlink an appointment from BCM by deleting it from the account, business contact, opportunity, or business project history section of a record. Deleting an appointment from BCM doesn't delete it from Outlook; the appointment remains in the Outlook calendar.

1. **Click the Communication History folder in the Folder List.**

2. **Double-click the meeting that you want to unlink.**

   Click the Link To Record button on the Ribbon. When the Link to Business Contact Manager Record dialog box appears, remove the record.

3. **Click OK to close the dialog box and then click Save & Close to record your changes.**

Chapter 9

Multitasking with the Task List

In This Chapter

▶ Creating tasks and linking them to contacts

▶ Completing a task

▶ Delegating work to teammates

▶ Searching the task list

*I*n this chapter, you find out how Business Contact Manager keeps track of tasks. These are the same tasks that are part of Outlook, except you can link them to contacts, accounts, or opportunities in BCM.

Why do you want to use tasks, you ask? You remember things you have to do — you have a memory like an elephant, right? Well, time management gurus have said for decades that the way to reduce stress in your life, be more productive, and accomplish more with greater efficiency centers around managing tasks. The number one rule: Get stuff out of your head and into a task management system, either on paper or on a computer. If you choose to do this on a computer, you have BCM to help! After you enter a task into BCM, your head is lighter, and BCM helps you keep track of what needs to be done and when it's due. And even after you've completed a task, you have a record of it in BCM's communication history so that you can refer to it when necessary.

So, if you want to lose weight in your head and be more effective in life, discover how to use tasks!

In Chapter 19, you find out about tasks that are part of projects. Those show up differently from the tasks we discuss in this chapter. Project tasks are designed for working with teams of users and are linked to specific projects. These tasks are the same tasks that are in Outlook with one exception — they can be linked to contacts.

Creating Tasks

You can create a new task in BCM from a lot of places. The big decision you make is whether to link the task to the contact, account, or opportunity. We suggest you always link your tasks because one of the secrets of contact management is to keep track of your interactions with people and to maintain a history of those interactions. Communication history in BCM is where this history is kept. You can find communication history from the Outlook menu bar by choosing Business Contact Manager⇨Communication History.

In this section, we show you how to create a task linked to a contact, how to create a task without linking it to a contact — for those rare times you might not want to link — and how to create a task from an e-mail.

Creating a task linked to a contact

If you want to create a task and link it to a BCM contact, we recommend starting from the contact record so that the task is part of the contact's communication history. Follow these steps:

1. **From the Outlook menu bar, choose Business Contact Manager⇨ Business Contacts.**

    Or you can get to the Contact List view by doing one of the following:

    - From the Outlook menu bar, choose Go⇨Contacts⇨Business Contacts in Business Contact Manager.

    - From the Business Contact Manager toolbar, choose Display⇨Business Contacts.

2. **Right-click a contact record and choose Create⇨New Task for Business Contact, as shown in Figure 9-1.**

    Starting from a contact record automatically links the task to it.

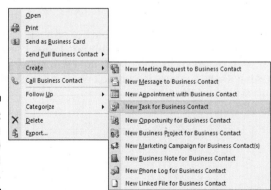

Figure 9-1:
Right-click a
contact to
create a
linked task.

The Task window opens, as shown in Figure 9-2.

3. **Enter a subject for the task in the Subject field.**

   A subject is all that is required to create a task. Actually, the subject isn't really required, but why would you enter a blank task? The rest of the fields are optional but useful.

4. **Enter a start date and due date.**

   If you enter a start date, the due date is automatically entered as the same day, which you can change.

   Click the drop-down list for a date field, and a calendar appears so that you can choose a date. For a really cool experience, you can enter dates such as **today** and **next Friday,** and BCM figures out the date for you!

5. **Choose a status from the Status drop-down list.**

   You can choose from Not Started, In Progress, Waiting on Someone Else, Deferred, and Completed.

6. **Choose a Low, Normal, or High priority from the Priority drop-down list.**

7. **Enter a number in the % Complete field, or use the arrows to increase/decrease the number.**

   This field is tied to the Status field. If you change the status to Completed, the % Complete field changes to 100%, and vice versa.

8. **Select the Reminder check box to set a reminder to alert you.**

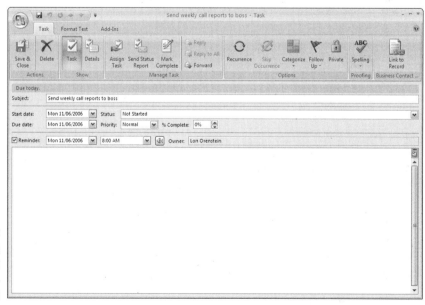

Figure 9-2:
The Task window.

Click the speaker icon to the right of the Time field to choose a different sound file.

You can set the default time to be different than 8:00AM by choosing Tools⇨Options⇨Reminder Time from the Outlook menu bar.

9. **Enter any comments or an agenda in the large text field.**

10. **Click Save & Close to save the task.**

Your task now shows up in the task list (look ahead to Figure 9-5) and in the contact's Communication History window.

These other options are available from the Ribbon and give you more powerful functions for your tasks:

✔ **Track the completed date of the task, mileage accumulated, and other billing information:** Click the Details button in the Show group. The Details window for the task opens.

✔ **Assign a task to a category:** Click the Categorize button in the Options group. The Categories dialog box opens. For a more detailed discussion of categories, flip to Chapter 6. You can have some categories for contacts or accounts, others for tasks, and still others for opportunities or projects.

✔ **Follow up with a flag:** Click the Follow Up button in the Options group. Your task appears on the To-Do bar and has a follow-up reminder set.

✔ **Mark your task as recurring:** Click the Recurrence button in the Options group. We discuss the Task Recurrence dialog box in detail in the "Making a task recur multiple times" section, later in this chapter.

✔ **Hide your task:** Click the Private button in the Options group. Others in your workgroup can't view that task.

✔ **Spell check your task:** Click the Spelling button in the Proofing group.

✔ **Link the task to a contact:** Click the Link to Record button in the Business Contact Manager group. The Link to Business Contact Manager Record dialog box opens. See Chapter 10 for more information about how to link a task (and other communication histories) to a contact.

If you created the task by right-clicking a contact record, it's already linked to a contact.

Creating an unlinked task

Sometimes you want to enter a task quickly and don't care whether it's linked — you're getting it out of your head and into BCM. Here are some easy ways to enter a task:

✔ Press Ctrl+Shift+K from anywhere in BCM or Outlook.

✔ From the Outlook menu bar, choose Go⇨Tasks. In Task view, click New on the Outlook toolbar.

A Task window opens. You can enter as little or as much of the data as explained in the previous section. Then, click the Save & Close button on the Ribbon when finished.

Creating a task from an e-mail

If you're asked to do something through e-mail (and who isn't, these days?), you want to create a new task directly from the e-mail. Fortunately, BCM gives you a cool way to transform the e-mail into a task with a drag of the mouse. Follow these steps:

1. **From the Outlook Inbox, highlight the e-mail.**

   These steps don't work from the Preview pane, so be sure to turn it off before Step 1.

2. **Drag the e-mail over the Navigation pane and drop it on top of the task bar.**

   A task is automatically created and the Task dialog box opens. The subject of the e-mail becomes the subject of the task, and the body of the e-mail is automatically copied into the Comments section of the task.

   The task is not linked to a contact. If you want to link the task to a contact, account, or opportunity, click the Link to Record button in the Business Contact Manager group on the Ribbon. The Link to Business Contact Manager Record dialog appears. Choose which record(s) you want to link this to and click OK.

3. **Click Save & Close to record the task.**

   The task appears in the task list.

Making a task recur multiple times

Sometimes you need a task to recur multiple times. An example is a weekly sales report you have to prepare. You can create one task and set it to recur weekly. The task is active until you mark it complete, then another task is active for the next week until you mark it complete, and so on. Follow these steps to make a task recur:

1. Open your task.

The Task window opens. (Refer to Figure 9-2.)

2. Click the Recurrence button in the Options group on the Ribbon.

The Task Recurrence dialog box opens. (See Figure 9-3.)

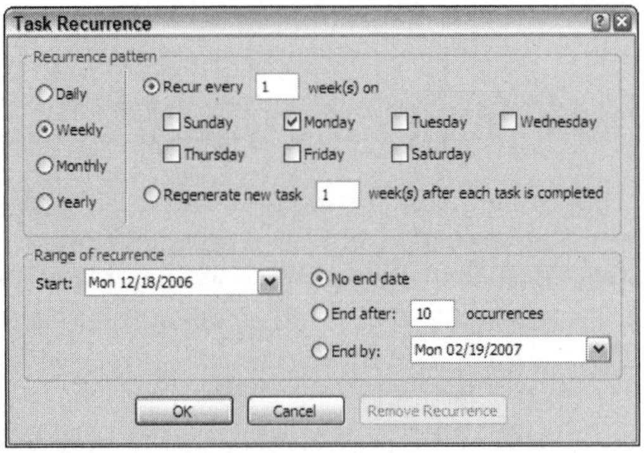

Figure 9-3:
The Task
Recurrence
dialog box.

3. Choose your recurrence pattern.

Your choices are Daily, Weekly, Monthly, or Yearly. The date options to the right change, depending on what you choose from that list:

- *Daily:* Choose the option for Every *X* Days and specify how many days apart this task should recur. Choose Every Weekday if this is something that you want to recur Monday through Friday (the work week).

- *Weekly:* Choose Recur Every *X* week(s) On to have the task recur every week on a specific day. For example, to have a task recur every Wednesday, enter **1** in the Recur Every Week(s) On box and select Wednesday. If you want a task to recur on Tuesday and Thursday every other week, you enter a **2** in the box and select Tuesday and Thursday.

- *Monthly:* Choose Day *X* of Every *X* Months(s) to have the task recur on the same date every month. To have a task recur on the 25th of each month, enter **25** in the Day box and **1** in the Month box. To have a task recur on the 10th of every quarter, enter **10** in the Day box and **3** in the month box.

- *Yearly:* Choose Every (Month) (Day) to specify a yearly date — this is great for birthdays or renewal dates of insurance policies where you know exactly which date you want each year.

4. **Select the Regeneration New Task option and enter when you want the task to recur.**

   Regeneration is your best choice when you don't want the next reminder for a task to appear until the previous one is marked as complete. If you don't mark the item complete, the next reminder is never regenerated. If you don't use regeneration, the next task recurs whether the first one is marked complete or not.

5. **Choose a range of recurrence.**

   • *Start:* This date is automatically filled with the start date of the task. You can choose a different one from the drop-down list.

   • *No End Date:* Select this radio button if this task goes on ad infinitum.

   • *End After X Occurrences:* Enter how may times you want the task to recur. This is handy for things like a class that meets weekly for 10 weeks or your kid's soccer league that has eight weekly games and that's the end of the season.

   • *End by (Date):* You can specify an end date, after which the task doesn't recur. Think about setting a task to take inventory every Tuesday and Thursday until the end of the quarter — you'd set the end-of-quarter date so the task would stop recurring.

   To remove the recurrence, click the Remove Recurrence button.

6. **Click OK to save your recurrence options and return to the Task window.**

To skip the current due date and reset the date to the next scheduled recurrence, click the Skip Recurrence button in the Options group on the Ribbon.

Managing Your Tasks

Part of your daily routine should involve managing your tasks — seeing what needs to be done today, what's coming up in the near future, and of course, marking completed tasks as completed to get them off your list and acknowledge your accomplishment in getting them done! This might involve opening a task and editing comments or rescheduling the due date to reflect the inevitable delays in life. Or, you may want to delete a task that isn't needed any longer.

You open a task by either double-clicking it or right-clicking it in a list and choosing Open. You find a list of tasks in two places in BCM and Outlook:

✔ **The task list:** Choose Go➪Tasks from the Outlook menu bar.

✔ **Communication history:** From within a contact window, click the Communication History button on the Ribbon. Tasks are mixed in with other items in this list.

Editing a task

From time to time, you want to change options for a task or update your comments in the task to reflect your progress. Follow these steps:

1. **From any view where you can see the task, double-click it to open it for editing.**

   Or you can right-click the task and choose Open.

2. **Make your changes.**

3. **Click the Save & Close button to save your edits.**

Completing tasks

Entering all your tasks in BCM is just the first part of improving your efficiency. You have to accomplish those tasks to get any benefit from them! The time management gurus all tell you that the act of completion, of marking a task complete, generates energy for you. You've done it; you've accomplished something; you're closer to your goal! So, relish the completion and go get more completions!

Marking the task as complete moves it to a status of Complete and changes the % Complete to 100%. A task that isn't marked as complete is considered active, and you should still be working on it.

The act of marking a task complete is similar to the other functions in BCM. And, as with other functions, you have multiple ways to do it.

✔ From any task list, right-click the task and choose Mark Complete.

✔ From within an open task, click the Mark Complete button on the Ribbon in the Manage Task group. Click the Save & Close button.

✔ From within an open task, change the Status to Completed or change the % Complete to 100%. Click the Save & Close button to complete this function.

If you're in a list view of tasks, the font changes to strikethrough and a light gray color. It might also remove the task from that view if the view is filtered to show only uncompleted tasks.

Deleting a task

You have a few reasons to delete a task: because it's old and you don't need to do it anymore, because you completed it, or because setting up the task was a mistake.

Two of these scenarios are valid reasons to delete a task. We recommend deleting tasks because you don't need them anymore and when they're a mistake. But if you complete a task, we recommend marking the task complete. (See the "Completing tasks" section.)

To delete a task, right-click it and choose Delete.

You aren't asked to confirm the deletion. It's removed from your task list and appears in the Deleted Items folder in the Navigation pane.

Assigning a Task to a Co-Worker

BCM gives you a powerful function to assign tasks to others on your team and monitor their progress. If you're the boss, this is a better way to delegate tasks to your workers than sending them e-mails. Assigning workers a BCM task creates a record on their task list, and they can easily send you status reports.

If you assign a task, you're not the owner anymore and any reminder to you is turned off.

Follow these steps to assign a task to someone else and send them an e-mail notifying them:

1. **In the Task window, click the Assign Task button in the Manage Task group on the Ribbon.**

   If you don't have the task open, you can right-click it and choose Assign Task.

   The Task window changes to give you a To field to enter the e-mail address of the person you're assigning the task to, as shown in Figure 9-4.

2. **Enter the person's e-mail address in the To field or click the To button to select it from your address books.**

3. **Choose your other options.**

   Fill in the start and due dates, along with a priority. If you'd like, you can also select these two check boxes:

- *Keep an Updated Copy of This Task on My Task List:* The task stays on your task list and its status keeps getting updated automatically when the assignee sends updated status reports.

- *Send Me a Status Report When This Task Is Complete:* You receive a notice when the assignee completes the task.

4. **Click the Send button to finish the assignment and send the e-mail.**

When creating a task, it's a good idea to do this step last — when you click the Send button, BCM records the task and sends the e-mail. It assumes that you've already chosen all the other options for this task.

5. **To cancel the assignment, click the Cancel Assignment button in the Manage Task group on the Ribbon.**

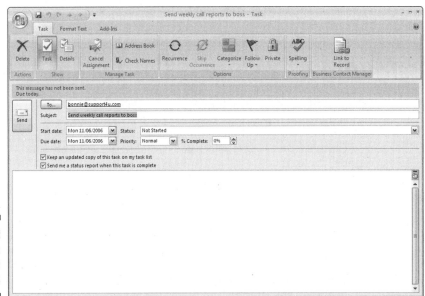

Figure 9-4:
Assign a
task to a
co-worker.

Sending a status report

When you send the task to the assignee, he receives a task request e-mail with Accept and Decline buttons. When the assignee clicks the Accept button, the task is added to his task list and the e-mail is gone. If he clicks the Decline button, BCM sends an e-mail to the original sender to say "no thanks."

The assignee can update notes in the task and send a status report at any point. Follow these steps if you're keeping a boss apprised of the status of a task:

1. **Open the task from any view.**

   The Task window opens. (Refer to Figure 9-2.)

2. **Update any of the information in the Task window.**

   You can write notes about the task in the Comments area. Also, you might want to update the % Complete field or change the status.

3. **Click the Send Status Report button in the Manage Task group on the Ribbon.**

   An e-mail is generated to the person who assigned it and the comments and basic information of the task are copied into the e-mail body. The e-mail adds a prefix to the original subject that says "Task Status Report." Here is a sample of the body of the e-mail — note that it shows the Actual Work field from the Details part of the task record.

   —Original Task—

   Subject: Prepare weekly call report for the boss

   Priority: Normal

   Start Date: Mon 11/6/2006

   Due Date: Mon 11/6/2006

   Status: Not Started

   % Complete: 0%

   Actual Work: 0 hours

   Requested By: Lon Orenstein

   I did the first step in this task . . . . Bonnie

4. **Enter any other information or message you want at the top of the e-mail window (like any other e-mail you'd write) and click the Send button to complete the process.**

   The e-mail is sent.

5. **When you complete the task and change the status to Completed (and save the record), BCM immediately sends an e-mail to your boss.**

   The subject of the e-mail has a prefix of "Task Completed."

Waiting for results

After you assign a task to a co-worker, you can't edit it on your own PC. If you selected the Keep an Updated Copy of This Task on My Task List check box when you assigned it, you see a copy in your task list. It also shows the new owner of the task when you open the task.

The first indication you get that this process is working is an e-mail you receive from the assignee. The phrase "Task Accepted" is entered as a prefix to the original subject. If you open the original task, you see at the top that the task was accepted and the date and time it was accepted.

When the assignee sends you a status report, you see how she's doing because the status report updates the original task — how cool is that? The Status, % Completed, and Comments fields are all updated in the original task.

Using Tasks Day to Day

The Task view of BCM gives you great flexibility to track your tasks as you move through your day. Hopefully, you're marking lots of them completed and creating new ones as you speak with people on the phone or after you leave meetings and have new tasks to deal with. You, most likely, have BCM open all day long and can easily get to your task list quickly. Now, customizing it gives you some great automation tools that enable you to see at a glance what's going on with your activities.

Opening a Task view

To get to the Task view, do one of the following:

- ✔ From the Navigation pane, click Tasks or the Tasks button.
- ✔ From the Outlook menu bar, choose Go➪Tasks.
- ✔ Press Ctrl+4 from anywhere in BCM or Outlook.

Figure 9-5 shows the Task view. The Navigation pane has a section for My Tasks and, under that, Business Contact Manager. This is where you find opportunities, marketing campaigns, projects, and project tasks. By clicking one of those choices, you see the list of those records (tasks associated with each type of data).

BCM stores opportunities, marketing campaigns, projects, and project tasks as types of tasks. This idea might be confusing at first, but the more you work with tasks, the more sense it makes.

Business Contact Manager tasks

My Tasks

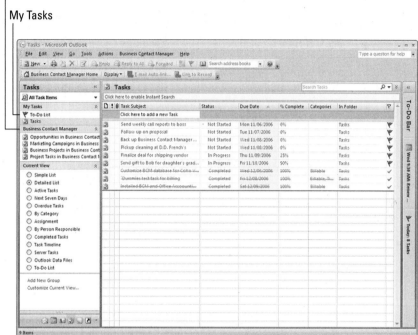

Figure 9-5:
Task view.

In this chapter, we're concerned with just tasks instead of opportunities, marketing campaigns, projects, or project tasks. When you click the Tasks button under My Tasks in the Navigation pane, the choices you see under Current View allow you to see your tasks presented in these formats:

- **Simple List:** This view contains all your tasks with no filters or grouping — just the subject and the due date. If you've lost a task somewhere, here's a good place to find it.

- **Detailed List:** This view also contains all your tasks with no filters or groupings, but it contains more columns of information. By default, it shows columns for Icon, Priority, Attachment, Task Subject, Status, Due Date, % Complete, and Categories.

- **Active Tasks:** This view contains the same columns as the Detailed List, but it's filtered to include those tasks with a status of Not Started, In Progress, or Waiting on Someone Else.

- **Next Seven Days:** This view contains the same columns as the Detailed List, but it's filtered to include only those tasks with due dates within the next seven days.

✔ **Overdue Tasks:** This view shows the same columns as the Detailed List, but this one is filtered for all tasks that are not completed with a due date on or before yesterday.

✔ **By Category:** This view shows the same columns as the Detailed List, and this one isn't filtered at all. Tasks are grouped by category and this view shows you how powerful categories can be. If a task is assigned to multiple categories, the task appears in each group. Sorting by a column heading still keeps the tasks grouped — they're just sorted within that group by the column you click.

✔ **Assignment:** This view displays the Icon, Priority, Attachment, Task Subject, Owner, Due Date, and Status columns, plus it's filtered to include only those tasks assigned by you to others. This is a great place to keep track of what you've assigned and which ones are completed.

✔ **By Person Responsible:** This view's columns are similar to Assignment, but it's grouped by the Person Responsible — the person you assigned the task to. The person responsible is really the owner of the task because the owner changes to the person you assigned it to.

✔ **Completed Tasks:** This view is a great way to see all that you've accomplished, grouped by date completed and filtered to show only tasks marked as complete (Status Is Completed).

✔ **Task Timeline:** This is a Gantt chart type of view that shows the time along the top and the tasks underneath. By default, it has no filtering and shows all tasks.

✔ **Server Tasks:** If you've integrated a SharePoint task list with Outlook, this is where your SharePoint tasks will appear.

✔ **Outlook Data Files:** If you use multiple Outlook files, you can group your tasks by file to see what is active in each file. The format is similar to the Simple List view and shows all tasks with no filters or groupings.

You can sort the records by clicking any column heading. The records are sorted in ascending order with the first click and then in descending order with the next click of the column heading. For example, if you want to see all of your tasks sorted by due date, click the Due Date column heading.

Searching for information in tasks

Many times, you enter some information in a task and can't remember the subject, so you can't find it. BCM gives you a great way to find words or phrases by searching through views of tasks quickly. Maybe you entered some information in a task that dealt with a competitor, and you know you wrote down the pricing for their new CX800 machine, but you can't remember which task you entered it into. In that case, you can use BCM's search function to find the phrase "CX800," in this example.

Follow these steps to search your tasks for a specific word or phrase:

1. **Enter a word or phrase in the Search Tasks text box (see Figure 9-6) and click the magnifying glass (or press Enter) to start the search.**

    BCM searches through the tasks contained in the current view. If it finds tasks that contain that word or phrase, it displays them in the grid below the Search Tasks text box and highlights the word if it appears in one of the visible columns. If it doesn't appear in a visible column, you have to double-click each task to open it and find the word.

2. **To restore the search field to its original state, click the X that replaces the magnifying glass.**

    The Task view returns to its original state. BCM creates a new filter for each view under your Current Views using your search term. To clear the filter and return to the settings for each view, click the X.

Figure 9-6:
Search
options in
Task view.

Clicking the drop-down arrow to the right of the search entry field gives you options for searching.

-   *Recent Searches:* See the last few searches you've performed to make it easy to rerun the same search. Select the search, and BCM immediately reruns that search.

-   *Search All Task Items:* Search through all your tasks, not just the ones in that view.

-   *Indexing Status:* BCM continually indexes your tasks and tells you their current statuses. BCM builds a separate file, or *index,* that makes searching super fast. BCM knows not to do indexing when you're busy doing other things — it waits until there's not much going on with your PC to update the indexes.

-   *Search Options:* Set up various options for your PC to use when indexing.

Using the query builder to find information

BCM has a query builder capability — to the far right of the Search Tasks field you find two arrows *(chevrons)*. Clicking the chevrons displays an expanded search field, as shown in Figure 9-7.

To use the query builder, you have to enable Instant Search with Office 2007. If you see a Click Here to Enable Instant Search link under the title bar, you haven't done so. Click the link to get Instant Search working.

The purpose of this capability is to let you construct a query that finds data without having to remember all the syntax and rules for searching. This can be quite extensive, and if you do a lot of searching, you can keep the criteria fields visible from one BCM session to the next. Unfortunately, you can't save and reuse the query that it builds, but it is available as a Recent Search from the Search Tasks drop-down list. The best part of this view is the capability it gives you to do interactive searches. You can change the criteria *on the fly* and see your results almost instantly! And because the items are indexed, it's a lightning fast way to find your information.

Figure 9-7:
Query builder options in Task view.

Follow these steps to search using a query:

1. **Click the two chevrons to the right of the Search Tasks text box to display the query builder area. (Refer to Figure 9-7.)**

   You see some criteria entry boxes by default, and BCM remembers the boxes you used the last time you built a query.

2. **Choose the criteria you want to use to build the query.**

   Depending on the type of field, you have different choices.

3. **To add a field that isn't included, click the Add Criteria button and enter the field.**

A box appears for you to use to enter criteria to select data from that field.

4. **As you define criteria, watch what happens to the Search Tasks box.**

   The search box fills with the different phrases as you string together different criteria.

5. **Depending on options you set in Search Options, you either see the results or you must click the magnifying glass to start the search.**

   The results of the search appear in the grid below the Search Options area. The complete query that's built appears in the list of Recent Searches.

6. **When you're finished with queries, click the chevrons to collapse the query builder pane.**

   The view returns to its original state.

Chapter 10

Creating Business Histories

• •

• •

*I*n this chapter, you find out how Business Contact Manager keeps track of the history of your interactions with contacts and accounts. Did you ever have a conversation with someone where you discussed pricing, and, later on, you thought you agreed to $123 per pound, but the other person remembered $132 per pound? Or have you spent time searching for that letter you sent them telling them that the widgets wouldn't be shipped until October? If you're paper-based, you have to page through slips of paper or your journal book looking for where you wrote it down. If you use BCM and diligently make notes of conversations and link them to the appropriate contact, it takes just a few seconds to find the answer. This kind of history may not be as interesting as the kind you learned in high school, but it makes your business life a lot smoother.

Notes that you write about your conversation and negotiations with contacts, tasks that you create and complete, appointments you schedule, opportunities you track, and files (such as spreadsheets or graphics) you create that relate to a contact — all these can be linked to the contact or account record and are called *communication history*. Linking these to a BCM record gives you an easy way to find everything in one place.

E-mails also are linked into communication history — mostly automatically, although you have a way to link a specific e-mail to a record. This is one of the great advantages of BCM being a part of Outlook — you can look at a contact or account record and see all the e-mails that you've exchanged. It's easy to find what you need, it's all in one place, and you're much more organized than before you started using BCM.

In this chapter, you also discover how to customize the views of your history so that you can see it just the way you want. Using the power of views (jump to Chapter 7 for more information), you can organize your history in the way that works best for you.

Keeping Track of Your Histories

The most important idea to remember about histories is *linking*. You want to make sure that the note you write or task you create is linked to the appropriate record *before you start it*. That way, you can always find what you're looking for by searching the history of a specific contact. If you forget which record you linked to originally, you can search all history items to find it. We show you how to do this in the section, "Recording and linking a history item," later in this chapter.

You aren't required to link a history to a contact, but we recommend it. You can schedule an appointment or create a task that is not linked to a contact, and you can still find it in communication history. Our recommendation comes from years of experience — when you need to find some piece of information, you tend to remember it best by recalling the person it related to most closely. Linking it initially makes it that much easier to find later on.

Four kinds of records in BCM allow histories: contacts, accounts, opportunities, and projects. The Ribbon on each of these windows has the History button in the Show group (shown in Figure 10-1). Clicking this History button shows you the history for the record you are viewing — just for that contact, account, opportunity, or project.

Types of history items

You can link the following history items:

- ✔ **Business Note:** You use this to keep track of all kinds of information such as negotiations, pricing offers, meeting notes, snippets of information you copy from the contact's Web site or press releases — in short, any information you want to keep track of.

- ✔ **Opportunity:** This is a record of what kind of business deal you're working on, when it will close, which products it consists of, and so on. It is linked to either a contact or an account, depending on whether you're using account records.

History button

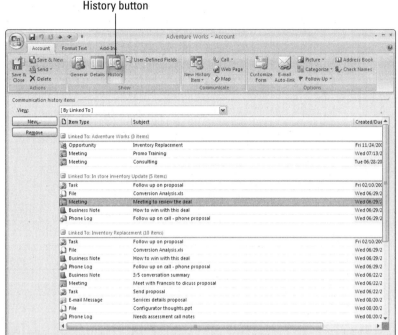

✔ **Task:** A task is a to-do, an activity you want to accomplish. Time management gurus will tell you that every task is related to someone: either you or the person who's involved in the task. If the task is "Get car fixed," for example, link the task to your car dealer's account record or mechanic's contact record.

✔ **Appointment:** Where does your body have to be at what time? Because you always have an appointment with another person, link it to that person's contact or account record instead of your own. You can enter an agenda for a meeting in the Details section, or maybe use a business note to keep track of it, and update either one with the notes during the meeting. The key is *linking* the record!

✔ **Phone Log:** This is another way of keeping track of calls. You could write a business note about it instead, or use the phone log for only calls and notes for other types of information.

✔ **File:** BCM allows you to link files from your hard drive or network server to a record to keep easy track of them. This might be a spreadsheet you created for pricing scenarios, the document you sent the prospect for a proposal, or pictures you took of the customer's house.

Table 10-1 shows the type of history item and to which record types it can be linked.

Table 10-1	Where to Find History Items
Type of Item	*Found in This Type of Record*
Business Note	Account, Business Contact, Opportunity, Business Project
E-mail	Account, Business Contact, Business Project
Opportunity	Account, Business Contact
Task	Account, Business Contact, Opportunity
Appointment	Account, Business Contact, Opportunity, Business Project
Phone Log	Account, Business Contact, Opportunity, Business Project
File	Account, Business Contact, Opportunity, Business Project

Recording and linking a history item

When you know what types of history items you can use, how do you actually do the linking? We recommend you link at the time you create the history item because fewer clicks to do it are needed that way. It also keeps you in the habit of thinking about linking. ("Thinking about linking" — there's a catchphrase to memorize!)

Linking at the time you create the history item

Say you're sitting at your desk and a call comes in (or you initiate a call). Seeing the other party's name on caller ID, you know this conversation is one that you will make notes about. Follow these steps:

1. **Choose Business Contact Manager⇨Business Contacts (or Accounts) to go to your contacts.**

   Or, on the BCM toolbar, choose Display⇨Business Contacts.

   You find that person's name in the list of names.

2. **Right-click the name and choose Create and then make a selection from the submenu that appears (see Figure 10-2).**

   A submenu appears with choices of history items to create that will be *automatically linked* to that contact or account's record. In our example, you would select New Business Note for Business Contact or New Phone Log for Business Contact. See the example in Figure 10-2.

A window appears depending on the type of record you chose to create.

3. **Fill in the information and click Save & Close.**

   This now links that history item to the contact or account you selected initially.

Figure 10-2:
Creating a
new history
item by
right-
clicking a
name.

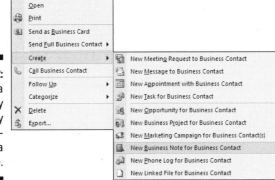

Linking an existing history item

If you already created the history item, you may want to link it to a contact, account, opportunity, or project.

Linking an item is always easiest when you create the item.

If you need to link an item to an account or contact after you've already created it, follow these steps:

1. **For an appointment or task, click Link to Record from the Ribbon. For a business note, phone log, opportunity, or project, click the Link To: button.**

   The Link to Business Contact Manager Record dialog box appears, as shown in Figure 10-3. This gives you the way to link that item to other contacts, accounts, opportunities, and projects — or all of those types.

2. **Select Accounts, Business Contacts, Opportunities, or Business Projects from the Folder drop-down list.**

3. **Select a record to link that item to.**

   To add more than one record at a time, hold down the Ctrl key and select different records. You can select a group of records by highlighting the first record in the range, then pressing Shift, and clicking the last one in the range.

Figure 10-3:
The Link to
Business
Contact
Manager
Record
dialog box.

Type the first few characters of the entry you're searching for in the Search field to move through a long list of contacts, accounts, opportunities, or projects. The grid moves to that part of the list that matches the characters you type.

4. Click the Link To button.

The record(s) are added to the Linked Records field next to the Link To button.

You can also double-click the record to enter it into the Linked Records field.

5. To add other links, repeat Steps 2–4.

By selecting a different record type (opportunities instead of contacts, for example), you can link this same item to accounts, opportunities, or projects.

6. Click OK to link that item to those records.

7. Click Save & Close on the Ribbon to save your changes.

That item is linked to all those records and shows up in the Communication History area for each and every one.

Editing an existing history item

In the preceding example, we showed you how to write a business note with details of your conversation and link it to the contact that called you. Now, imagine that you just clicked Save & Close, and the person calls again with more details he forgot to tell you. Editing the note or any other item involves the same steps as editing any other record:

1. **Open the record by either double-clicking it or right-clicking it and choosing Open.**

2. **Make changes to the information in the dialog box.**

   If it's a note or phone log, you can add, change, or delete text. You have the ability to change any other information also.

3. **From the Ribbon, click Save & Close to save your changes.**

   The record is saved and linked to the contact or account (unless that was one of your changes).

Deleting an existing history item

Usually, we recommend that you keep history and not delete it. If you believed the item was important enough to enter originally, it probably is worth keeping. The BCM database can hold hundreds of thousands of records, so don't worry about filling it up! However, it's also appropriate at times to delete some entries. Here's how:

1. **In whatever view you find the history item, right-click the item and choose Delete.**

   You could be within the contact's history or on the Communication History view (see "Customizing the Communication History view," near the end of this chapter).

2. **BCM sometimes asks for confirmation that you want to delete — click Yes.**

   BCM doesn't always ask you to confirm (depending on the type of item you're deleting).

   That history entry is now deleted from communication history

If you didn't mean to delete the item, you can drag it back to its appropriate place from the Delete folder in the Navigation pane.

Automating the E-Mail Connection

Just like in the old days of filing cabinets and paper folders, keeping all your information about contacts in one place has great value. Filing cabinets are easy to locate, easy to search, and make it easy to see the history of your interactions. In today's digital world, BCM provides that filing cabinet experience. This section explains what BCM does with e-mails and how the linking works, both automatically and manually.

In today's world, e-mail has become the most important medium for communication among people and companies. Outlook has become the most widely used e-mail program, and now BCM fits tightly into Outlook. How many times have you said, or heard someone say, "I just can't find that e-mail?" If they used BCM and Outlook and linked their e-mails correctly in communication history, they could go to that contact's record and have a much easier time finding what they were searching for. To make this work, you have to link both the incoming and outgoing mail to the contact's or account's record using the e-mail address.

The e-mail auto-linking settings that you make remain the same until you change them. Be aware that, when you share a Business Contact Manager database, any user with access to the database can also view your auto-linked messages.

Linking outgoing mail

You need to make sure that all the e-mails you send to contacts are linked to their contact record. Obviously, every conversation has two sides, and linking the outgoing mail gets one side of it linked to your communication history. When Outlook is installed, this feature is usually always turned on, but it's a good idea to verify it. With Outlook open, follow these steps to save outgoing e-mail to communication history:

1. **On the Outlook menu bar, choose Tools⇨Options.**

    The Options dialog box appears.

2. **On the Preferences tab, click the E-Mail Options button.**

    The E-Mail Options dialog box opens.

3. **Select the Save Copies of Messages in Sent Items Folder check box.**

    Outlook saves a copy of every e-mail that's been sent.

4. **Click OK.**

Outlook now not only saves a copy of each outgoing message in its Sent Items folder, but also each message is automatically linked to the BCM contact or account record's communication history.

Linking incoming mail

You get lots of e-mail. Some messages are important and should be saved in history, others you delete, and some are in between. You want to use the power of BCM and Outlook to automate the functions they can do best — link both incoming and outgoing e-mails to specific contacts with no action on your part.

We assume you've set up a set of folders or subfolders in Outlook to store your e-mails, and those are safely archived in Outlook. Because you have all the e-mails in Outlook anyway, do you really need a link to a business contact who sends you lots of jokes or with whom you endlessly discuss football statistics? You might want to turn off auto-linking for that contact.

But, sometimes you have legitimate business e-mails from those same contacts that you want to link to communication history, and those you have to do manually. In this section, you discover how to let Outlook *automatically* link the e-mails into communication history for those contacts or folders that are important to you.

Follow these steps to auto-link incoming e-mails to BCM contacts and accounts:

1. **Choose Business Contact Manager⇨Manage E-Mail Auto-Linking.**

   The Manage E-Mail Auto-Linking dialog box appears, as shown in Figure 10-4.

2. **Click the E-Mail tab.**

   This tab gives you options for managing connections between e-mail and communication history for all your BCM contacts and accounts. You see either e-mail addresses from the one e-mail you have highlighted or all contacts in BCM.

3. **Find the contacts and accounts for which you want to manage the e-mail linking.**

   You have several ways to choose the contact and account records:

   • *Click the Select All or Clear All button.* All your contact and account records are already selected. Click the Clear All button if you want to deselect all records (get rid of all the check marks).

- *Type the contact or account you're looking for in the Search For text box.* Type the first few letters of the name you're looking for, and BCM highlights the first record that matches.

- *Click a column heading to sort records by that column.* For example, clicking the Company heading is a fast way to locate all contact records for a particular company.

4. **Select the Link check box for your chosen records.**

You can also deselect the Link box so that e-mails from this person no longer automatically link to his contact or account record. The e-mails are still saved in your Outlook folder but don't show up in the contact or account communication history.

5. **Click OK.**

Figure 10-4:
Manage automated e-mail linking.

Linking old e-mail with new contacts

Another function BCM can use to help you link e-mails to contacts automatically is the Search and Link e-mails capability. Say that you're given new prospects or customers from a salesperson who left the company, you have some e-mails from these contacts stored in your Outlook folders, and you want to get those e-mails linked to the new contacts quickly. Follow these steps:

1. **Link the new contact to any incoming mail (after entering the contacts into BCM, of course).**

   See the previous section if you're not sure how to link incoming mail to a contact. Make sure you include the new contacts and be sure to select them in the list of e-mail addresses.

2. **Click the Folders tab in the Manage E-Mail Auto-Linking dialog box. Choose which folders to search for the old e-mails.**

   This step assumes that you have subfolders into which you move old e-mails after reading them in your Inbox. This practice is recommended for managing e-mails with Outlook. If you don't do this, you probably have thousands of e-mails in your Inbox, so make sure that folder is selected also!

3. **Click the Search and Link button.**

   The Link Existing E-Mail dialog box appears. This dialog box gives you the option, while searching and linking, to ignore e-mail older than a certain date. This tells BCM not to link any e-mails that are older than that date.

4. **Select the Ignore E-Mail Older Than box.**

5. **Select a date from the Date drop-down list.**

   You'll probably want to use your oldest date or one that you know includes mail stored in your Outlook file.

6. **Click the Start button.**

   BCM searches your database and finds existing e-mails to link to the contacts you chose. The progress bar shows you how long until the process finishes.

7. **When finished, click Close to return to the Manage E-Mail Auto-Linking dialog box.**

8. **Click OK to complete the process.**

Not linking Outlook folders to a contact

If you have a Personal Confidential folder where you store e-mails from your sweetie, your therapist, and your psychic, you can choose not to link those e-mails to the contacts.

Follow these steps to delink an entire Outlook e-mail folder:

1. **Choose Business Contact Manager➪Manage E-Mail Auto Linking.**

   The Manage E-Mail Auto Linking dialog box appears (refer to Figure 10-4).

2. **Click the Folders tab.**

   This tab gives you the choice of linking e-mails stored in these folders to their associated contact or account, or not linking them.

3. **Deselect the folders whose e-mails you do *not* want to link to contacts, accounts, or projects.**

   Those e-mails are not linked to business history in BCM.

4. **Click the E-Mail tab.**

   This tab gives you the choice of linking or not linking e-mails to or from these e-mail addresses. Select the e-mail addresses of whomever you don't want to link e-mails to BCM.

5. **Click OK to complete the process.**

Linking a specific e-mail

Sometimes you may get an e-mail from someone who's not in your BCM database — maybe a contact's assistant. You don't want to add the assistant to BCM, but you want to link the e-mail to that contact or to a project. BCM gives you a way to link or delink a specific e-mail message to one or more BCM contacts. Follow these steps:

1. **From your Inbox, highlight the e-mail message.**

   You could do this from another folder, but you'll typically do this from the Inbox when you're reading the e-mail.

2. **From the BCM toolbar, click Link to Record.**

   The Link to Business Contact Manager Record dialog box appears, as shown in Figure 10-5. This gives you the way to link that e-mail to selected contacts, accounts, opportunities, and projects — or all of those types.

3. **Select Accounts, Business Contacts, Opportunities, or Business Projects from the Folder drop-down list.**

4. **Select a record to link that e-mail to.**

   To add more than one record at a time, hold down the Ctrl key and select different records. You can select a group of records by highlighting the first record in the range, then pressing Shift, and clicking the last one in the range.

   Type the first few characters of the entry you're searching for in the Search field to move through a long list of contacts, accounts, opportunities, or projects. The grid moves to that part of the list that matches the characters you type.

Figure 10-5:
The Link to
Business
Contact
Manager
Record
dialog box.

5. **Click the Link To button.**

The record(s) are added to the Linked Records field next to the Link To button.

You can also double-click the record to enter it into the Linked Records field.

6. **To add other links, repeat Steps 3–5.**

By selecting a different record type (opportunities instead of contacts, for example), you can link this same e-mail to accounts, opportunities, or projects.

7. **Click OK to link that e-mail to those records.**

That e-mail is linked to all those records and shows up in the communication history for each one.

Linking an e-mail to a project

You can also link an e-mail to a business project. If you're using projects, especially when many people are working on them, you can keep everything linked together automatically in that project's communication history. Follow these steps:

1. **From your Inbox, highlight the e-mail message.**

2. **From the BCM toolbar, click the E-Mail Auto-Link button.**

   The E-Mail Auto-Link dialog box appears.

3. **Click the Business Contact Manager Projects tab.**

   You see a list of your projects displayed on that tab, as shown in Figure 10-6.

4. **Select the Link box of one or more projects and then click OK.**

   That e-mail address is linked to that project. Any future e-mails sent or received from that address automatically link to that project.

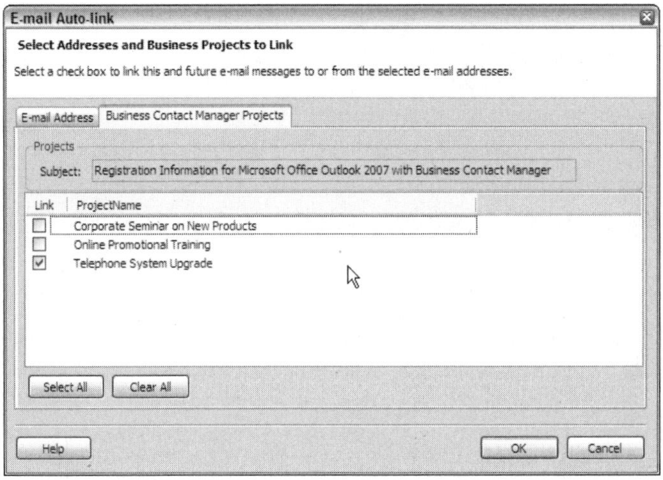

Figure 10-6:
Linking
e-mails to
a specific
project.

Creating a new contact and linking their e-mails

This happens a lot in business — you're working on a project or trying to sell a customer and a new player appears on the scene. You know you're going to work with this person in the future, so you want to add her as a contact and link all future e-mails to the record. And, while you're at it, you want to link her e-mail address to the project you're working on.

To create a new basic contact record (name and e-mail address) and link e-mails to the business project you're working on, follow these steps:

1. **From your Inbox, select the e-mail message.**

2. **From the BCM toolbar, click the E-Mail Auto-Link button.**

   The E-Mail Auto-Link dialog box appears, as shown in Figure 10-7, with the E-Mail Address tab showing.

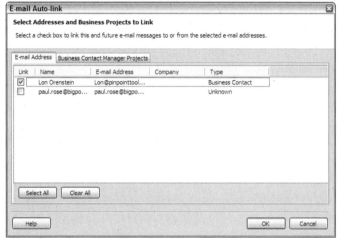

Figure 10-7:
Creating a new contact and linking it to a project.

3. **Select the Link check box of the new contact's e-mail address.**

4. **Click the Business Contact Manager Projects tab at the top of the dialog box.**

   You see the list of projects in BCM.

5. **Select the project with which this new contact is involved.**

6. **Click OK to complete the process.**

   A new contact record is created in your Business Contacts database. It links the selected e-mail message and any future e-mail messages — both incoming and outgoing — that contain the e-mail address to that new contact record. And it links those e-mails to the project they're involved with.

Keeping Track of Files Using Communication History

So, you've been working on a proposal for the hot new prospect, and you've created documents and spreadsheets, taken pictures of their factory and superimposed where your new machine would go on the production line, and received a contract back from Legal with their terms; and all these files are stored who-knows-where on your hard drive. You can use BCM to keep track of all these files in communication history. You can link the files to not only the contact but also to the opportunity you've entered to track the deal, plus the project.

Use the following steps to link to a contact record. If you want to link the files to an account, opportunity, or project, the concept is the same except you start by finding the record to link to instead of the contact.

1. **Go to a list of your contacts.**

2. **Right-click the contact record and choose New Linked File for Business Contact.**

   The Link File dialog box opens, as shown in Figure 10-8. This dialog box enables you to browse your hard drive to find the file you want to link into communication history.

3. **Click Open to finalize the process.**

   A link is established between the file and the communication history of that contact.

These steps work identically for linking files to accounts, projects, or opportunities.

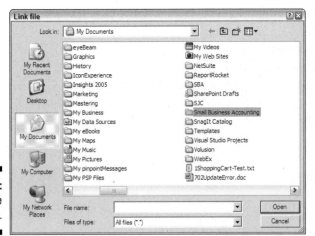

Figure 10-8:
The Link File
dialog box.

Viewing, Searching, and Managing Your Histories

After you use Business Contact Manager for a while, all your communication history starts piling up. You need a way to view and manage these histories. You can go to each record, click the History button on the Ribbon, and see a list of all the histories linked to that record. That works well every once in a while. If you want to repeatedly look at your communication history, you can become more productive by viewing and customizing the Communication History views.

Viewing history in Communication History view

You can see communication history for *all* records by going to the Communication History view. This can show every history record, and you can create customized views to see just the histories you want. Follow these steps to find a specific history item if you're not sure which contact or other record it's linked to:

1. **From the Outlook menu bar, choose Business Contact Manager⇨ Communication History.**

   Alternatively, from the BCM toolbar, choose Display⇨Communication History.

   In the event that you are viewing the Folder List first (choose Go⇨Folder List from the Outlook menu bar), you won't see the choices for views. You must get to Communication History by choosing Business Contact Manager⇨Communication History from the Outlook menu bar.

   The Communication History window opens, as shown in Figure 10-9. The current view on the Navigation pane shows your histories grouped and organized by different filters.

2. **Click one of the Current Views to see history displayed with those options.**

   Your choices are as follows:

   • **[By Linked To]:** This option is a good way to see history grouped by the contact, account, opportunity, or project that it's linked to.

   • **[Chronological]:** This option groups the records by date, such as Today, Last Week, Last Month, and Older. If you know when you entered a history, this is a good way to find what you're looking for.

Figure 10-9:
Communi-
cation
History
view.

- **[Communication History Item]:** This option shows you all records, with no grouping, and is a good view to see *all* history in one place.

- **[Created By]:** This option shows you histories grouped by which user of the database created it. This is a good way to see who has done what with whom, if you have multiple users using BCM over a LAN or remotely.

3. **Click the column headers to sort the records by that column.**

   The first click is in ascending order, and the second click changes it to descending order. This is an easy way to get to the record you're looking for.

4. **After you find the history record you are looking for, double-click it to open and view it.**

Customizing the Communication History view

Chapter 7 shows you more details about how to customize the Communication History view — it's just like all the other views in BCM and Outlook. In order to access the Customize View dialog box, follow these steps:

1. **While in the Communication History view, click Customize Current View in the Navigation pane.**

   The Customize View dialog box opens, as shown in Figure 10-10. The title bar reflects which current view you're customizing — in this example, the [By Linked To] view is the one.

2. **Click one of the buttons (Fields, Group By, Sort, Filter, Other Settings, Automatic Formatting, and Format Columns).**

   The choices you can use to customize the view or filter the records displayed in the view appear.

3. **When you finish customizing, click OK to save your options.**

Figure 10-10: Customizing the Communication History view.

If you have a specific way you want to see communication history, create your own view and name it. It then shows up in the Navigation pane like the standard views, plus it appears in the choices of views in each record (as we explain in the next section). Chapter 7 gives you more information on this, but the quick way to save a new view name is like this:

1. **From the Outlook menu bar, choose View⇨Current View⇨Define Views.**

   The Custom View Organizer dialog box appears.

2. **In the View Name column, click Current View Settings to highlight it.**

   It's probably highlighted by default.

3. **Click the Copy button. Enter a name for your new view and click OK to save it.**

   The current view that you have customized gets a unique name with unique settings. You can now modify this new view on its own and choose it from the Navigation pane whenever you choose.

4. **Click Close to exit the Custom View Organizer dialog box.**

Searching history in Communication History view

Sometimes, what you're looking for is embedded inside a note or phone log record, and you can't tell from the subject which one it is. To find the correct note, you use another function in BCM — Search. Searching the Communication History view is the ultimate way of finding something you entered into BCM and need to see again.

Say that you made a call on a prospect, and he was really rude to you. So rude, in fact, that you wrote a business note saying, "This person is not just rude, he is world-class rude, and we don't need him as a customer." It's six months later, you've forgotten the person's name, and another salesperson is relating a similar story with a new prospect. You remember that you wrote "world-class rude" and need to find that note to see if it's the same person.

Follow these steps to find an account or contact based upon a communication history item:

1. **From the Outlook menu bar, choose Business Contact Manager⇨ Communication History.**

   Alternatively, from the BCM toolbar, choose Display⇨Communication History.

   The Communication History window opens, as shown in Figure 10-11.

2. **Enter your search term in the Search Communication History box and click the magnifying glass or press Enter.**

   The window is populated with records with that phrase in the subject or in the note, task, appointment details, or phone log.

3. **Sort the results by clicking the column headings or choose another Current View to rearrange the search results in that customized view.**

   You see the search results until you do another search or move to another part of BCM and return to communication history. You can also click the X at the right side of the search box to cancel the search function and return to the original view.

4. **Double-click the item you want to open to see the contents.**

Enter a search term.

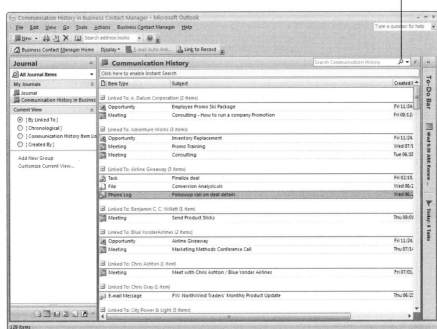

Figure 10-11: Searching from the Communication History view.

Viewing history in each record

The other way of seeing communication history is to go to an individual contact, account, opportunity, or project record and see the history for just that record. Many of us know that a note we wrote or an e-mail we sent was concerning *this contact* or *that project,* and it's more efficient to go right to that contact's history and find it. If this is a project or opportunity, this history view is like "action central" — the central repository of activities, notes, files you've created, and more concerning a particular project.

Follow these steps to find communication history in a contact, account, opportunity, or project record:

1. **From any one of a variety of views, find the contact, account, project, or opportunity record that you want to search and open it.**

2. **On the Ribbon, click the History button in the Show group.**

   You go to the Communication History Items window for that record.

3. (Optional) Choose a customized view from the View drop-down list.

Not only do you see the default views, but you also see the customized views you created. (See the "Customizing the Communication History view," section, earlier in this chapter.)

4. Sort the records by clicking the column headings.

This view doesn't provide a Search function — only the Communication History view offers a Search function.

5. Double-click the record to open and view it.

Two other functions are in this view: adding and removing history items. Here's how to add a new history item:

1. Click the New button in the Communication History Items window.

2. Choose which type of history item you want to enter.

3. Fill out the appropriate dialog box and click Save & Close to finish.

If you want to remove a history item, do the following:

1. Click once on the item to highlight it.

2. Click the Remove button.

The item is removed from history.

Part IV
Show Me the Money!

The 5th Wave   By Rich Tennant

"The top line represents our revenue, the middle line is our inventory, and the bottom line shows the rate of my hair loss over the same period."

In this part . . .

*E*ntering contact information in BCM is only half the fun. The other half consists of using those contacts to increase your bottom line. In this part, you find out how to share both your contact information and your sales opportunity info with the rest of your organization. You'll now have a little army that can go forth creating and managing sales opportunities. With a bit of hard work those opportunities will turn into quotes, sales orders invoices — and money in the bank!

Chapter 11

Sharing Your Data

*W*hy would you want to share your BCM data? Easy answer — so everyone can be on the same page with the same customers, prospects, sales opportunities, projects, and marketing campaigns. BCM gives your business the ability to see what everyone is doing and who is doing what to whom! When Mary, your best salesperson, has a conversation with your biggest customer and writes a phone log about the call, you can see it in BCM as soon as she saves it. If she's on the road and writes it on her laptop, you can see it as soon as she synchronizes with the master database. You'll see the date she entered it, what she entered, and that Mary is the user who entered it. Now you're starting to track all the touch points, and everyone can share. The next time that best customer calls in and asks a question, anyone in the office can be just as smart as Mary in answering it — just by looking in the communications history for the customer.

We assume you have co-workers with whom you want to share your BCM database. If you work by yourself and don't want anyone else to enter or change data, don't read this chapter — it's not for you!

Understanding How BCM Shares Data

It's good to be the king or queen! In this case, it's good to be the owner of the BCM database because you have all the power to decide who gets to see and change data in BCM. As the administrator or owner of the BCM database, you can do the following:

✔ Choose to share or not share your database with other users.

✔ Grant or deny access to your database for some users and not others.

✔ Delete the database.

✔ Back up the database.

✔ Restore a deleted database.

✔ Permanently delete a record by emptying the Deleted Items folder.

Further, if you're an administrator for the computer the BCM database resides on or for the domain in your office, you can

✔ Add new users to the computer or the domain.

✔ Access any shared database on that computer or domain, including databases created by others.

Well, now that you're the king or queen and can share the data, how do you? Without getting too technical, here are some things you should know about networks and domains and BCM:

✔ **In order to share a database with others, users must be able to access the database across a network.** That typically involves a wire running from each PC into a hub or switch. Or you can use wireless connections that accomplish the same thing — the signals go through some hub, switch, or router to get to the database.

✔ **You see two kinds of networks in most small businesses: a domain and a workgroup (also known as *peer-to-peer*).** A server controls a *domain* network. Many businesses use Microsoft's Small Business Server, and some run Microsoft Exchange on it for e-mail. A *workgroup (peer-to-peer)* is a collection of PCs without a controller. They still send their signals through a switch, but one domain controller doesn't manage the network. It's a loose confederation — and just fine if you're connecting one to ten PCs.

As an administrator, you have more functions to do if you have a domain instead of a workgroup. You might want to hire a consultant to advise you on the best way to proceed — thousands of Microsoft Certified Partners can help you with the questions you might have.

✔ **Regardless of the type of network you have, you need one PC onto which you load BCM and store the database you want to share.** We recommend a computer that is powerful enough to serve up data for all the users you want to access it. It's also a good idea restrict this PC from doing a lot of other work; let it just sit in the corner and be the

BCM server. If you have a domain controller and a network consultant, work with them so they can set this up for you.

✔ **All the users sharing the database must have the same version of Office 2007 and BCM installed.** You can't have some users on Office 2003 and some on Office 2007. Our assumption here is that you have Office 2007 loaded on all PCs with any service packs applied. To find out what version you're using, from the Outlook menu bar, choose Help⇨About Business Contact Manager for Outlook. Compare the version number you see there with the version numbers on other computers that share the database.

✔ **Users are either all in or all out.** You can't give someone permission to see some contacts or accounts but not others. You can turn off e-mail linking so they can't see e-mails sent or received, but all the data in the contact, account, opportunity, projects, and marketing campaigns is visible to everyone who shares the database.

If you need functionality that enables you to alter permissions, look at a software program such as Microsoft Dynamics CRM (www.microsoft. com/dynamics/crm/default.mspx) or ACT! (www.act.com).

✔ **You can choose how to share your database.** You can share the database within your office only, or you can allow people to take copies of it with them on a laptop, make changes while they're out of the office, and then synchronize their changes with the master database when they return. With the latter option, while you give up some security of your data, having your people constantly and consistently making notes about calls and visits and updating their opportunities daily makes for a more current system.

Sharing the Database Across a Network

When you've decided that you want to give others access to your database and you have a PC ready to be the server, you're ready to set up BCM on your network.

You have to take these three steps:

1. **Load the BCM software on the server PC.**

2. **Create the BCM master database on the BCM server.**

3. **Share your database.**

We discuss each of these steps in the following sections.

Step 1: Load the BCM software on the server PC

You can just load Outlook and BCM on that server PC. You don't need to load the rest of Office. We call this the *BCM server* on which the BCM master database is stored. It can be a PC sitting in the corner running Windows XP, or a domain controller, or a Microsoft Small Business Server, or Windows Server 2000 or 2003.

Step 2: Create the BCM master database on the BCM server

Launch Outlook on the BCM server PC. The first time you launch BCM, you go through the Microsoft Office Outlook 2007 with Business Contact Manager Wizard. (See Chapter 3 for details on this process.) Because this is a new installation, BCM takes you through this process on this PC. The new database you create is your shared BCM master database.

You might want to share the database you previously created on your PC with the other people in your group. You might expect to be able to just copy the files from your PC to the BCM server PC, but this is not the case. You must back up your BCM data from your PC's database and then restore it into the BCM server's master database.

Chapter 20 gives you all the details of the backup and restore processes — but here are the high points:

1. **On your PC, do a backup of your existing database.**

   When the backup wizard asks to which location to back up the database, choose the BCM Server PC's hard drive. This way, the data is already on that PC, ready to be restored to the BCM master.

2. **Go to the BCM server PC and restore that backup you just made.**

   The initial wizard created the BCM master database for you. It's empty of data, and you restore the data from your PC into that master. It's then populated with the data from your PC.

Step 3: Share your database

If you're using multiple BCM databases, you can choose which database to grant access to. But you must follow these steps for each database:

1. **From the Outlook menu bar, choose Business Contact Manager⇨ Database Tools⇨Share Database.**

   The first screen, Share Your Business Contact Manager Database, of the Share Database Wizard displays, as shown in Figure 11-1.

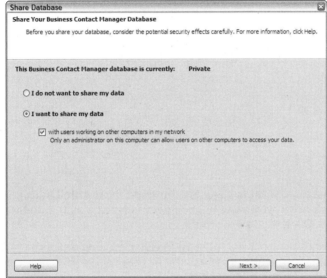

Figure 11-1:
Opening the
Share
Database
Wizard.

2. **Select the I Want to Share My Data option, specify whether that applies to a network, and click Next.**

   If this dialog box says, "This Business Contact Manager database is currently: Shared," the following changes affect the settings. It normally says "Private."

   If you're working with users on other PCs, select the With Users Working on Other Computers in My Network check box. If you want to share your data with users on this PC only, don't select that check box. This might be appropriate if you have only one PC (at a home office, for example) and your assistant uses your PC but logs in with her own login.

The second screen, E-Mail Auto-Linking Settings, of the wizard opens, as shown in Figure 11-2.

Share Database

E-Mail Auto-Linking Settings
To maintain your current settings, accept the default selection, and click Next.

☑ I want to keep my current E-Mail Auto-Linking settings

⚠ You may choose to change these settings when you share your database because e-mail messages can be shared accidentally and may result in confidential information being distributed unintentionally. To change your E-mail Auto-linking settings now or later, on the Business Contact Manager menu, click Manage E-mail Auto-Linking.

Help   < Back   Next >   Cancel

Figure 11-2:
E-mail auto-linking in a shared database.

3. **Select the I Want to Keep My Current E-Mail Auto-Linking Settings check box if you want to keep your current e-mail auto-linking settings. Click Next to continue.**

   While sharing e-mails is useful to give everyone a clear picture of interactions with contacts, you might have sensitive information in them that you don't want others to see.

   The third screen, Select Users, of the wizard opens, as shown in Figure 11-3.

4. **Select which users of this PC, or the domain's users, you want to grant permission to access your database. Click Next when finished.**

   Depending on your setup (peer-to-peer or domain), you might see all the users in your network. If you don't see the person you want to share the database with, you can add a new user to the list by following these steps:

   a. *Click the Add New User button.*

      The Select User dialog box opens.

   b. *Click the Browse button.*

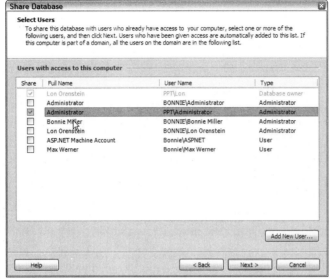

Figure 11-3:
Select users
who'll
share the
database.

c. *Enter the username in the Enter the Object Name to Select text box, and then click the Check Names button.*

The names of users are returned.

d. *Verify that the names are correct and click OK.*

e. *Click OK in the Add User dialog box to add that person to the list of users with whom you want to share the database.*

The fourth screen, Check Computer Settings for Database Sharing, of the wizard appears, as shown in Figure 11-4.

5. Choose whether you want to review the settings or if you'd rather leave it to BCM:

- *If you want to review the settings:* Select the I Want to Review the Settings That Will Be Changed check box, click Next, and you see the settings that you can review. Click Next to go to the next screen.

- *If you want BCM to handle the changes (the best idea!):* Deselect the I Want to Review the Settings That Will Be Changed check box and click Next.

The fifth screen, Grant Database Access, of the wizard appears, as shown in Figure 11-5.

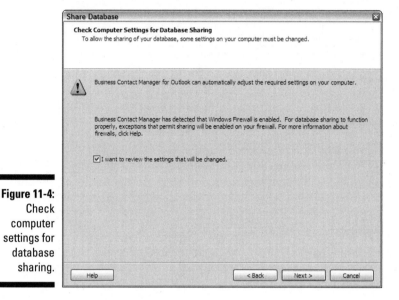

Figure 11-4:
Check
computer
settings for
database
sharing.

Figure 11-5:
Grant
database
access.

6. **Check whether the listed users are correct:**

   • *Click the Back button and move back through the wizard to correct your choices if any are wrong.*

   • *If all the users are listed correctly, click the Finish button and BCM shares your database with other users.*

   A new screen, Instructions for Using a Business Contact Manager for Outlook Shared Database, of the wizard appears.

7. **Print the customized page of instructions that BCM provides to your other users to show them how to connect to the shared database.**

   BCM puts the name of the computer and database into the instructions so your users have no doubt about how to connect. These instructions are also written to the hard drive of the PC you're working on, in the My Documents folder of the user you're logged in as. It's titled `Business Contact Manager Database Sharing Instructions for` *(name of the database you're sharing)*`.htm`. You can search for the filename on that PC to find it and then send it to the other users.

   You can also copy and paste the information into an e-mail that you send to users.

Connecting Each User's PC to the Database

When you've loaded the BCM server with Outlook and BCM, created the new BCM master database (and maybe loaded your existing data into it from your PC), and shared the master database with the correct users in your company, you can go to each user's PC and link its BCM to the BCM master database. This ensures that every time your users open BCM, the contacts, accounts, opportunities, projects, and marketing campaigns they see are the company's, and everyone is on the same page. An entry that a connected user makes is instantly available to other users and shows the user's name as the creator.

Follow these steps from each computer to connect it to the BCM database:

1. **From the Outlook menu bar, choose Business Contact Manager⇨ Database Tools⇨Create or Select a Database.**

   The Microsoft Office Outlook 2007 with Business Contact Manager Wizard starts. The Create or Select a Business Contact Manager Database screen appears, as shown in Figure 11-6.

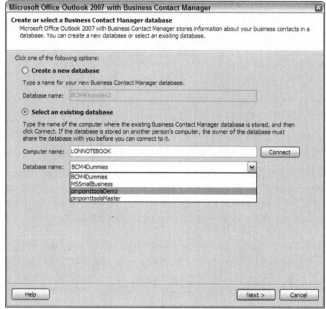

Figure 11-6:
Create or
select a
database.

2. **Choose the Select an Existing Database option.**

   You don't want to create a new database, so be sure that the Create a New Database option isn't selected.

3. **Enter the name of the BCM server in the Computer Name field and click the Connect button.**

   Your PC connects to that computer and shows you the BCM databases available for you to open.

4. **Choose the database you want to log in to from the Database Name drop-down list. Click Next to continue.**

   You receive a warning saying, "The automatic linking of e-mail will be turned off . . . ." This keeps your e-mail from automatically being linked into the shared database and able to be seen by all other users. If you want to enable that feature, check out Chapter 10 for more details.

5. **Click OK at the warning.**

   The Configure Database for Offline Use screen appears, as shown in Figure 11-7.

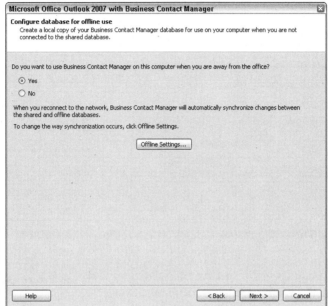

Figure 11-7:
Configure
database for
offline use.

6. **Choose how you want to set up the database for offline use.**

   - *If the PC you're connecting from is a desktop and never leaves the office, select No.*

   - *If you're connecting a laptop and you want to take the BCM database with you when you leave the office, select Yes.*

7. **(Optional) For more synchronization options, click the Offline Settings button.**

   The Offline Settings dialog box, shown in Figure 11-8, gives you the choice of how often to synchronize the BCM master with your local copy on your PC.

   This is applicable only when you're connected to the network, either physically in the office or via a VPN connection. Otherwise, skip to Step 10.

8. **(Optional) Decide what you want to do when the shared database is not available.**

   - *Switch Automatically to My Local Database:* Choose this option if you want BCM to automatically switch to the copy of the BCM master on your laptop.

   - *Don't Switch Automatically. I Will Switch Manually:* Choose this option if you want to decide when to switch to your local copy and when to reconnect online.

Figure 11-8:
Choosing
synchroni-
zation
options.

Most of the time, you want to automatically switch to your local database. The BCM master updates and saves your data as soon as you
reconnect, whenever that might be. Don't worry, be happy, enter data,
synchronize easily! Sometimes, you might want to choose not to connect
automatically — maybe you're working on your sales forecast and aren't
quite ready to send that data up to the boss.

 9. **(Optional) Click the Conflict Resolution tab to specify what you want
    BCM to do when two users enter conflicting data and click OK. (See
    Figure 11-9.)**

    Say you're on the road and find out that your customer has moved. You
    change the data on your laptop, then synchronize with the BCM master.
    In the meantime, a customer service person at headquarters finds out
    the same information while on the phone with the customer and makes
    similar changes. These options allow you to control which change
    wins — does the new change overwrite the existing data?

Figure 11-9:
Offline
Settings:
Conflict
Resolution.

10. **Click Next in the wizard.**

    The offline database is created, and your BCM is connected to the BCM master database.

    You see a progress bar for the creation of the offline database and then a new progress bar for the finalization of the BCM configuration.

To prove that you're now connected to the BCM master database, choose File➪Data File Management from the Outlook menu bar. You see the current Business Contact Manager database in the list of data files.

If you don't see the current database listed, click once to highlight the Business Contact Manager line, and then click Settings. Select the new BCM database in the Settings dialog box.

Your e-mail now connects to the BCM Contacts in the BCM master, not your local, personal BCM. If you still want to store you e-mail on your local copy, make changes in these settings by choosing Business Contact Manager➪ Manage E-mail Auto Linking from the Outlook menu bar.

Removing Access to a Shared Database

Say you decide that someone shouldn't have access to a database anymore. Maybe you've terminated the user. Or maybe you've consolidated databases and created a new master database so that this database can become a single user — you only! By removing sharing from a database, you make it more secure because someone would have to be logged in as you to access it.

Keep your login information secure and change your password often if you want to administer a more secure environment.

Follow these steps to remove access to a database:

1. **From the Outlook menu bar, choose Business Contact Manager➪Database Tools➪Share Database.**

   The Share Your Business Contact Manager Database screen of the Share Database Wizard opens. (Refer to Figure 11-1.)

2. **Select the I Do Not Want to Share My Data option. Click Next to continue.**

   The Removing Database Access Permissions screen appears.

3. **Click Finish.**

   BCM removes sharing access from this database. No users other than you can log in to the database. All the entries past users made in the database stay there with references to their user IDs in the records.

Chapter 12

Working with Opportunities

*I*n this chapter, we lead you through the entire sales process using BCM. We show you how to create an initial opportunity, make changes to it as the sale makes its way through the sales funnel, and view your opportunities by using the dashboards. For good measure, we even show you how to link your BCM opportunities with your Office Accounting opportunities — unless, of course, you would rather duplicate your efforts.

Taking Advantage of Opportunities

In BCM, an *opportunity* is a potential sale to a business contact or account, and each opportunity must be associated with either a business contact or account. When you create an opportunity, you actually create a brand-new item in much the same way that you create a new business contact or account. You can include the names of your products or services, specify a sales stage and forecasted close date, and even add a bunch of your own user-defined fields. If you prefer, you can create a new opportunity directly from a business contact or account record.

After creating an opportunity, you can go to the Opportunities folder in the Folder List, where you can see all your opportunities listed together. Or you can view the business contact's or account's Communication History tab. As if that isn't enough, you can choose from a slew of opportunities reports or access any of the neat opportunities dashboards. Whew!

Creating a new opportunity

So why are you sitting around reading a book? It's time for you to go out there and make some money — or at least track all those eggs that are going to hatch some time in the very near future.

There are a number of ways to make your first million — and track it in BCM:

- ✔ From either the business contacts or accounts folder, right-click the business contact or account and choose Create⇨New Opportunity for Business Contact (or Account).
- ✔ From the business contact or account record, choose New Communication History Item⇨Opportunity.
- ✔ From the business contact or account record, choose Office Button⇨ New Business Item⇨New Opportunity.

Whatever your method, the Opportunity window opens with the General button showing on the Ribbon, as shown in Figure 12-1.

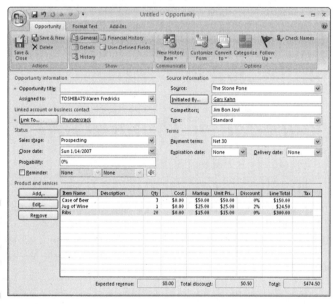

Figure 12-1:
Entering
a new
opportunity
record.

If you didn't know better, you might think that you're looking at a business contact or account record; some of the information you enter for an opportunity is very similar. Here's a rundown of the information you want to add:

✔ **Opportunity Information:** These are pretty much the must-have fields that you need to fill in with opportunity information:

- *Opportunity Title:* This field is mandatory so that you can identify your opportunities. Feel free to name the opportunity with an important tidbit of information like, "This one will finance my kids' education."

- *Assigned To:* You can access a list of the salespeople in your company and tie one of them to the opportunity.

- *Link To:* This field is required — it links the opportunity to a business contact or account. Click the Link To button to get to the Link to an Account or a Business Contact dialog box. (See Figure 12-2.) Select an account, click the Link To button, and then click OK. If you prefer, select Business Contacts from the Folder drop-down list and link one of your business contacts to the new opportunity.

Figure 12-2: Linking an account or business contact to a new opportunity.

✔ **Status:** You track the deal in this section as it moves through the sales process. It consists of four fields:

- *Sales Stage:* You can select a sales stage from the drop-down list.

- *Close Date:* You can indicate the date that you think your red-hot opportunity will convert into cold hard cash.

- *Probability:* This is the probability that the deal will close. You enter the probability based on the stage you're in.

  If you indicate that the Sales Stage is "Closed Won," the probability changes to 100%. If you indicate that the Sales Stage is "Closed Lost," the probability automatically changes to 0%.

- *Reminder:* You might want to set a reminder to follow up with the people who're trying to give you some of their hard-earned money. The Reminder field consists of a date, time, and alarm field. Click the alarm button and you can choose the alarm sound of your choice — a loud "ka-ching" is certainly appropriate.

  Sometimes it seems that BCM has reminders of its reminders. Case in point is the Follow-Up flag that is located on the Ribbon. It really doesn't make a whole lot of difference which one you choose, as long as you're reminded to follow up on this once-in-a-lifetime, money-making opportunity.

✔ **Source Information:** You can record where this opportunity came from in this section — and what little devil might be lurking in the background just waiting to snatch it away from you:

- *Source:* This is the main marketing source that helped you to reel in the big *kahuna.* If you're spending money on any type of marketing effort — Web site optimization, direct mail campaigns — fill in this field to track if you're getting any bang from your marketing buck.

- *Initiated By:* Just like the Link To field, this field lets you indicate the business contact or account who handed you this deal on a silver platter. This information might prove useful to you at holiday time when you're trying to decide who gets the great gift basket and who's going to have to contend with the lousy fruitcake.

- *Competitors:* Win or lose, you might want to know who your competition is.

- *Type:* You might think of this as a do-it-yourself field, as the choices can help you analyze your business a wee bit better. Maybe you differentiate between Commercial and Residential sales, or Wholesale and Retail products. Here's where you want to track that important information.

✔ **Terms:** In this section, you indicate the payment terms you're going to extend; the Expiration Date field lets you know at a glance how long that special pricing is good for. The Delivery Date field helps you remember when your client should receive your product.

Click Save & Close when you finish entering the opportunity information. Or if your business is really on a roll, click Save & New and forge on to your next opportunity.

You want to fill in as much information as possible. When you start to look at the dashboards, reports, and opportunity lists, you can use this information to perform searches, filters, and sorts.

Wrapping a ribbon around an opportunity

Just like in other records in BCM, the Ribbon at the top of the window gives you a few more places to store your data as well as a few more functions to help keep track of your opportunities. Chapter 4 talks about the Business Contact Ribbon, and Chapter 5 gives you the skinny on the Account Ribbon, so now we tell you what's specific to opportunities. You can accomplish these tasks from the Ribbon:

- ✔ **Add time-stamped comments:** Click the Details button in the Show area.

- ✔ **Add custom fields:** Click the User-Defined Fields button in the Show area. Tune in to Chapter 7 for more details!

- ✔ **Assign the opportunity to a category:** Click the Categorize button in the Options area. This button isn't specific to opportunities; you see its identical twins when working with business contacts and accounts. However, the concept of using categories is so important that we've devoted Chapter 6 to it.

Editing an opportunity

You might need to edit an opportunity for two reasons:

- ✔ You forgot to add some information the first time or some of your original information requires a bit of tweaking. (That's an official computer term.)

- ✔ You want to track the progress of the opportunity as it makes its way from freezing cold to super hot.

Here's all you have to do to make a change to an existing opportunity:

1. **Click the Opportunities folder in the Business Contact Manager area in the Folder List.**

    The Opportunities list appears, as shown in Figure 12-3.

2. Double-click the opportunity that you want to edit.

Not sure how to find the opportunity you're looking for? You can type your search criterion in the Search box at the top of the Opportunities list.

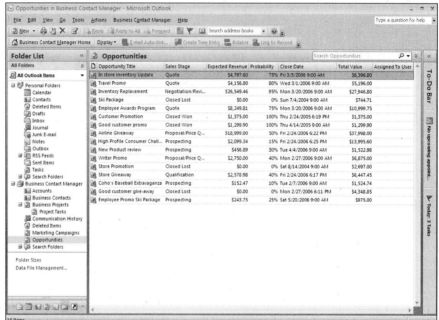

Figure 12-3:
Choose an opportunity to edit.

The Opportunity window for that record opens. (Refer to Figure 12-1.)

3. Make any changes you need.

In addition to adding information that you might have left off the first time, you want to make sure that you change the information in the Sales Stage field. This helps keep you on top of the opportunity as it follows along the path of your sales pipeline. As you work your way through the stages, the probability of closing becomes higher and higher.

4. Click Save & Close when you finish making all your changes.

Closing the deal

And now, the moment you've waited for — drumroll please — you're ready to close the deal. All those hours of sweating and chasing that prospect around are going to (hopefully) pay off in spades.

You close a deal in the same way that you edit one. Start with opening an existing opportunity. At that point, you select either Closed Won (yippee) or Closed Lost (gasp) from the Sales Stage drop-down list. As you make this change you'll notice these things:

- ✔ All the existing fields gray out, which means you can no longer enter additional information in them.

- ✔ The probability changes to 100% if you select Closed Won or 0% if you select Closed Lost.

- ✔ The boss greets you with a cigar and a slap on the back or a pink slip.

Deleting an opportunity

In general, you'd mark an opportunity as Closed Lost rather than just deleting it. (See the preceding section.) You can often gain valuable insight from a Lost Opportunity: Maybe one of your competitors is offering a brand-new product, or someone else is selling a comparable product for half the price. Other times, you might just want to get rid of the evidence: Perhaps the company you were selling to closed its doors for good, or maybe you inadvertently entered the same opportunity twice. Whatever the reason, the procedure for removing unwanted opportunities is as simple as choosing one of these methods:

- ✔ Right-click the opportunity record in the Opportunities Folder List and choose Delete.

- ✔ Double-click the opportunity record in the Opportunities Folder List to open it and then click the Delete button on the Ribbon.

- ✔ Highlight an opportunity record in the Opportunities Folder List and press Ctrl+D.

As soon as you perform one of those actions, your opportunity disappears. Quickly. Without further warning. Fortunately, when you delete an opportunity, it's gone but certainly not forgotten. It's sitting in Business Contact Manager's Deleted Items folder just waiting to be rescued. To do so, just drag it back to the Opportunities folder. To delete it permanently, right-click it in the Deleted Items folder and choose Delete.

Adding Products to Your Opportunity

The previous sections of this chapter show you how to create a basic opportunity. In this section, you find out how to add specific products and services to an opportunity. If you're like most people, this part is fun because those products and services come with a price tag — which, hopefully, translates into money in your pocket.

Show me the money!

You can add even more information about an opportunity in the Product and Services area that runs along the bottom of the General tab. Here's where you get to count the cash, bill for the beans, dream of the dollars . . . . In any event, the Products and Services portion of the General tab is where you get to add all the line items for your opportunity and sit back while BCM crunches the numbers for you.

Here's how you start counting those beans:

1. **Open an existing opportunity and click the Add button in the Opportunity window.**

   The Add Product or Service dialog box, shown in Figure 12-4, opens.

2. **Select the name of the product from the Item Name drop-down list.**

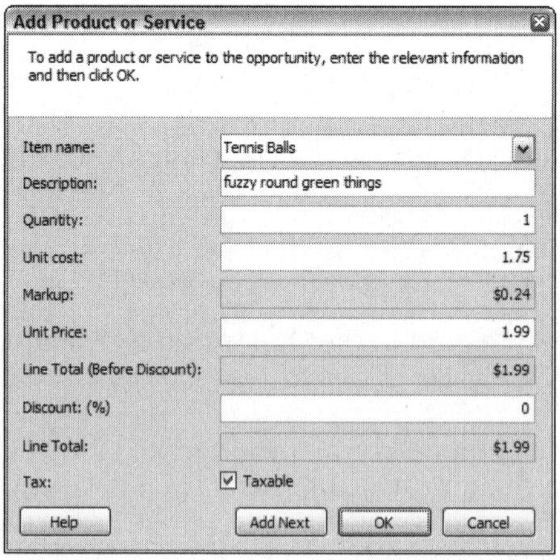

Figure 12-4:
Add a product or service.

You can simply type the first letters of a product name if you're already familiar with the items in your product list. If you find the product you need, move on to Step 3.

If you don't find the product that you need, choose Edit This List from the Item Name drop-down list.

The Products and Services dialog box opens. You see all the products and services that you've created in both BCM and Office Accounting proudly displayed in the Products and Services dialog box. Follow these steps to add a product:

>   a. *Click the Add button.*

>   The Add Product or Service dialog box opens.

>   b. *Fill in the juicy details about your product and then click Save.*

>   You have to add a unit price, but don't worry — you can override the amount every time you create a new opportunity if you need to.

>   c. *Click OK to close the Products and Services dialog box.*

 3. **Enter the quantity of the item you're selling.**

    When you set up your product list, you can set up a default quantity. Feel free to change it each time you create a new opportunity. As you change the quantity, the Line Total (Before Discount) field changes as well.

 4. **(Optional) Change the amounts in the Unit Cost and the Unit Price fields.**

    You can't enter anything into the Markup field because BCM is doing the math for you.

 5. **(Optional) Type a Discount percentage.**

 6. **Ooh and aah as the Line Total totals up for you.**

    Okay, you don't have to ooh and aah — or if you do, do it quietly so that the rest of the office doesn't think you have a stomachache.

 7. **Click OK if this is the only product you're entering, or click the Add Next button if you want to add another product.**

When you return to the Opportunity Detail tab, you might want to check out a couple of other options:

✔ Highlight a line item and click the Edit button to make a change.

✔ Highlight a line item and click the Remove button to remove an item from the opportunity. You're asked if you're sure you want to remove the item — the answer is Yes.

✔ Notice that the Total discount and the Total of the opportunity totals up at the bottom of the Product and Services table.

✔ Also notice an Expected Revenue field. This field is calculated based on the probability percentage and the total of all your line items.

Importing a CSV product list

In the preceding section, you find out how to add a product on-the-fly as you enter a new opportunity. That's great if you have only a product or two to add. However, you might find yourself with hundreds of products to add.

BCM imports .csv (comma-separated values) files, so make sure your product list is in that format. The file must contain three columns: Product Name, Description, and Unit Price, and they must be in that order. If you'd like, you can add a field for Default Quantity.

By definition, a .csv file uses the comma to determine where one field stops and the next one starts. Therefore, avoid using commas in the Unit Price column. Also, avoid dollar signs and any other symbols that might confuse the issue.

You have to return to the scene of the crime — or at least to your products database — in order to import your list of products. Follow these steps:

1. **Click Opportunities in the Business Contact Manager Folder List.**

2. **Open an existing opportunity by double-clicking it.**

   Don't have any existing opportunities? Then you'll have to click New on the Outlook toolbar and start a new one. Don't worry — once you've imported your list you can exit the opportunity without saving it.

3. **Click the Add button in the Product and Services area.**

   The Add Product or Service dialog box opens. (Refer to Figure 12-4.)

4. **Select Edit This List from the Item Name drop-down list.**

5. **Click the Import button.**

   The Import Product and Service Items Wizard opens, as shown in Figure 12-5.

6. **Click the Browse button, navigate to the file that contains your product list, and click Open.**

7. **Choose your import option.**

   You can add the items in the .csv file to your existing product list, or you can replace the existing product list with the items in the .csv file.

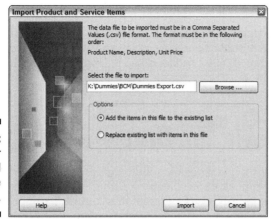

Figure 12-5:
Import your
product and
service
items.

8. **Click the Import button.**

   If the import is successful, you get a congratulatory message and you can sneak out to the driving range for a few hours. If BCM encounters errors, it points them out to you.

9. **(Optional) Correct any errors and try again.**

Editing or deleting a product or service

If you need to edit or delete a product or service, you do that in the same dialog box you add it in: the Product and Service dialog box. Follow these steps to make changes to your products or services:

1. **Click Opportunities in the Business Contact Manager Folder List.**

2. **Open an existing opportunity by double-clicking it.**

3. **Click the Add button in the Product and Services area.**

   The Add Product or Service dialog box appears.

4. **Select Edit this List from the Item drop-down list.**

   The Products and Services dialog box opens.

5. **Select a product and service and then do one of the following:**

   • *Click the Edit button to change the item name, description, default quantity, unit cost, or unit price of a product of service.*

   You can't edit an item that was synchronized to BCM from Office Accounting — you have to do your editing in Office Accounting.

• *Click the Delete button to remove a product or service.*

When you delete a product, it doesn't end up in the Deleted Items folder. When BCM asks if you want to delete the product, be absolutely sure. The product disappears permanently from the product list when you click the Yes button.

You Can Quote Me on That

The only thing better than making a lot of money is having plenty of time in which to count it. If you enable the link between BCM and Microsoft Office Accounting (see Chapter 13), you can transform your BCM opportunity into a quote, sales order, or invoice without having to re-input any data.

Here's all you need to do to make that happen:

1. **Click Opportunities in the Business Contact Manager Folder List.**

2. **Open an existing opportunity by double-clicking it.**

3. **Click Convert To in the Options group of the Ribbon.**

4. **Choose Quote, Sales Order, or Invoice from the drop-down list.**

   After a moment of thinking, Office Accounting opens the appropriate form with your information already entered into it. You might pause and give thanks for this wonderful feat.

If your information doesn't fill in automatically, you didn't do anything wrong — the business contact or account that is linked to your BCM opportunity doesn't exist in Office Accounting.

Business contact and account information needs to originate in Office Accounting and then get synchronized to BCM — the process doesn't work in the opposite direction.

Keeping an Eye on Your Opportunities

After you create an opportunity, you'll want to track your progress — and BCM has a variety of methods to do just that.

Checking the dashboard for sales information

By definition, a dashboard is the panel of dials, compartments, and instrument controls under the windshield of a vehicle. In case you're wondering why a book on Business Contact Manager is talking about car parts, it's because dashboards in computer software are very cool areas that contain several snapshots of your information. Dashboards appear on BCM's Home window. A *dashboard* is a graphical representation of your data. If a picture is worth a thousand words, then surely a dashboard is worth a million. Whereas a report might list your opportunities in plain, boring text format, a dashboard more typically depicts the information in the form of a colorful chart or graph.

Figure 12-6 shows two of the opportunity charts that are found in BCM.

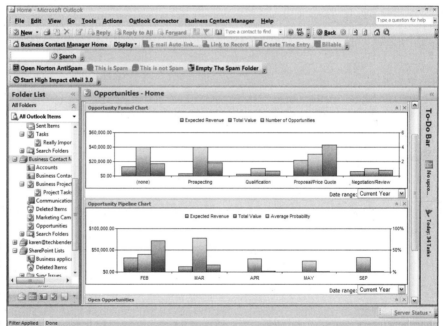

Figure 12-6:
Analyze your opportunities.

The Opportunity Funnel Chart shows the expected revenue, total value, and number of opportunities grouped by sales stage. The Opportunity Pipeline Chart shows the expected revenue, total value, and average probability grouped by month.

BCM comes with lots of dashboards that you can use to help you analyze your opportunity data. Follow these steps to add a dashboard to the BCM Home window:

1. **Click Business Contact Manager Home on the Business Contact Manager toolbar.**

2. **Click Add/Remove Content at the top of the Home window.**

   The Add/Remove Content dialog box opens, as shown in Figure 12-7.

3. **Select the check boxes for dashboards that you want to test drive and click OK.**

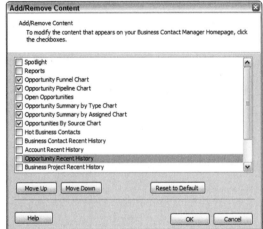

Figure 12-7:
Choose your
dashboard
content.

Reporting on your opportunities

Chapter 18 talks about the various BCM reports — suffice it to say, there's a bunch of them! Eight of the reports are specific to opportunities; they're listed on the Reports section of the Business Contact Manager menu, as shown in Figure 12-8.

These reports are based on the various information that you include for each of your opportunities. You might want to get a feel for some of those reports, so here's the lowdown:

✔ **Opportunities by Account:** Your opportunities are grouped by the accounts that they're linked to.

✔ **Opportunities by Business Contact:** Your opportunities are grouped by the business contacts that they're linked to.

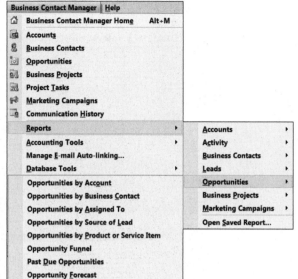

Figure 12-8:
The BCM
Reports
menu.

✔ **Opportunities by Assigned To:** Your opportunities are grouped by salesperson.

✔ **Opportunities by Source of Lead:** Your opportunities are grouped by the source of the lead — in other words, your marketing effort. If you're paying money for your marketing efforts and want to see your Return on Investment (RoI), this report is very useful.

✔ **Opportunities by Product or Services Item:** Your products and/or services are listed along with a total of how many are sold. This report can be particularly valuable to you if you carry an inventory or manufacture products.

✔ **Opportunity Funnel:** Your opportunities are sorted and grouped by Sales Stage.

✔ **Past Due Opportunities:** Compares the expected closing date to today's date and gives you a list of the opportunities that are more than 90 days old.

✔ **Opportunity Forecast:** Shows the opportunities that are expected to close within the next week.

Reporting is one of the times when less *isn't* more. If you want these reports to work for you, make sure you fill in each opportunity as thoroughly as possible. If you have insufficient opportunity data, the report is empty, as shown in Figure 12-9.

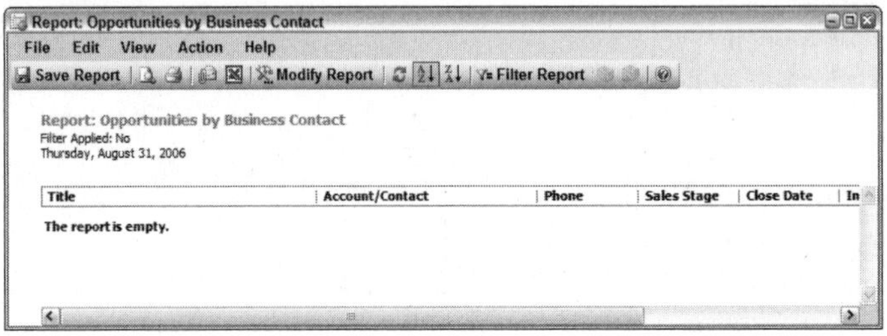

Figure 12-9:
An empty
report.

Report: Opportunities by Business Contact

File   Edit   View   Action   Help

Save Report   Modify Report   Filter Report

Report: Opportunities by Business Contact
Filter Applied: No
Thursday, August 31, 2006

Title	Account/Contact	Phone	Sales Stage	Close Date	In
The report is empty.					

Chapter 13

Accounting We Will Go

● ●

In This Chapter

▶ Granting permissions

▶ Linking BCM to Office Accounting

▶ Using BCM to feed money data into Accounting

▶ Seeing Accounting's data in BCM

● ●

*O*ne of the best benefits of using BCM is that it links directly to Microsoft Office Accounting. If you purchased BCM in the Small Business Edition, Accounting is included in the suite. Microsoft Office Accounting is competitive with QuickBooks — QuickBooks has some functions that Accounting doesn't, and vice versa. Accounting imports your existing QuickBooks file and re-creates all your accounts and transactions. And, the Express version is *free!* You can get the details at www.ideawins.com.

Here are some of the things you can do after BCM is integrated with Accounting:

✔ View the financial history of accounts in BCM that are the same as Customers in Accounting. This is both a summary of data (balance and sales information) and the transaction level (date, type, and amount of each transaction).

✔ Edit the individual transaction in BCM's screen, and it's updated in Accounting.

✔ Refresh your products and services from Accounting to use in opportunities — opportunities become Quotes, Sales Orders, or Invoices in Accounting.

✔ Track billable time using BCM's project tasks, phone logs, tasks, and appointments. Send them over to Accounting so you can bill your clients without reentering the data. You can use the same entries to pay your employees or workers for the time they've billed, too.

✔ Get a 360-degree view of your whole relationship with your customer by seeing all their data in one place — BCM!

In this chapter, you discover how to share the BCM and Accounting databases, link them, set up users' permissions to access the data, and move data both ways between them.

Setting Up Your Network

Because of the increased security necessary in today's world, you need to specify which users get to view, add, or change your data. That's why there are all these rules. Here are some tasks to do while you're setting up BCM and Accounting to work together:

- ✔ **If you have multiple users, set up the Accounting program and BCM on a dedicated PC.** This PC doesn't necessarily have to be a Microsoft Small Business Server or other, beefier PC. It does need to run Windows XP Professional SP2 or Windows Server 2003 SP1 (or higher).

- ✔ **Set up the Windows Administrator of the PC (or Administrator's Group in a domain) on which you're loading Accounting.** Those Administrators are needed to create users, assign roles, change users' roles, and remove users' access in Accounting.

- ✔ **Set up User Accounts to belong to a Windows Group.** The Users have to access the PC holding the Accounting data.

- ✔ **In a non-domain workgroup, you must add each user as a Windows user to each PC the user is going to use.** Make sure each user has the same password at each PC also.

- ✔ **Be careful when you remove a user from Accounting.** If you remove a user from Accounting who is a member of the Windows Administrator Group, the user still retains Accounting privileges until he's also removed from the Windows Administrator Group.

- ✔ **Allow all members of the Windows Administrator group to have full access to Accounting.** This access includes installation, setting up the company, and managing users. To safeguard your company records, make sure that only appropriate users are listed in the Windows Administrator group on the computer or in the domain where Accounting is installed.

  When one user accesses Accounting and works with the same data as another user, all other authorized users are locked out of the data in use. When there is any conflict, the last user to write data in the area updates that data. This way, one user can't change information while it is being accessed by another user.

- ✔ **Run Windows Vista in order to take advantage of the security features.** If data security and access is a concern for you, check out Microsoft's Web site for Microsoft Office Accounting www.ideawins.com.

Sharing the Accounting Database

If you're putting both BCM and Accounting on the same PC, don't worry; it's a cinch. If you're sharing these databases across a LAN with multiple users, you don't have to be a network guru to get the programs linked together, but it might help to have a consultant close by if you're not network savvy. All you need are these two programs — you don't have to perform any voodoo on your network or hardware.

This section details what you do on the PC where Microsoft Office Accounting is installed. You have two steps here:

1. **Setting up users and roles.**
2. **Integrating the database.**

Setting up users and roles

In Microsoft Office Accounting, you can define which users in the company can see which data. Financial data is much more sensitive than phone numbers and addresses, so Accounting has roles that you can create for your different users. A *role* is a set of permissions you assign that permits a user to access certain parts of the Accounting data and keeps them out of others. Setting roles is how you can maintain the security of your data and not let the wrong people see the payroll information, for example.

You're probably the Owner role. Your assistant might have the Office Manager role. Salespeople can have Sales roles. You can even create ten different customizable roles. This is how Accounting knows which data to make available to which user.

Each user in Accounting is either a user in the domain or a user on the PC where the database is stored. That person is also the same user you allow to share the BCM data. To give that person permission in the soon-to-be-shared, integrated database, follow these steps:

1. **From Microsoft Office Accounting, choose File⇨Manage Users and Roles.**

    The Manage Users dialog box opens, as shown in Figure 13-1. You must have Administrator privileges in order to make these changes.

    If users are entered, make sure they're the ones you want to access data from the integrated BCM and Accounting database and that their roles are correct.

- *To remove users:* Click the user's name once to highlight the record and then click the Remove button. Confirm the deletion, and the user is removed from accessing Accounting data.

- *To edit a user's settings*: Click once on the user's name to highlight the record and then click the Edit button. You can change their role or remove their status as an Application Administrator. Click OK to save your changes or Cancel to quit without saving changes.

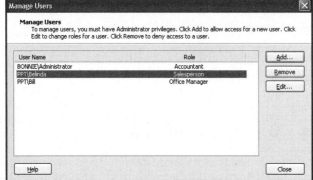

Figure 13-1:
Manage
Users
dialog box.

2. **To add a User to Accounting, click the Add button.**

   The Add User dialog box, shown in Figure 13-2, opens.

3. **Fill in the User Name field:**

   - *If you know the user's name*: Enter it in the User Name field.

Figure 13-2:
Add User
dialog box.

- *If you don't know the user's name:* Click the Select User button and then click the Locations button. Choose the domain by clicking its name; then click OK. In the Enter the Object Name to Select text box, enter the user's name and click the Check Names button. This verifies that you entered the correct name by displaying all user names that are close and enables you to choose the right user. Make sure the correct user is there, and then click OK. The name is entered in the User Name field.

4. **Enter a domain name in the Domain field.**

5. **Choose a role from the Role drop-down list.**

6. **If you want the user to be an Application Administrator, select the Application Administrator check box.**

   An Application Administrator has the permissions needed to set up this integration and the ability to control the SQL Server Accounting database.

   For more choices on configuring the roles, click the Manage Roles button. You can customize the ten roles so that your user groups have different types of access — Full Control, Read Only, or No Access, and so on — to the various types of data in Accounting.

7. **Click OK in the Add User dialog box to finalize the setup and add the users to the list of users in Accounting**.

Now that you have the users set up, you can run the wizard to actually link BCM and Accounting together.

Integrating the database

When you first install Accounting, a wizard sets up your company, and you can choose to integrate with Business Contact Manager. If you didn't integrate, follow these steps to run the wizard to integrate BCM with Accounting:

1. **From Microsoft Office Accounting, choose Company➪Integrate with Business Contact Manager.**

   The Integrate with Business Contact Manager for Outlook Wizard launches.

   It explains in the first screen that after this integration is completed, BCM and Accounting share the same physical database. This is good! Changes made from within BCM update Accounting, and vice versa. In the event that you disable this integration later, the data stays in the Accounting database for that company.

2. Click Next to continue.

The Select a Business Contact Manager for Outlook Database screen appears, as shown in Figure 13-3.

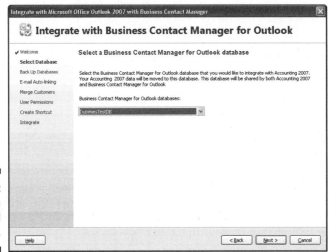

Figure 13-3:
Select a
BCM
database.

3. Select the BCM database to integrate with Accounting from the Business Contact Manager for Outlook Databases drop-down list. Click Next to continue.

The Back Up Databases screen appears, as shown in Figure 13-4.

4. Specify where you want to back up your databases. If you want to password-protect the databases, enter the passwords in the fields provided. Click Next to continue.

This wizard requires that you make a backup copy of both the BCM and Accounting databases before it integrates them — grand idea, and we concur!

The Business Contact Manager for Outlook E-Mail Auto-Linking screen appears, as shown in Figure 13-5.

5. Choose whether to link your Outlook e-mail and then click Next to continue.

   • *Keep Current Business Contact Manager for Outlook E-Mail Auto-Linking Settings:* This means that you have decided to share some or all e-mails with the rest of the users, depending on the settings in effect. You can see the settings by choosing Business Contact Manager⇨Manage E-Mail Auto-Linking from the Outlook menu bar.

- *Disable Business Contact Manager for Outlook E-Mail Auto-Linking:*
  This setting means that e-mails are not shared with other users of
  the BCM database.

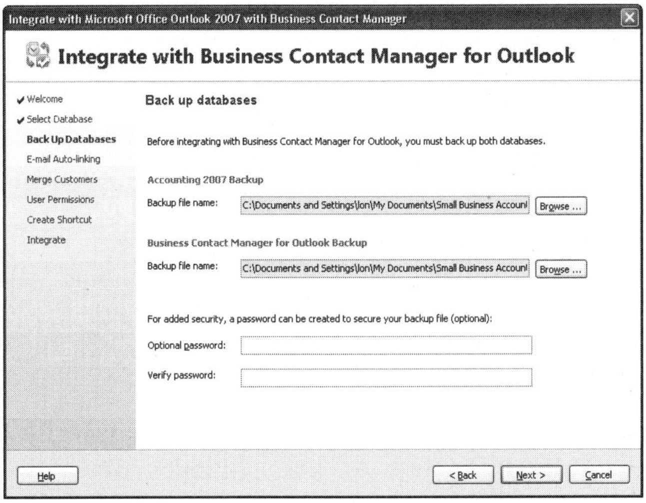

Figure 13-4:
Back
up your
databases.

Because BCM automatically links e-mails and every user of the BCM database can see these, you might want to rethink how much data you want
to share. See Chapter 10 for more explanations about these settings.

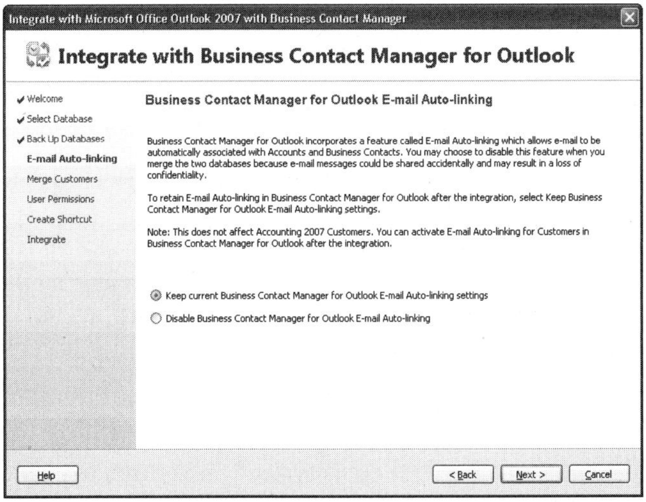

Figure 13-5:
Link your
e-mail.

The Merge Duplicate Customers and Accounts screen appears, as shown in Figure 13-6.

6. Choose whether to merge duplicate customers and accounts and click Next.

BCM's accounts are integrated with Accounting's customers — note that the accounts integrate, not the contacts, in BCM. If two are the same, do you want them merged together or both added to the integrated database? If you're not sure which data is being combined, you might choose Keep Duplicate Accounts and Customers, then review the data after the merge, and delete what you don't want.

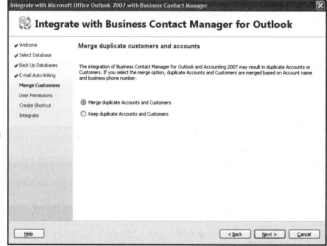

Figure 13-6:
Merge
duplicate
customers
and
accounts.

The Review Accounting 2007 Permissions screen appears, as shown in Figure 13-7.

7. Review Accounting 2007 permissions and click Next to continue.

These are the users you set up. All users can access BCM, but only those listed here can create documents in Accounting or view financial data in BCM. One nice thing here is that you can change a user's role by choosing a different role from the Accounting 2007 Role column.

The Create Shortcut screen appears.

8. Create a new shortcut and click Next to continue.

This creates a new shortcut that Windows uses to tell Accounting where the database is located. There is typically no reason to change this because Accounting knows what it's doing!

The Ready to Integrate screen appears, as shown in Figure 13-8.

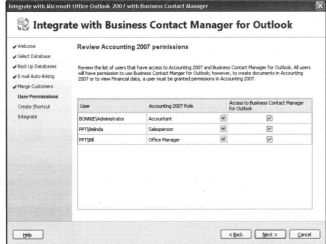

Figure 13-7:
Review
access to
Accounting
2007.

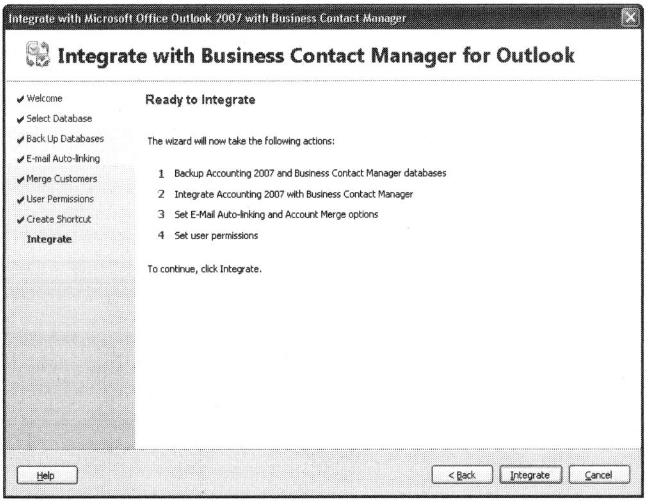

Figure 13-8:
Ready to
integrate!

9. **Review your choices and click the Integrate button to continue or Cancel to start over.**

The linking process might take a while to complete, especially because you're doing a backup first, so just be patient. "A watched database never integrates," is the saying.

During the integration, all account records in BCM are copied into Accounting as customers; however, these customer records don't become active in Accounting until you select each customer from a drop-down list or from the Customer list. All locations where customers appear reflect the integrated list of account and customer records (for example, the Customer Name Field on quotes, sales orders, or invoices).

If you delete an account record in BCM, the change in Accounting depends on whether the customer is active. If the customer isn't active, the customer record is deleted; if the customer is active, the customer status changes to inactive.

If you delete a BCM account record that is related to an active Accounting customer, the contacts that have been added to the customer record during the integration are removed from that customer record.

Disconnecting BCM from Accounting

So, you've had a change of heart or mind and don't want your BCM and Accounting linked anymore?

If you disable integration, whatever information you added to Accounting from the integration remains.

Follow these steps to unlink BCM from Accounting:

1. **From the Accounting menu bar, choose File⇨Utilities⇨Data Utilities.**

   The Data Maintenance dialog box opens.

2. **Click the Advanced Tools tab.**

3. **Click the Disable button.**

   A list of BCM databases displays.

4. **Select the database once to highlight it and then click the Disable button.**

   The integration between BCM and Accounting is removed but leaves all the data in the Accounting database.

Flowing Data from BCM into Accounting

Entering data into BCM in your normal course of activity gets you big benefits by having data show up in Accounting. Just by keeping track of your billable time in a task or appointment or phone log makes that show up in an invoice in Accounting that you send to your client. Tracking opportunities in BCM through the sales process and then having a Sales Order created in Accounting without having to reenter data is a huge timesaver, not to mention more accurate!

In this section, you discover how to go with the flow of data and use BCM with Accounting on a daily basis to get your data entered and moved into Accounting.

Creating a quote, sales order, or invoice

Start with an opportunity. Add three tablespoons of product data integrated from Accounting. Stir well and send into Accounting as a quote, sales order, or invoice. That's what's available for you when you use BCM and Accounting in tandem. Tracking opportunities as they move through the sales process is valuable enough in itself — and even more so when you can send it right into your accounting program.

So, assume you're working on a new deal for an existing customer. You have an opportunity that you've been modifying for a couple of months — adding items, changing quantities, adjusting prices as you're beat up by the customer. Now the customer gives you the okay to send an official quote. This process is exactly the same for converting the opportunity to a Sales Order or Invoice, just with different options.

For more information about creating and modifying opportunities, see Chapter 12.

Follow these steps to turn an opportunity in BCM into a quote in Accounting:

1. **From any view of opportunities, open the opportunity you want to convert to a quote.**

   Double-click the opportunity in the list, or right-click it and choose Open.

2. **From the Ribbon, in the Options group, click the Convert To button and then choose Quote from its drop-down list.**

The Quote window opens, as shown in Figure 13-9.

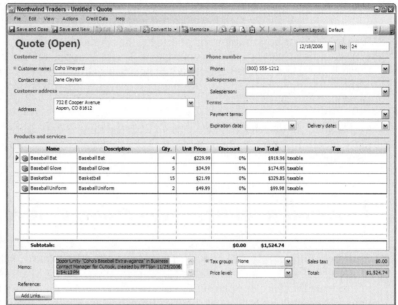

BCM copies all the data it can into the Quote window.

At this point, you're in Microsoft Office Accounting, not BCM. So, if you want to change quantities or pricing or add and delete items, go ahead and modify the quote.

3. **Review and enter necessary information.**

Note that the Memo field shows which opportunity the quote comes from. This is a handy way to keep track of how your quotes were generated.

4. **When finished modifying data, click the Save and Close button to save the record in Microsoft Office Accounting.**

The quote is stored in Accounting and is visible in BCM in the Financial History view (see Figure 13-13).

The opportunity is still showing in BCM — the quote is a separate record stored in Accounting. You should continue to track the opportunity through to the end of the sales process.

Creating time entries

Creating time entries is our favorite feature of using BCM and Accounting because you can easily keep track of your billable time. Staying on top of what work you do for a client, detailing the description of the work you perform, and getting it into your accounting program might be one of the most tedious tasks you have to do. If you don't keep up on your accounting (which is all too common), you have no cash flow — no billing leads to no payments from customers, which leads to no cash in the bank. Sound familiar?

You can create billable entries for Accounting from appointments, tasks, phone logs, and project tasks. So, just by scheduling an appointment on your calendar and updating the time worked, you have your billing handled!

Follow these steps to create a time entry for an appointment, phone log, or task:

1. **Open a task, appointment, or phone log.**

   This can be from a list of tasks, a calendar view, or a history view within an account record.

2. **Link your task, appointment, or phone log to an account record.**

   If you didn't link your item when you initially created it, click the Link to Record button on the Ribbon.

3. **Enter the Start Date, End Date, and the Time, if appropriate.**

   BCM and Accounting use these dates to calculate the time to bill for appointments and phone logs.

4. **Enter a good description of the work you did so that it flows through to Accounting.**

   Enter this description as close to the time you do the work as possible so that it's fresh in your mind — when you submit these as time entries into Accounting, you'll be glad you did.

Here are the specifics about each item type and what data flows into Accounting in what form:

✓ **Project tasks:** In a project task, you enter the description of the work performed in the Comments field, and you can add a time stamp to each entry. When the project task becomes a time entry in Accounting, the entire Comments field is copied into the time entry's Comments field. The subject of the project task becomes the description in the time entry record.

✔ **Task:** In a task, the Billing Information field on the Details tab becomes the description on the time entry. You can track how much total time (in the Total Work field) you spent on this task and then bill the client less or more (the Actual Work field). It's the Actual Work total that flows through to be the billed amount. If you plan to deduct mileage on your income tax return, fill in the Mileage field. The IRS loves documentation on how much you drove for each client on each day.

✔ **Phone Logs:** If you bill the time you spend on phone calls, the phone log is the place to enter the time and description of your conversations. Enter comments in the Comments field and click the Add Time Stamp button to record repeated entries. The subject of the phone log becomes the description of the time entry.

✔ **Appointments:** Enter a subject that becomes the description. Enter any comments in the big white box at the bottom, which becomes the Comments section on the time entry.

Submitting time entries to Accounting

You have two different ways of submitting the time entries to Accounting: one at a time as you enter them (or review them later) or in a group or batch. There's no right or wrong method here — it's up to your business style and practices.

Creating time entries as you enter them

Creating time entries as you enter them is especially handy for the times when you do some work and immediately want to generate an invoice or get the time worked into Accounting immediately. Follow these steps:

1. **From the Ribbon, click the Create Time Entry button in the Business Contact Manager group.**

   The Time Entry window opens. Figure 13-10 shows a Time Entry window for a task.

   The Time Entry window is part of Accounting, not BCM. If you enter the data correctly in the original task or other item, the data flows into the time entry.

2. **Make any further modifications to the time entry.**

   Depending on the type, other fields such as Billing Item and Pay Type can link to payroll so that you can pay the worker for the time worked.

   Select the Billable check box to bill the entry or leave it blank to not bill it immediately but keep it in the Accounting database.

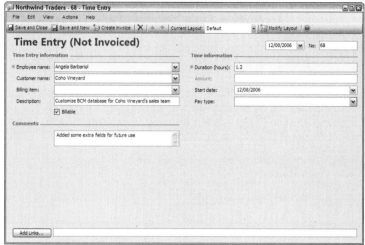

Figure 13-10:
Creating a
time entry in
a task.

3. **Click Save and Close to save the record in Accounting.**

4. **(Optional) To create an invoice, click the Create Invoice button.**

   An Invoice dialog box from Office Accounting opens. You have the
   option of changing any of the data and then clicking Save and Close.
   An invoice from the time entry is created. You can now send the invoice
   to the customer as appropriate, collect the money, and go to the bank!

Creating time entries in a group

Creating time entries as part of a group is the more routine way of billing
time. As you enter these items into BCM, you mark each one as billable in
BCM. At the end of your billing period (weekly, twice a month, monthly, or
whenever you run out of cash), you review the entries marked as billable and
then send the group over to Accounting all at once. You can then generate
and send invoices in Accounting in a batch. Follow these steps:

1. **Mark the item as billable with one of these methods:**

   • On the Ribbon, in either the Business Contact Manager or Options
     group, click the Billable button.

   • On the BCM toolbar, click the Billable button.

   The Billable button is highlighted, so you can tell at a glance whether an
   item is marked as billable. A Billable field is under the Ribbon to show
   you that it's marked.

2. **To send the marked items to Accounting, choose Business Contact Manager⊅Accounting Tools⊅Submit Billable Time from the Outlook menu bar.**

   Alternatively, from the BCM Home window, click the Projects tab and then click the Submit Billable Time button.

   The Submit Billable Time dialog box opens, as shown in Figure 13-11. All items marked as Billable appear in the grid, filtered by the Look For time frame chosen (This Week, Previous Week, This Month, Previous Month).

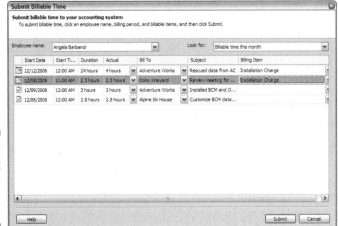

Figure 13-11:
The Submit
Billable
Time dialog
box.

3. **Choose your name from the Employee Name drop-down list, if it's not already showing.**

   If your name isn't here, you must add it in Accounting in order for it to show up. It's necessary to have your name showing here so that the items are linked to you when they land in Accounting. In Accounting, you can add a new employee by choosing Employee⊅New Employee from the main menu.

4. **To change the items based on billing date, click the Look For drop-down list and choose another time period.**

   The items displayed in the grid change appropriately.

5. **(Optional) Assign a service item from Accounting to an item from the Billing Item drop-down list.**

You can keep track of what kind of work you're doing and get a report that breaks this down for you in Accounting.

6. **Modify the Actual time submitted or even change the account you're billing to.**

   If you have changes you want to make to the item, click Cancel, go back to the item, make the changes, and start over at Step 2.

7. **Click Submit to send these items into Accounting.**

   A Time Submitted field is added to the right of the Billable field on the Ribbon.

Using Data from Accounting in BCM

Due to the amount of work you do in Accounting, you might think Accounting is in charge of this relationship with BCM; for the most part, that's true. Some key functions are available in BCM to make use of the Accounting data without having to run the Office Accounting program. The main purpose of keeping the data inside BCM is to give you and your team a 360-degree view of the customer — all the data concerning that entity in one place.

The customer in Accounting is an account in BCM.

You access the Accounting data from within the account record, and that's exactly how it works. Even though your opportunity or quote is now stored on the Accounting side, you can see it and modify it from within BCM.

Looking at financial history and summary information inside BCM

Where is this 360-degree view? It's in the account record. Open the Account window by choosing Display⇨Accounts.

Click the Financial Summary button in the Show group on the Ribbon. The financial data appears, as shown in Figure 13-12. These fields are read-only — they can't be changed. They're stored in Accounting and are displayed in real time. If you make changes in Accounting, the data is refreshed in the Account window.

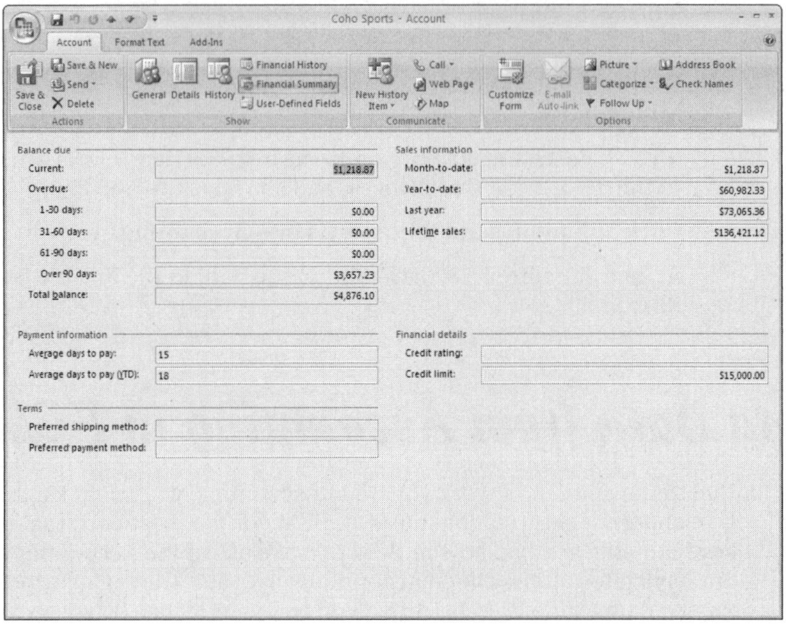

Figure 13-12:
The
Account
window
shows the
financial
summary.

The Financial History window gives you more capabilities for interacting with the data. In this display, you see individual transactions for that account — invoices, payments, quotes, and more. To see the financial history, follow these steps:

1. **From the Ribbon, in the Show group, click the Financial History button.**

   The Account window changes to a grid display showing transactions in Accounting that are linked to this account record (customer in Accounting), as shown in Figure 13-13.

2. **Double-click any line in the grid display to show the details.**

   At this point, you see the item displayed in the form from Accounting that is appropriate. For example, a customer payment shows in the Customer Payment dialog box from Accounting, and an invoice displays in the Accounting Invoice dialog box.

   You are *live* in the Accounting application, and any changes you make affect that data.

3. **If you make changes, click Save and Close on the menu bar of the dialog box.**

To cancel without making any changes, click the X in the upper-right corner and click No when asked to save changes.

To find information in the grid display, you can click the column headers of any column, just like in other BCM displays. The data sorts in ascending and then descending order by Date, Document #, Type, Business Contact, or Total Amount. This makes it handy to find data — but there's no search function in this dialog box, as in other BCM dialog boxes.

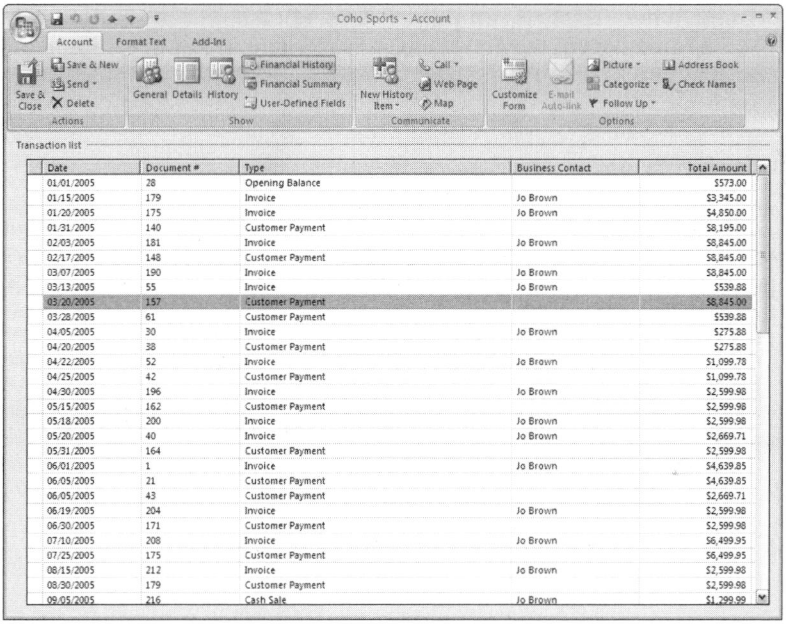

Figure 13-13:
The
Account
window
showing
Financial
History.

Running reports in BCM using Accounting data

Another useful integration between BCM and Accounting is the ability to run financial reports from within BCM. After you do the integration, you get a new menu option enabling you to run reports that show Accounting data. Follow these steps to run a report with Accounting:

1. **From the Outlook menu, choose Business Contact Manager➪Reports➪ Financial Reports.**

   The Financial Reports dialog box, shown in Figure 13-14, opens.

2. **Select a report group in the Report Group column.**

   The reports available in the Reports column on the right change accordingly.

3. **Select a report from the Reports column and then click the Open Report button.**

   The report runs and appears in a report viewer window. For more information on reports, check out Chapter 18. You can choose from many options to filter the data, format the report, group the data, and more.

4. **When finished running reports, click the Close button or X in the upper-right corner to close the Financial Reports dialog box.**

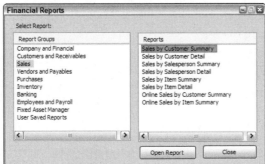

Figure 13-14:
The Financial Reports dialog box.

Part V
Communicating with the Outside World

The 5th Wave   By Rich Tennant

"We should cast a circle, invoke the elements, and direct the energy. If that doesn't work, we can see what BCM says the probability of our making a sale is."

In this part . . .

You've added contacts and accounts into BCM and hopefully started selling your widgets. However, you might be getting impatient at your progress and want to kick up your sales to the next level with a bit of marketing. In this part, you find out how to reach an audience of one or thousands through the use of snail mail or e-mail. You'll use E-Mail Marketing Service to help you run a full scale marketing campaign. Finally, as you dash from customer to customer, you check your information from your mobile device, laptop — or from the nearby Internet café.

Chapter 14

Merging BCM with Word

. . . .

. . . .

*T*he idea of using BCM to send marketing e-mails, letters, or postcards is one of the key concepts of customer relationship management. Staying in touch with your prospects and customers on a regular basis can keep your business at the tops of their minds.

In this chapter, we show you how to use the mail merge feature to create personalized letters — as well as mailing labels and envelopes — from the data in your account or business contact records. In Chapter 15, we show you how to create marketing campaigns with letters you create.

The terms *mail merge* and *mass mailings* are used interchangeably in BCM and Office 2007, even though *mass* can be just two or three people. They both denote merging some of the data in BCM into documents (e-mails, letters, postcards, labels, flyers, newsletters, and anything else you can format).

Merging BCM data into documents and e-mails is a dance between Word and BCM. Word leads the way, and BCM supplies the oomph to make the final outcome exciting. The basic data coming from BCM, such as First Name, is easy — *Dear <<FirstName>>.* But because you can add fields of data to BCM, you can construct sentences such as *You know, <<FirstName>>, since we met at <<Last Trade Show Attended>>, we've improved the value proposition on our <<Product Interested In>> to the point where you can't ignore it any longer.* By adding fields of data to BCM such as <<Last Trade Show Attended>> and <<Product Interested In>>, you make the merged document more personal and important to the recipient. That's what BCM and Word can do for your mail merges.

Setting Up Your Document

You might be familiar with the term *template*. This is similar to what Word calls the *main document*. It's the place where you put your text — "We're pleased to invite you to our Spring Golf Tournament, Bob, and hope you'll be able to attend." You include merge codes (such as <<First Name>>) so that the e-mail or letter is personalized for Bob.

If you don't want to start from scratch, check out templates you can use as a starting point for your letter at `http://office.microsoft.com/en-us/templates/default.aspx`.

You're now working in Word, not BCM!

Follow these steps to set up your document for fast merging:

1. **In Word, from the Mailings tab on the Ribbon, click Start Mail Merge.**

   You're presented with the types of documents you might want to use to create the main document.

2. **Select the type of document you want.**

   Choose from Letters, E-Mails, Envelopes, Labels, or *Directory* (which is like a catalog where you're listing contacts and information about them).

Save the document often. You can return to this main document whenever you like and resume what you were doing. When you link the document to BCM's contacts, you're asked whether you want to retrieve data. These data selections are also save in the document.

Selecting Contacts from BCM

The connection from the document to the contacts is actually saved inside the document. In this section, you select where to get the contacts you want to merge — your answer is BCM (at least in *this* book).

Follow these steps to select your contacts:

1. **In Word, from the Start Mail Merge group on the Ribbon, click the Select Recipients button, and then choose Select from Outlook Contacts.**

   If you don't have Outlook open when you start this, you're first asked to choose your profile from the Choose Profile dialog box.

a. Choose from the Profile Name drop-down list.

If you have only one profile, it's named Default.

b. Click OK to continue.

If you're already logged into Outlook, it knows which profile is active and shows you the various lists of contacts in that profile.

The Select Contacts dialog box opens (as shown in Figure 14-1), listing the various BCM account and contact lists, address books, and personal contacts.

Figure 14-1:
The Select
Contacts
dialog box.

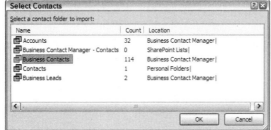

2. **Select a contact folder to import and click OK.**

The Mail Merge Recipients dialog box (shown in Figure 14-2) shows all your BCM contacts (and accounts).

3. **Select the contacts you want to include in this mail merge.**

You have a couple of ways to choose the contact or account records:

- *Select all or clear all:* Select the check box in the column header to select all of your contacts, or deselect it to exclude all of your contacts.

- *Select individual recipients:* Select the check box for each contact you want to include in the merge.

  If you want to include a few people, deselect all of the check boxes first; then select the few records to send your document to.

  If you're sending e-mails to most of the list, select all the check boxes and then deselect the ones you don't want to send to.

You can sort the list by clicking the name of the field in the column header. The arrow shows you whether it's in ascending or descending order.

To rearrange the columns, grab the header field with your mouse and drag the column to another position. Unfortunately, when you leave this dialog box, the columns revert to the default.

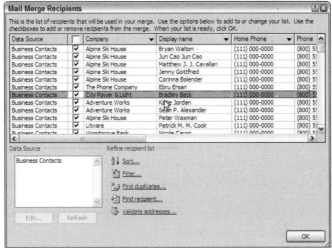

Figure 14-2:
The Mail
Merge
Recipients
dialog box.

4. **(Optional) Further refine your contacts.**

In the Refine Recipient List area in the bottom half of the Mail Merge Recipients dialog box, you find the following tools for refining your merge list:

- Sort
- Filter
- Find Duplicates
- Find Recipient
- Validate Addresses

We discuss how you can use these tools in the four sections that follow this one.

5. **Click OK when you're done.**

6. **Save your document.**

Sorting your fields

In order to choose which contacts you want to include in the mail merge, it's sometimes handy to sort the list in different ways to see that data differently. These Sort and Filter functions allow you to include or exclude people from the final merge. To sort your fields, follow these steps.

1. **Click the Sort link in the Mail Merge Recipients dialog box.**

   The Filter and Sort dialog box opens, as shown in Figure 14-3. You see two tabs: Filter Records and Sort Records.

2. **Click the Sort Records tab.**

Figure 14-3:
Sorting your
records.

3. **Choose the field you want to sort from the Sort By drop-down list.**

4. **Choose Ascending or Descending order from the radio buttons to the right of the Sort By field.**

   Word sorts the records first by this choice.

5. **(Optional) Pick two other fields to sort from the Then By drop-down lists.**

   For example, you can sort by Company first and then by Display Name so that you see all the contacts for each company in order.

6. **Click OK.**

Filtering your contacts

Use filtering to select multiple criteria you want to specify to include the contacts for the merge. This is another function to allow you to specify who will receive the final merged document.

The results of filtering are the contacts you include in the merge, not the contacts you want to exclude.

To filter your fields, follow these steps:

1. **Click the Filter link in the Mail Merge Recipients dialog box.**

   The Filter and Sort dialog box opens, with the Filter Records tab showing, as shown in Figure 14-4.

Figure 14-4:
Filtering
your
records.

2. **Select your first field from the top Field drop-down list.**

   In Figure 14-4, we chose the Company field. You can choose any other field to use.

3. **Choose your condition from the top Comparison drop-down list.**

   In Figure 14-4, we chose Equal To.

   You have other choices for comparison: Not Equal To, Less Than, Greater Than, Less Than or Equal, Greater Than or Equal, Is Blank, Is Not Blank, Contains, and Does Not Contain. These Boolean expressions allow you to filter data in almost every way imaginable.

4. **Enter the name of a BCM field in the top Compare To field.**

   In this example, we entered **XYZ Inc.** because we're filtering for a specific company.

5. **Choose And or Or from the first drop-down list in the second row.**

6. **(Optional) Repeat Steps 2 and 4 in the rows that follow to add more criteria, if necessary.**

7. **Click OK to finalize your filter selections.**

   You return to the Mail Merge Recipients dialog box. (See Figure 14-2.)

Finding duplicates

You certainly don't want to send a letter to the same person twice. You can go through the contacts you've selected for a merge and delete any duplicates you find. Follow these steps:

1. **Click the Find Duplicates link in the Mail Merge Recipients dialog box.**

    The Find Duplicates dialog box opens, as shown in Figure 14-5. It immediately starts searching through the contacts currently selected in the Mail Merge Recipients list.

    Duplicates are shown together in the grid display.

2. **Decide which contact you want to exclude from the merge and deselect the check box.**

    The duplicate record is removed from inclusion in the merge.

3. **Repeat Step 2 for all duplicate records.**

4. **Click OK when you're done.**

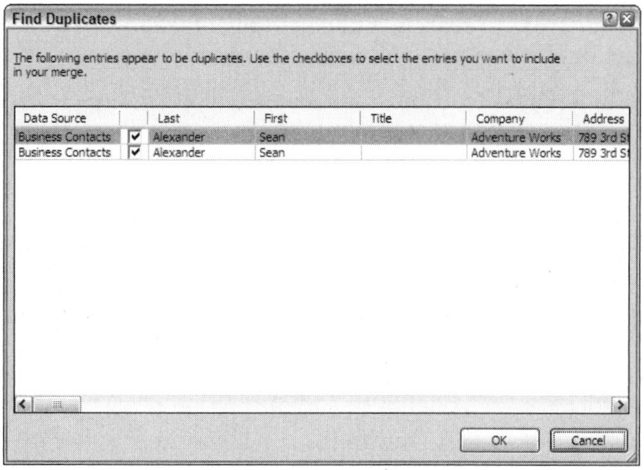

Figure 14-5:
The Find
Duplicates
dialog box.

Finding recipients in a large list

The Find Recipients tool is an easy way to find a contact from a large list. It's especially useful if you want to search through your list looking for a partial name or phrase.

Validating addresses

You can link to Microsoft Office Online, where you can buy services that can validate your addresses. Validating can save you a ton of money on postage by making sure the letters or postcards you mail have the correct U.S. postal addresses on them (or getting the nine-digit zip codes that allow you to send in a carrier route sort order). There will be more offerings when Office 2007 has been on the market longer. Just click the Validate Addresses link in the Mail Merge Recipients dialog box to start the process.

Follow these steps to find a contact:

1. **Click the Find Recipient link in the Mail Merge Recipients dialog box.**

   The Find Entry dialog box appears.

2. **Enter a value in the Find field.**

   You can choose to look in All Fields or pick a field from the This Field drop-down list.

3. **Click Find Next to search, and click Cancel when you've found your contact or if you want to abandon the search.**

   When BCM finds the contact you're searching for, the contact remains selected. Choosing Cancel makes the Find Entry dialog box go away.

Placing Merge Codes in the Document

You might notice that your document, so far, doesn't have any characters — never fear, we show you how to remedy the situation. This is where you start writing your letter or e-mail and add the merge codes that pull data from BCM to personalize each document (or label or envelope).

Follow these steps to write your letter:

1. **Place the cursor in your blank Word document.**

   You're now in a position to start composing your letter or message.

2. **On the Ribbon, click the Address Block button in the Write & Insert Fields group.**

   The Insert Address Block dialog box opens, as shown in Figure 14-6.

3. **Format the address block as you need to.**

   - *Specify Address Elements:* Choose the format for the recipient's name from a list of choices.

   - *Insert Company Name:* You can include the contact's company name in the document by selecting the check box. Or, if you'd rather not include the company name, deselect that check box.

   - *Insert Postal Address:* Selecting this check box adds the postal address for each contact in the appropriate document. Use the radio buttons to adjust how that address is displayed. Or deselect the Insert Postal Address check box to exclude postal addresses from the merged documents.

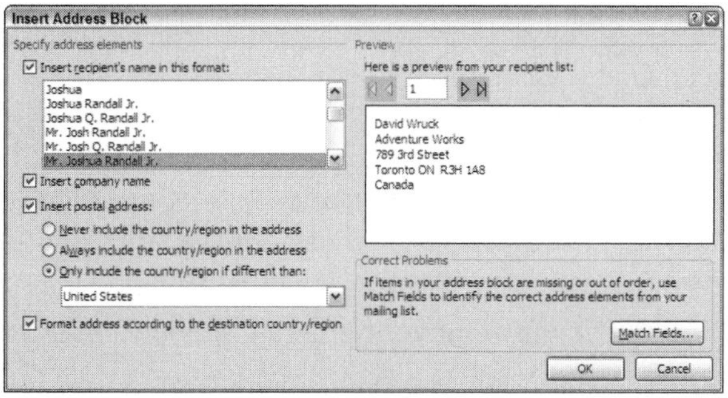

Figure 14-6:
Insert
Address
Block
dialog box.

   - *Preview:* Check out how the address will look when merged into your document. Use the arrows above the Preview window to move through your selected recipients to see how they'll look after merging.

   - *Correct Problems:* Click the Match Fields button to match your customized fields or addresses in BCM with what Word wants to use.

4. **Click OK to finalize the Address Block and insert it into the Word document.**

   Back in the document, you see only <<AddressBlock>>, which is Word shorthand for "merge the lines in the address at this point of the document."

5. **Click the Greeting Line button in the Write & Insert Fields group on the Ribbon to add a greeting.**

   The Insert Greeting Line dialog box opens, as shown in Figure 14-7.

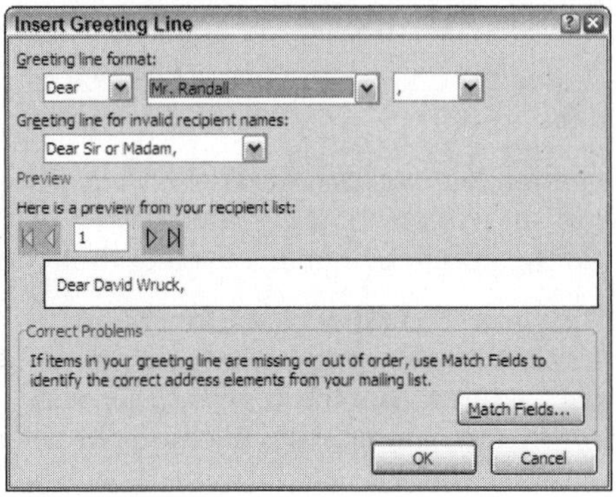

Insert Greeting Line

Greeting line format:

| Dear | ▾ | Mr. Randall | ▾ | , | ▾ |

Greeting line for invalid recipient names:

Dear Sir or Madam, ▾

Preview

Here is a preview from your recipient list:

◁◁ ◁ 1 ▷ ▷▷

Dear David Wruck,

Correct Problems

If items in your greeting line are missing or out of order, use Match Fields to identify the correct address elements from your mailing list.

Match Fields...

OK   Cancel

Figure 14-7:
The Insert
Greeting
Line dialog
box.

6. **Format the greeting.**

   • *Greeting Line Format:* From the drop-down lists, choose a saluta-tion, the form of address you'd like to use, and the punctuation at the end of the greeting.

   • *Greeting Line for Invalid Recipient Names:* If your BCM data is miss-ing some data, choose one of these options from the drop-down list, and Word will use that greeting instead.

   • *Preview:* Check out what your greeting will look like.

   • *Correct Problems*: Click the Match Fields button to match your greeting fields to your BCM fields.

7. **Click OK when you're done.**

8. **Start typing the letter.**

9. **When you come to the point in a sentence where you want to include a merge code, click the Insert Merge Field button in the Write & Insert Fields group on the Ribbon.**

   The Insert Merge Field dialog box appears, as shown in Figure 14-8.

10. **Highlight the field name and then click the Insert button to embed the merge code into the main document.**

   In this example, we typed **You know,** and then inserted the <<First>> field to insert the contact's first name at that point. We continued typing **, all of your coworkers at** and then we inserted <<Company>> (following the instructions in Step 9) to insert the contact's company name at that point in the document.

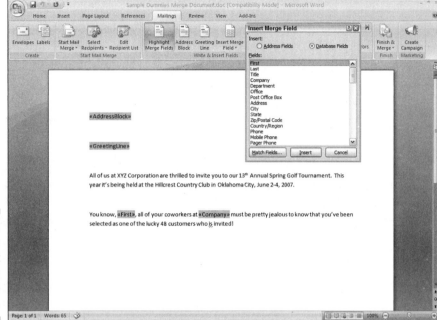

Figure 14-8:
A sample
document
showing
merge fields
inserted.

11. **Click Cancel or the red X in the upper-right corner of the Insert Merge Field dialog box to close it.**

You're now back in the Word document and can continue to modify it with text, graphics, or other elements.

Completing the Merge (And Preview)

When you finish your letter with all the merge codes inserted, click the Finish & Merge button in the Finish group on the Ribbon. Choose one of these options from its drop-down list:

✓ **Edit Individual Documents:** The Merge to a New Document dialog box opens. Instead of sending the document directly to the printer or e-mail outbox, you can see the merged document in Word, change it, and then send it on its way.

This is a great way to add a personal message to an almost completed merge. For example, maybe you did a week's trip on the road and made ten personal visits. You can send each person you visited a Thank You letter that merges most of what you want to say, and then you can add a special line to each one, such as "Wasn't that Steak Diane at Jacques' Internationale the best you've ever had?" The person who ate there with you will know that this thank you is *really* special!

You can choose to edit from All, the Current Record, or a Range of records to merge into a new document.

✔ **Print Documents:** The Merge to Printer dialog box opens. You can choose which records to merge, do the merge, and send the output to the default printer.

✔ **Send E-Mail Messages:** The Merge to E-Mail dialog box opens, where you can choose which contacts to send the letter to. You can specify which e-mail address to send it to, the Subject line, and the format (HTML, plain text, or whether to send the document as an attachment to an e-mail).

After choosing your options, click OK, and the merge starts.

Other options available to you on the Ribbon are as follows:

✔ **Highlight Merge Fields:** If you need to look in your main document and see where all the merge codes are, click the Highlight Merge Fields button on the Ribbon in the Write & Insert Fields group, and they all light up. This makes it easy to keep track of where you've placed them.

✔ **Preview Results:** You can see the real letter just as it will be printed by clicking the Preview Results button on the Ribbon in the Preview Results group. You can scroll through different recipients by using the arrows — the double arrows take you to the beginning or end of the list of recipients; the single arrows move you one recipient at a time through the list.

✔ **Auto Check for Errors:** Click the Auto Check for Errors button on the Ribbon in the Preview Results group to have Word check your merge settings. This gives you a great way to simulate the merge and have Word tell you what it thinks will go wrong. Alternatively, you can just do the merge and Word gives you an error report.

✔ **Find Recipient:** If you want to see how the document will look for one specific recipient, click the Find Recipient button and search for that person to see what her document will look like.

✔ **Create Campaign:** BCM lets you save your document in a marketing campaign. Check out Chapter 15 for all the information about campaigns.

Using the Create Campaign option is a fabulous way to avoid having to duplicate the effort — you can go into the campaign stored in BCM and make modifications easily instead of starting over from scratch.

Making Merged Documents Look Special

Here are some ideas for making merged documents better and more personalized for your contacts so that they really seem to be written directly to them:

- ✔ **Use merge codes to fill in the blanks, as if you were talking directly to the person.**

    You know, <<First Name>>, our XR9000 machine can outperform any of the competitors' machines — and that was proven by the XYZ Testing Lab.

    Instead of saying, *This would help your company do a better job*, use a merge code to say, *This would help <<Company>> do a better job.*

- ✔ **Use the correct merge code for the tone of your message.**

    If you're a casual person, use <<First Name>> instead of <<Title>> <<Last Name>>. This merges into *Bob* instead of *Mr. Smith.*

- ✔ **Know what merge codes you want to use and enter data into BCM so that it merges intelligently.**

    If you know you'll be using the <<Company>> merge code, enter the company name into BCM as **XYZ Co.** instead of **XYZ Company, Inc., division of ABC Conglomerate Worldwide**. That would look strange when merged into a conversational letter or e-mail.

    If you want to address your letters in a specific way, you can add a field to BCM called Salutation. Every time you enter a new contact, make sure that the Salutation field contains precisely the words you want to use as a salutation in a letter or e-mail. Then, in the main document, use the merge code <<Salutation>>, and you know the data will merge correctly. Flip back to Chapter 7 to find out more about adding custom fields to BCM.

- ✔ **Use emphasis, when appropriate, to make merged data stand out.**

    If you have a field in BCM called Yearly Revenue, you can put that in bold and italics when merging into a letter, for more emphasis: *Whenever a customer of ours, like <<Company>>, exceeds* ***<<Yearly Revenue>>*** *in successive years, we raise your discount by 2% to thank you for your business! Buy more, and get more discounts!*

- ✔ **If you use labels, get creative by using Word's formatting capabilities.**

    Consider using a larger label and then adding your logo and maybe some text, such as *This is a special invitation for <<First Name>> <<Last Name>>*. You can print these to a color printer and use Word's ease of formatting to do some special effects with your merged text. When selecting labels, you'll find that Word provides virtually all of Avery's and Dymo's labels already laid out correctly.

✔ **Envelopes can become part of the letter using merge codes.**

The same rules apply to envelopes — they're just another place to use merge codes to get emphasis and personalized text in front of your prospect or customer. Increase your open rates with more customized envelopes!

Chapter 15

Creating and Tracking Marketing Campaigns

In This Chapter

▶ Finding out about BCM marketing campaigns

▶ Setting up a marketing campaign

▶ Using E-Mail Marketing Service to send promotional e-mails

▶ Tracking the success of your campaigns

*M*arketing campaign creation and management is one of the new features in BCM. It can help you generate sales through sending e-mails or printed materials and then tracking the resulting leads and opportunities all the way through to a sale. If you're using Microsoft Office Accounting 2007, you can even track them into the invoice and, ultimately, the bank account!

In Chapter 14, you discover how Word can create mail merges to take data from BCM and merge it with a document template. That's the basis of a *marketing campaign* in BCM — you send a document (or e-mail) to multiple people, and each document is customized with each person's individual information. In this chapter, you find out how to create a campaign and track the results using BCM.

Staying in contact with your prospects and customers is a critical part of marketing and advertising your business. BCM makes it easy to do! You can create a marketing campaign from almost anywhere in BCM. For example, after you've run any of the reports, you can create a new marketing campaign using the contacts shown on that report. Also, if you create a document in Microsoft Office Publisher or Word, you can turn it into a new BCM marketing campaign from within that program.

Creating a New Marketing Campaign

Imagine that you're a consulting firm specializing in single malt scotches. You go around to restaurants and bars to produce tastings and educational seminars in conjunction with scotch importers and distributors. Then, you hire the foremost authority on Russian vodka and you want to announce that your firm can produce vodka-tasting events as well as scotch tastings. If this works well, you'll branch out to bourbon tastings also. (Branch and bourbon — get it?)

So, you're going to use BCM to create a marketing campaign to send e-mails to all your restaurant and distributor contacts to announce the vodka expert's availability. You're very excited to be able to track the results of this campaign to see what kind of new business you generate from your new hire.

You can create a marketing campaign from lots of places in BCM. Here are a few:

- ✔ From the Outlook menu bar, choose Business Contact Manager⇨ Marketing Campaigns⇨New.

- ✔ From the Business Contact Manager toolbar, choose Display⇨Marketing Campaigns⇨New.

- ✔ From the Business Contact Manager toolbar, click Business Contact Manager Home, click the Marketing tab, and then click New Marketing Campaign.

- ✔ From a Contact or Account list view, right-click the record, and choose Create⇨New Marketing Campaign for the account (or contact).

The Marketing Campaign window opens, as shown in Figure 15-1. Here's where you enter the details of your campaign.

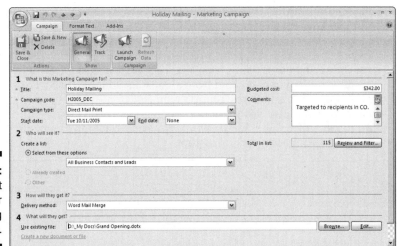

Figure 15-1: Document your marketing efforts.

The Marketing Campaign window consists of five areas (each conveniently numbered), which we describe in depth in the following sections.

At any time in this process, you can click the Save & Close button on the Ribbon to save the campaign and come back to it later.

Entering basic information about your campaign

You enter basic information about your campaign in the What Is This Marketing Campaign For? section (1) of the Marketing Campaign window. This data displays by default in lists of marketing campaigns, making it easier for you to sort and organize your campaigns:

- ✔ **Title:** Enter the title or name of the campaign. You might call this *Vodka-Tasting Announcement Campaign.* Other examples might be *Spring Promotion on XR9000 Machine — 30% Off,* or, *Widget2006 Trade Show Follow-Up — Hot Prospects.* The title is a required field for a campaign. The title becomes the subject of the message if you e-mail your campaign.

  You can always change the subject of an e-mail before you send it on its way.

- ✔ **Campaign Code:** This field is also required and is designed as a short description of your campaign. BCM automatically enters the date and time that you create the campaign in this field; you can erase it if you don't like it.

- ✔ **Campaign Type:** Select the type of campaign you have from the drop-down list. Depending on what you select here, different options become available to you in the How Will They Get It? section (3) of this form.

- ✔ **Start** and **End Date:** These fields allow you to keep track of when you ran this campaign.

- ✔ **Budgeted Cost:** Enter an amount that reflects the cost of this campaign, if you want to track this information.

- ✔ **Comments:** This field allows you to enter a description or notes about this campaign.

Deciding who'll receive the e-mail or letter

The Who Will See It? section (2) is where you choose the contacts that you want to receive the merged documents. BCM gives you some preselected choices, or you can select your own group.

To choose a preselected group, choose the Select from These Options radio button and choose a group from the drop-down list:

- ✔ **All Accounts, All Business Contacts and Leads, All Business Contacts, or All Leads:** You designate whether contacts are leads in each of their contact records. (See Chapter 4 for instructions on entering contact details.)

- ✔ **Search Folder:** Opens the Folder Picker dialog box, where you can choose one of the search folders you've created in the Folder List view of Outlook. Flip over to Chapter 17 to find out more about how Search Folders work.

- ✔ **Existing Campaign:** You can reuse a list you created in a prior campaign. The Select a Campaign dialog box opens and you can select from another campaign's recipient list.

- ✔ **New List:** Opens the Filter Business Contacts dialog box. Turn to Chapter 17 to find out how to use this Contacts dialog box.

If you've started this campaign from a report, the Already Created button is selected. This is a way that you can run a report, filter the report's contents to your liking, then use those contents as the recipients of a marketing campaign. Chapter 18 tells you all about reports.

If you select Telemarketing, Printed Flyer, Seminar/Conference, Mass Advertisement, or Other as the Campaign Type in the What Is This Marketing Campaign For? section (1), BCM automatically chooses the Other radio button for you. This is because BCM assumes that you want to track the cost of the campaign but aren't specifying which contacts or accounts are involved — think of printing flyers you're handing out at a trade show or printing a mass advertisement to insert into the local newspaper.

When you've selected the contacts who will receive this marketing campaign, BCM automatically populates the Total in List field with the number of recipients you've chosen.

Choosing how your recipients get your campaign

In the How Will They Get It? section (3) of the Marketing Campaign window, the Delivery Method drop-down list gives you choices for sending the campaign to its recipients. The choices available are dependent on what you choose in the Campaign Type drop-down list in the What Is This Marketing Campaign For? section (1).

✔ **If you chose Direct Mail Print as the Campaign Type:** BCM gives you the choice of using Word or Publisher to do the mail merge.

✔ **If you chose E-Mail as the Campaign Type:** BCM gives you Outlook, Word E-Mail Merge, Publisher E-mail Merge, or E-Mail Marketing Service as available methods of generating the e-mails and/or sending them out.

Other options as a Campaign Type gray out the choices in Delivery Method because BCM assumes that you have other methods in mind for the campaign.

If you want to use E-Mail Marketing Service, skip ahead to the "Sending E-Mails with E-Mail Marketing Service" section in this chapter. E-Mail Marketing Service is a subscription service from Microsoft that allows you to send thousands of e-mails at a time and track who opens them, who clicks links in them, and more.

Choosing what to send

The What Will They Get? section (4) is where you choose which document the recipients receive for this campaign. The type of template depends on whether you use Word, Publisher, or another program to design the message to send. Here are some tips for filling out this section:

✔ **If you're sending a file:** Click the Browse button to find the file you want to send out. If it's a Word or E-Mail Marketing Service delivery, it browses for a .doc extension. If it's Publisher, it looks for a .pub extension.

✔ **If you're sending the campaign through Outlook:** Enter the e-mail subject you want to use, and then click the Create button to create the e-mail message.

✔ **If you need to edit the document you're sending:** Click the Edit button to open the document in its appropriate program. When you're done editing it, save and close the document and you return to the Marketing Campaign window.

Launching the Marketing Campaign

After you have everything set correctly and ready to go, click the Launch button in the Are Your Ready to Launch the Marketing Campaign? section (5) — and up, up, and away goes your campaign.

Sending E-Mails with E-Mail Marketing Service

Microsoft E-Mail Marketing Service is a fully integrated online service that allows you to target your e-mail campaigns more precisely and track the open rates and click rates from the campaign. It also keeps you compliant with the CAN-SPAM Act of 2003 and allows your recipients a way to unsubscribe or opt out of receiving your messages.

The CAN-SPAM act (the clever acronym stands for Controlling the Assault of Non-Solicited Pornography and Marketing) in the United States specifies what constitutes a spam e-mail, compared to a legitimate one. Each infraction can cost the sender a fine of up to $11,000 per e-mail. The three basic rules are:

- ✔ The e-mail must clearly state who sent it, including the physical address of the company. This is usually entered at the bottom footer in small type.

- ✔ The e-mail must give the recipient a way to unsubscribe or opt out. Creating a link in the e-mail template or footer that takes the user to your list service (such as E-Mail Marketing Service) satisfies this requirement. (E-Mail Marketing Service marks which contacts have unsubscribed when it updates BCM.)

- ✔ Your subject line must be clear and not deceptive. You should also be sure that the From name is clearly linked to your company.

The best function that E-Mail Marketing Service provides is sending thousands of e-mails at a time, something many Internet service providers (ISPs) keep you from doing in order to keep spam in check. Most ISPs allow you to send 100 e-mails per day — if you're sending more than that, you should look at E-Mail Marketing Service.

There are two plans to choose from when you sign up for E-Mail Marketing Service — 1,000 e-mails for $9.95 per month or 10,000 e-mails for $19.95 per month. The total cost is still very low, when compared to other services, and the ability to integrate so tightly with BCM's marketing campaigns makes it a great value.

The pricing plan might change after this book goes to print, but all the terms and conditions are explained when you sign up for your account. Click the E-Mail Marketing Service Privacy Policy link to read Microsoft's assurance that your information is kept private.

To go to Microsoft's Web site, get all the information, and sign up, click the Learn More About E-Mail Marketing Service link to the right of Delivery Method in the Marketing Campaign window.

You must have chosen E-Mail as the Campaign Type and E-Mail Marketing Service as the Delivery Method in the Marketing Campaign window. If you still need to fill in your campaign detail, see the earlier section, "Creating a New Marketing Campaign."

When you click Launch in the Marketing Campaign window, the E-Mail Marketing Service Wizard starts. (See Figure 15-2.)

Click Next to continue. The Set Up E-Mail Tracking screen appears.

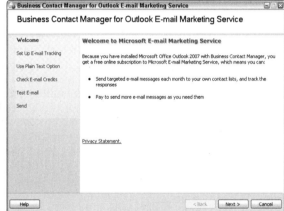

Figure 15-2:
Welcome to
the E-Mail
Marketing
Service
Wizard.

Setting up e-mail tracking

On the Setup E-mail Tracking screen (see Figure 15-3), you can choose whether you want to track the e-mails sent. *E-Mail tracking* tells you how many messages bounced and how many people clicked which links in the e-mail you sent them. This is the first step to analyzing how effective this message is, compared to others you send out. Select Yes or No.

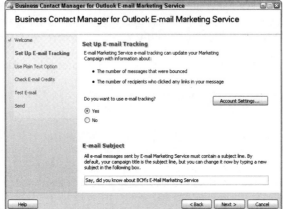

Figure 15-3:
Setting up
e-mail
tracking.

Click the Account Settings button to log in with your Windows Live ID creden-tials. This is where you save your information so that E-Mail Marketing Service remembers who you are. If you don't have a Live ID, the signup process guides you through linking your e-mail address to Windows Live. Windows Live is a free service from Microsoft that allows you to log in to multiple sites on the Internet using one ID and password.

Enter your login information, choose whether to save this login on the PC (so you don't have to reenter it next time), and click Sign In. You'll see a progress bar while you're connecting to the E-Mail Marketing Service. If this is your first time and you don't have an account set up, it asks you if you want to set it up and takes you through the signup process. If you already have an account, it connects and then returns you to the wizard.

In the E-mail Subject field, enter the subject of the e-mail. You need to enter a subject regardless of whether you entered the subject in the Marketing Campaign window. Actually, E-Mail Marketing Service uses the title of the campaign, which you'll certainly want to change.

Click Next to go to the next screen, Use Plain Text Option.

You can choose whether to use plain text in your e-mail. The purpose of plain text is to send a text-only message (no graphics, pictures, or special fonts) to people who can't view HTML e-mails. If you choose to use plain text, re-create your e-mail message here, using only text. When E-Mail Marketing Service determines that a recipient can't view graphical e-mails, this e-mail is sent instead.

Depending on your audience, you might not need the text-only message, as more and more people are capable of viewing graphical e-mails now.

Click Next to go to the next screen, Check E-Mail Credits.

Checking e-mail credits

The Check E-Mail Credits screen (see Figure 15-4) of the E-Mail Marketing Service Wizard is where you pay for the e-mails you send. You get *X* number of e-mail credits each month (based on your level of service — 1,000 or 10,000), and you can buy more. If you don't have enough credits for the campaign you've just launched, the Next button is grayed out — no further e-mails for you without more credits purchased! Click the Buy More E-Mail Credits button to stock up your account.

Figure 15-4: Checking e-mail credits.

Click Next to go to the next screen, Send Test E-Mail.

Sending your e-mail

On the Send Test E-Mail screen in the E-Mail Marketing Service Wizard, shown in Figure 15-5, you can (and should!) test the e-mail to make sure it looks okay before you blast it out. Enter an e-mail address and click the Send Test E-Mail button. Send one to yourself first — if it doesn't look good to you, back to the design studio! You can repeat this process to let other co-workers proof your message before you unleash it on the public. If you're sending to recipients who will use different e-mail programs, such as Lotus Notes or GroupWise, you might want to test sending to those programs too.

Stay on this screen until you receive the e-mail and have a chance to review it. If you find it has errors, click Cancel on the Send Test E-Mail screen, fix the e-mail message, and start the process again in the Marketing Campaign window.

Figure 15-5:
Sending a
test e-mail.

Click Next to advance to the next screen, the Send E-Mail screen.

The last screen is where you finally, after all this time, get a button that says Send. Click the Send button, and away the campaign goes through E-Mail Marketing Service. Of course, there's also a Cancel button to use if you just aren't ready to pull the trigger.

Tracking Your Marketing Campaign

So, want to find out if you received any business from that marketing campaign you sent out? Easy enough with BCM. One of the toughest problems for small businesses is measuring the effectiveness of advertising and marketing expenditures. Where should I put my dollars? What medium is the most effective? BCM has these answers — if you do just a few things to help it along. Effectively spending your money and getting measurable results is invaluable in building your business. This is the final piece of marketing — what's your return on your marketing efforts!

Linking the campaign to the contact, account, or opportunity

When you create and launch a marketing campaign, you give it a name that will show up in the Initiated By drop-down list in a contact, account, or opportunity record. Entering the marketing campaign value in the Initiated By field for every new contact record (or account or opportunity) allows you to link that contact as coming from that marketing campaign and then reporting on the results. Make sure you and your other users enter how this person or opportunity was generated — from which marketing campaign was it initiated? This is a key requirement in analyzing your results!

You can use the Opportunities window to track which deals result from which campaigns. Click the Initiated By button in the opportunity record to show which campaign the opportunity was generated from. The value in this is to measure the dollar amount of return (sales!) versus the cost of the campaigns.

Unfortunately, BCM doesn't have a report that calculates this total, but you can run multiple reports to find those numbers and create your own spreadsheet to measure the return on investment (ROI) for each campaign.

You can see exactly which leads, opportunities, accounts, and contacts come in from a campaign right in the Marketing Campaign window. Click the Track button in the Marketing Campaign window to see the results of your campaign. (See Figure 15-6.)

The list of recipients is shown in the middle, and the far right column shows delivery status. Double-clicking a name brings up the contact or account record.

From the Ribbon, click Track in the Show group to view almost all the statistics you would ever want — and the ability to run reports. If you use E-Mail Marketing Service to send out the campaign, the tracking results are at the bottom of the window in the Number Not Sent, Bounces, Unsubscribes, Clicks, and Replies fields. You don't have to do a thing to see these — E-Mail Marketing Service enters the data for you!

You can keep this window open, enter data in BCM, and then click the Refresh Data button in the Campaign group of the Ribbon. Your BCM database refreshes the Campaign Results fields at the top of the window.

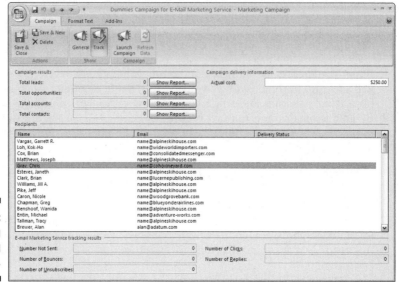

Figure 15-6:
Tracking
marketing
campaigns.

Reporting on marketing campaigns

To see additional results of a campaign, you have to run a report. While still on the Track window of a marketing campaign (from previous section), click one of the Show Report buttons to see a report showing which contacts, accounts, or opportunities are included in each total shown:

- **Total Leads:** Clicking the Show Report button produces the Business Contacts by Marketing Campaign report, filtered for Leads only.

- **Total Opportunities:** Clicking the Show Report button produces the Opportunities by Marketing Campaign report.

- **Total Accounts:** Clicking the Show Report button produces the Accounts by Marketing Campaign report.

- **Total Contacts:** Clicking the Show Report button produces the Business Contacts by Marketing Campaign report, filtered for business contacts only.

Alternatively, from the Outlook menu bar, choose Business Contact Manager⇨ Reports⇨Marketing Campaigns. You can choose from these three reports, which are the same, but not filtered. You can specify which campaign you want to report on, and the report shows which opportunities, accounts, or contacts were generated from that campaign:

✔ Opportunities by Marketing Campaign

✔ Business Contacts by Marketing Campaign

✔ Accounts by Marketing Campaign

If you and your users don't choose the campaign from the Initiated By field, you won't get the proper results on these reports.

Chapter 18 includes more details on reports, creating filters for the reports, changing the columns displayed on reports, and other options.

Following up with the next campaign

These marketing reports show you the results of your campaigns. For many businesses, these produce great data that help you analyze what's working and what needs more fine-tuning to reach the people and get them to respond. One more BCM function can help with this fine-tuning — you can create a new marketing campaign from the data in a report.

1. **After you run a report, on the Report Viewer window's menu bar, choose Actions⇨Launch Marketing Campaign (see Figure 15-7).**

2. **Select All Items or Selected Records.**

   A new Marketing Campaign window displays. (Refer to Figure 15-1.) The Already Created option in the Who Will See It? section (2), is selected. You can change the contacts or accounts that are a part of this campaign by clicking the Review and Filter button.

3. **Fill in the rest of the fields and click Save & Close to save your new marketing campaign.**

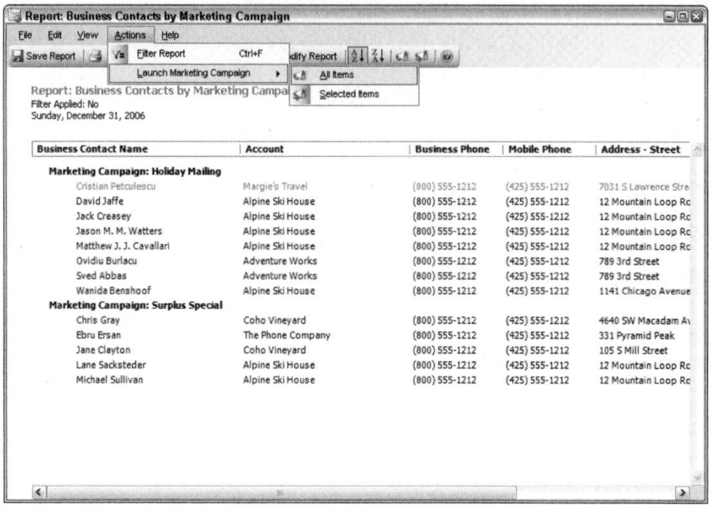

Figure 15-7:
Launch a
marketing
campaign
from a
report.

These contacts then become the recipients of the new campaign. This is a
great way to follow up on responses from one campaign with a follow-up
campaign to target them further.

Chapter 16

Taking the Show on the Road

· ·

In This Chapter

▶ Synchronizing remote and mobile databases with the mothership

▶ Taking bite-sized data with you

▶ Accessing your data from the road

· ·

*I*f you're like millions of other modern businesspeople, you are on the go, mobile, and remote. You might spend some of the day at the office, some traveling, and sometimes working at home or at a hotel on a laptop. You want access to your e-mail, your calendar, your contact database, and your task list. You want the away-from-office experience to be as close to an in-the-office environment as it can be. This is a holy grail of sorts for the road warrior class.

BCM and a laptop (or a Tablet PC) give you a good way of making this happen — not perfect, but good. Because it is integrated into Outlook and separate from it, you can take BCM with you and access e-mail in other ways. We don't have room to cover how to access your e-mail on the road in this book. Check out *Outlook 2007 For Dummies,* by Bill Dyszel (Wiley Publishing) for information on that.

The Big Question to ask yourself is "How much data do I want (or really need) with me?"

If your answer to the Big Question is, "I want most of the same data as I have at the office," you need a full-fledged PC with you, in laptop or Tablet PC sizes. You can synchronize your BCM database onto the laptop, take the entire database with you, make changes, and add new data; and when you reconnect to the master database, it synchs all the changes made to both databases. You can even synch while you're away from the office, using a virtual private network (VPN) to connect. We show you how to set up synchronization in the "Creating an Offline Database" section, later in this chapter.

If your answer to the Big Question is "just the basics" — names, addresses, phone numbers, e-mails, calendar, and tasks — consider using a handheld device such as a Pocket PC, Palm, or smartphone. We discuss those options in the "Putting Your Business in Your Pocket" section.

If your answer to the Big Question is "I'd ideally like to unplug my desktop and carry it with me everywhere I go," check out "Connecting to Your Office Instead of Taking BCM with You," later in this chapter, to discover how to connect to your desktop while you're away.

Creating an Offline Database

If you want your entire BCM database with you, synchronization is your answer. BCM makes an exact copy of the master database (the main shared database for your company) onto your laptop (called the *remote database*). While you're away from the office, you add, change, or delete data in this remote database. Microsoft calls the status of your remote database *offline*. When you connect the remote BCM to the master database *(online status)*, BCM is smart enough to figure out which changes you've made to which records and *synchronizes* the two databases. At the precise moment you disconnect from the master, all data is exactly the same.

People at the office might be making changes while you're synchronizing. Some of those changes might make it into this synch, and some are stored for the next time you connect. But the timing is close enough for most small businesses. Later in this chapter, you find out how BCM reconciles data conflict — for example, what if you change a phone number and the inside sales rep changes the same phone number?

What name does your computer go by?

Before you can create an offline database on your laptop, you need to know the name of the PC where your master database is stored. Don't remember the name you gave your computer? Follow these steps:

1. **Choose Start⇨Control Panel⇨System on the computer that stores your master database.**

If you're using a different operating system than Windows XP, these steps might differ slightly.

The System Properties dialog box opens.

2. **Click the Computer Name tab.**

You see the full computer name in the middle. This is the name that other PCs use to identify this PC.

Follow these steps to create an offline database on your laptop:

1. **From the Outlook menu bar, choose Business Contact Manager➪ Database Tools➪Create or Select a Database.**

   The Microsoft Office Outlook 2007 with Business Contact Manager Wizard opens with the Create or Select a Business Contact Manager Database screen, as shown in Figure 16-1.

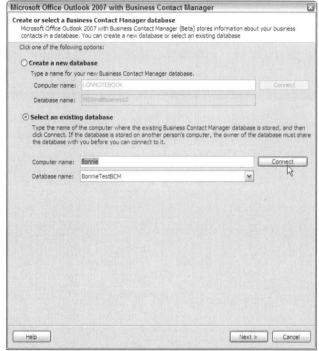

Figure 16-1:
The Create or Select a Business Contact Manager Database screen.

2. **Choose the Select an Existing Database option.**

3. **Enter the name of the BCM Server in the Computer Name field and click the Connect button.**

   If you're not sure of the name of your BCM Server or how to find out, check out the sidebar, "What name does your computer go by?"

   Your laptop connects to that computer and shows you the BCM databases available to you.

4. **Choose a database from the Database Name drop-down list and click Next to continue.**

5. **Click OK at the warning message saying that the automatic linking of e-mail will be turned off.**

While sharing e-mails is useful to give everyone a clear picture of interactions with contacts, you might have sensitive information in them that you don't want others to see.

The Configure Database for Offline Use screen appears, as shown in Figure 16-2.

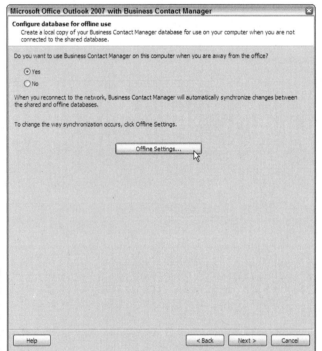

Figure 16-2:
Configure
database for
offline use.

6. **Select Yes to configure the database for offline use.**

7. **Click the Offline Settings button.**

The Offline Settings dialog box with the Synchronization tab showing opens. (See Figure 16-3.)

Figure 16-3:
Offline
Settings:
Synchroni-
zation.

8. **Choose how often to synchronize the BCM master with your local copy on your PC and then what to do when the shared database isn't available:**

   • *Switch Automatically to My Local Database:* Choose this option if you want BCM to automatically switch to the copy of the BCM master on your laptop.

   • *Don't Switch Automatically. I Will Switch Manually:* Choose this option if you want to decide when to switch to your local copy and when to reconnect online.

   Most of the time, you want to automatically switch to your local data-base. The BCM master updates and saves your data as soon as you reconnect, whenever that might be. Don't worry, be happy, enter data, synchronize easily!

9. **Click the Conflict Resolution tab (see Figure 16-4) and decide how to resolve conflicts:**

   • *Ask Me:* If there's a conflict of data, BCM displays a message box asking you to choose whether the remote or master's data wins. This is the safest way to guard against bad data in a very small workgroup, but it's tedious when synching many records.

   • *Always Accept the Latest Changes:* This is easy for BCM to figure out — it knows the date and time of the modifications on both databases. If you updated the data more recently than what's stored in the master database, the latest date wins. This is a good choice if you have good agreements with other co-workers or if you're the only one making changes — you know for sure who made the latest change: you!

- *Always Accept Changes Made in the Shared Database:* This is a good choice if you have more work going on in the office than on the road. Outside salespeople might be more useful in front of customers or hunting for business than entering address changes. So, the agreements your co-workers make are that those changes happen at the office, and, if there's a conflict, the remote guy is usually wrong.

- *Always Accept Changes Made in the Local Database:* This is the best choice for single users or small teams where you're all out of the office more than in (and mostly work on your own contacts). The chance for conflicting changes in the master is low.

Decide amongst yourselves who's going to handle these types of situations and try to review the data regularly for errors. Make new agreements and try again!

Figure 16-4:
Offline
Settings:
Conflict
Resolution.

10. **Click OK in the Offline Settings dialog box and then Next on the Configure Database for Offline Use screen.**

The offline database is created, and your BCM offline database is created as a copy of the BCM master database.

You see a progress bar for the creation of the offline database and then a new progress bar for the finalization of the BCM configuration.

What physically happens on your hard drive is that a copy of the BCM master database is created on your hard drive with YourName_ offline added to the name. For example, if the name of your BCM master database is XYZCorpMaster.mdf, the database on your hard drive is XYZCorpMasterJaneDoe_offline.mdf in the same folder.

You're now ready to hit the road with a copy of your master BCM database on your laptop's hard drive. Make changes just as though you're connected at the office and synchronize when you can. If you want to synch while still on the road, see the next section. If you want to synch when you get back to the office, skip to "Synchronizing when you return to the office."

Synchronizing while you're out of the office

When you disconnect your laptop from the network at the office, you're in *offline* mode. You leave town, call on customers, or attend a trade show, and that night you want to connect to the office from your hotel room and synchronize your data.

BCM is pretty smart about lots of things — one of them is knowing where you are. Not physically where you are, like the Hilton versus Motel 6, but whether you're online and connected to the master BCM database or offline.

Look at the Status button on the BCM toolbar. If it says Offline, you're working offline; if it says Online, you're synched with the master database.

If you're connected to the local area network (LAN) or via a virtual private network (VPN), you can change your status. Here's how:

✔ **To work online:** If you're offline, choose Work Offline from the Status button to toggle back to online status. You see the Synchronizing progress bar and receive status messages as it applies changes. The button changes to Status:Online and the synch is completed.

When the synchronization process starts, the only thing for you to do is stand back and watch. BCM finds the master and synchs. That's it — you're back in synch.

Depending on how often you synchronize and how many changes you make daily, synching shouldn't take more than a few minutes. If you or someone at the office has just imported 2,000 names from a trade show you just attended, it takes much more time to update. But, for a daily synch, it shouldn't be more than five minutes over a reasonably fast DSL connection.

✔ **To work offline:** If you're online, choose Work Online from the Status button to go in offline mode. You can change your offline settings in the Offline Settings dialog box. (Refer to Figure 16-3.)

Outlook doesn't have to be connected to a mail server when you synchronize BCM. You just have to be connected the BCM database server. Getting e-mail remotely is a topic outside the scope of this book. Check out *Outlook 2007 For Dummies,* by Bill Dyszel, for lots more information on how to get e-mail while you're away from the office.

Synchronizing when you return to the office

The process when you return to the office is just as easy as when you synch away from the office. (See the previous section.)

If you told BCM to automatically detect whether you're online or offline, BCM automatically starts the synchronization on its own.

If you told BCM that you'd connect manually, choose Work Offline from the Status drop-down list. BCM toggles back to online status and starts synching. It doesn't get much easier than that!

Putting Your Business in Your Pocket

Maybe having some or all of your data with you is important and necessary to do your business. But maybe you don't need all the BCM data with you. Maybe you can do just fine with names, addresses, and phone numbers. Maybe getting e-mail instantly is most important for you. Maybe seeing your calendar and tasks is most important, but you really need to see only what's current — you don't want to enter a lot of changes while you're away from the office.

Deciding on a mobile device

The computer and mobile phone industries have made major strides in giving you devices that solve the problem of what to take with you. That said, you always have a trade-off in function and with choices in size, touch screens, keyboards, all-in-one-converged devices, and more. Generally, the devices are now grouped like this:

✔ **Cell phone:** This is mostly a phone (even though most phones now have 43 other functions, such as camera or media player). It has limited storage for names, addresses, phone numbers, and the like. It usually doesn't have a touch screen, and the keyboard is a phone keyboard, so writing notes or e-mails is hard if you're over the age of 20.

✔ **PDA:** PDAs are at the opposite end of the spectrum from cell phones. They have big screens that you can write on, and they translate your handwriting into text. They run programs just as PCs do and store lots of data. Some have keyboards, and others can connect to a full-sized keyboard through Bluetooth wireless or a docking station. The Microsoft Windows Mobile devices have pocket-sized versions of Word, Excel, Outlook, and PowerPoint, so you can create and edit files away from the office. If you want to take more data with you than fits on a cell phone but don't want to lug a laptop around, consider this category.

✔ **Smartphone:** This is a generic name for a category of *converged devices* that combines parts of cell phones and PDAs. This category has a wide range of functions and capabilities, and each device seems to be slanted to one main function or another. Blackberry phones have keyboards and are optimized to enter text, so you can write e-mails. Others are slanted more to the phone side, have smaller keyboards that are more functional than a cell phone, but aren't too good for answering e-mail. Still others are slanted more to data entry, like Microsoft Mobile Pocket PC with a touch screen, but their form factor is more like a cell phone.

Getting data into your device

All the data that is Outlook-based — e-mails, contacts, tasks, and appointments — synchronizes to your mobile device just fine. Every device out there synchronizes this basic information. Okay, a few of them can't synch, but very, very few — Outlook is *the* program with which the mobile devices interface.

But the BCM data doesn't make the trip so easily (as of this writing). So, the contacts that Outlook synchs are the Outlook contacts in the basic address book, not the business contacts that are in BCM.

Microsoft has a free application called Business Contacts for Pocket PC that synchronizes Business Contact Manager contacts into a Windows Mobile Pocket PC (but not a Windows smartphone — Microsoft is still working on that). To find it, follow these steps:

1. **From the Outlook menu bar, choose Help⇨Business Contact Manager for Outlook⇨Use Business Contact Manager for Outlook with Mobile Devices.**

   The Help dialog box opens, with the Use Business Contact Manager with Mobile Devices page displaying.

2. **Click the Microsoft Office Online Web site link.**

   Your browser launches the Microsoft Web site where you can download and install Business Contacts for Pocket PC.

3. **Click the Download button to start the download.**

   You can either run the install from the dialog box that appears or save the file (named BCMV3PPC.EXE) to your desktop, My Documents folder, or other folder on your hard drive.

4. **Put your Pocket PC in its cradle and connected to your PC, then run the installation of Business Contacts for Pocket PC.**

The Business Contacts for Pocket PC application is not very robust. It synchronizes only business contacts, and it stores them in a separate database from the main contacts on a Pocket PC. You don't get any accounts, opportunities, projects, or project tasks, and only the last five to ten communication history items for each contact. But, it's better than not getting any of them. One indirect benefit of this is that you can have a different group of contacts in your Outlook address book and synch those to the contacts application on the Pocket PC.

So, what's a BCM user to do? As of this writing, your best bet is PocketMirror from Chapura (www.chapura.com). Chapura has been synchronizing Business Contact Manager contacts longer than any other company. PocketMirror allows you to map the BCM contacts into the main Pocket Outlook database on the Pocket PC and accomplish getting the basic information out of the office and onto your device.

Tricking BCM into synchronizing contacts

You can synch your BCM Contacts easily with any mobile device. Because Outlook synchs contacts as part of its basic data, almost all the devices synch your basic name and address information successfully, assuming that they're in Outlook, not just BCM. So, you trick BCM by copying your BCM contacts into Outlook's contact address book.

This requires a couple of decisions about using the Outlook address book. Here are some things to consider:

✔ **You can't have separate address books, one for BCM and one for Outlook.** Your BCM Contacts invade the Outlook list. They can co-exist just fine, but you don't have a separate list of Outlook-only contacts. You might want to assign your personal, non-BCM contacts to a category such as Personal or Friends so that you can find them quickly.

✔ **You're responsible, not BCM or Outlook, for updating the data.** After you copy the BCM contacts into Outlook initially and you (and others) make changes to the BCM contacts, you have to manually copy those changes to Outlook. You now have, literally, two John Doe records — the real, original one in BCM and the new copy in Outlook. Changing one does not update the other one — they are not linked in any way. So, making changes on your mobile device doesn't update the BCM one after you synch. The synch updates the copy in Outlook.

We recommend not updating contacts on the handheld — wait to do it in BCM when you return. You could make a note or task on your handheld with the changes to be made and then you'd transfer that into BCM.

As long as you understand these points, this is a decent solution, especially if you have a cell phone and don't need to carry a lot of data with you. Follow these steps to copy some or all of your BCM contacts into your Outlook address book:

1. **From the Outlook menu bar, choose Business Contact Manager↪ Business Contacts.**

   You see a list of all your contacts in Outlook and BCM, as shown in Figure 16-5. On the left is the Navigation pane that shows the My Contacts folder near the top, with the Business Contact Manager folder below it.

2. **Choose a view from Current View that gives you access to all or to the group of contacts you want to copy.**

3. **Press Ctrl+A to select all of your contacts.**

   All of your contacts displayed on the right side are highlighted.

   If you want to select some, but not all, of these contacts from the list, Ctrl+click to select records that aren't contiguous. For contiguous records, highlight the first one, then Shift+click to select the last one, and all the ones in between are highlighted.

4. **Drag the contacts from the right pane and drop them into the Contacts folder under My Contacts near the top of the Navigation pane.**

   This makes a copy of the BCM contacts in the Outlook contacts folder. All the basic information is copied across accurately.

Drop your contacts in this folder.

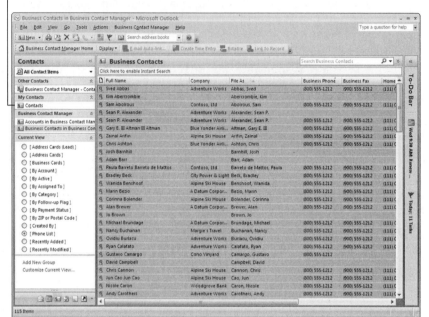

Figure 16-5:
Business
Contacts
screen.

Connecting to Your Office Instead of Taking BCM with You

If you want to unplug your desktop and carry it with you, you need to do just that, but remotely. You can connect to your office PC from a remote PC so that you can operate it just as though you're sitting in front of it. There is almost no functional difference in working remotely versus working at your desk.

You might choose this solution for the following reasons:

✔ You're not adept at synchronizing and don't feel comfortable moving data.

✔ You like that the data stays in one place.

✔ You back up your data regularly so it's safe. (You do, don't you?)

✔ You don't typically make a lot of changes while you're out of the office.

Here's what you need in order to accomplish remote connecting:

✔ **A high-speed connection to the Internet at the office:** If you have just one PC, that's easier. If you have multiple PCs in the office, you want to configure access to your personal PC. Regardless, you must have a firewall and protection in place so that you can securely connect and keep out the bad guys. It's safe to do, but you might need some help.

We recommend consulting with a Microsoft Partner or local networking consultant to help you get the infrastructure and firewall settings correct.

✔ **A laptop to carry with you:** This laptop usually needs just the latest browser software. You don't need to store any data on it — all data stays on your desktop. It needs to connect to high-speed connections in hotels, airports, or the like. You can also just bum some time on someone else's PC or rent one at a kiosk because you just need a browser to connect back to your office.

✔ **Some sort of connection software or program to make it all work:**

- *Remote Desktop:* This is the cheapest solution because it comes with Windows. It's easy to configure and allows you to control your office PC, copy files to and from the PC you're working on, and even print documents from the office on your local printer.

- *WebEx:* This is one part of a complete meeting service from the pioneer in remote meetings (www.webex.com). If you can use the WebEx service for online meetings, its Access Anywhere is a great benefit to allow you to control your desktop from out of the office.

- *GoToMyPC:* Citrix knows how to connect to networks because it powers lots of networks, and GoToMyPC is a cinch to connect to your PC while you're out. It doesn't have the same meeting functions as WebEx, but you can add that function for more bucks (www.gotomypc.com).

- *pcAnywhere:* This is the granddaddy of remote access software, and it works flawlessly. You do need to load this software on both your office PC and your remote PC to make it work (www.symantec store.com).

Part VI
Digging In a Bit Deeper

The 5th Wave   By Rich Tennant

"We can monitor our entire sales force from Business Contact Manager. We know what the 'Wax Lips' people are doing, we know what the 'Whoopee Cushion' people are doing, we know what the 'Fly-in-the-Ice Cube' people are doing. But we don't know what the 'Plastic Vomit' people are doing. We don't want to know what the 'Plastic Vomit' people are doing."

In this part . . .

On the surface, BCM is a deceptively easy program to master. However, you'll want to explore a few more advanced features including querying your data and running a few reports. As your business grows, you might start organizing your players into teams to help you work on your various projects. Finally, this section has your back covered; when you need to maintain or troubleshoot your database, just turn to this section for help.

Chapter 17

Seek and Ye Shall Find Your Data

In This Chapter

▶ Querying for filters, or filtering for queries — finding your data

▶ Search folders: Your best friend for creating subsets of data

▶ Applying filters to your everyday job

*M*ost of the earlier chapters in this book deal with how to enter data into BCM and how to use the different functions available. In this chapter, you find out how to dig into all the data you collect, how to find it, and how to create subsets of data that you can use for reporting, mail merging, or managing.

BCM uses the terms *filter* and *query* interchangeably. In most of the dialog boxes, buttons, and menus, you see *filter* used, but when you save a filter to your hard drive it's stored as a BCM query with the .bcmq extension. So, in this chapter, we use the word *filter;* if you see *query,* just know that it's the same concept.

A *filter* is the way you select a subset of data from BCM to view. If you have 1,000 contacts in your contact database and want to see only your leads, you filter the report or view to show you only the contacts whose Classification field is marked as Lead. Or maybe you want to see only those contacts you met at the Spring Trade Show in 2006 (the Source field shows "Spring Trade Show 2006"). Now, instead of seeing all 1,000 contacts, you see only the 89 people you met at that show.

Filtering Your Data

BCM has a simple way to create a filter by just selecting check boxes and choosing a date range. BCM also has some powerful, advanced capabilities that you can use to construct complex queries with up to 20 different criteria. You can save simple or advanced queries and reuse them in multiple parts of BCM to deliver consistent data on demand.

BCM has created one dialog box that lets you create and apply filters — the Filter dialog box, shown in Figure 17-1. If you're filtering business contacts, it's called the Filter Business Contacts dialog box (which is what's shown in Figure 17-1). If you're filtering project tasks, it's called the Filter Project Tasks dialog box. No matter what it's called, you get the same options.

Getting to the Filter dialog box is pretty easy. Anywhere you see a Filter button, click it to open the Filter dialog box. Reports have a Filter Report button. Search folders have a Filter button.

When you're customizing a view, the Filter button uses a different scheme to allow you to select records. If you don't see the Filter dialog box, you know you're in the right place to customize the view.

The Filter dialog box has three tabs:

- ✔ **Simple Filter:** The choices on this tab change depending on the type of data you're filtering. Figure 17-1 shows the choices for contacts.

    You can create filters for these data types: business contacts, accounts, opportunities, business projects, project tasks, business contact history, account history, opportunity history, and business project history. Each one of these filters has different options on the Simple Filter tab.

- ✔ **Advanced Filter:** This tab doesn't change, regardless of the data you're filtering. This is where you can create complex queries with up to 20 criteria.

Figure 17-1:
The Filter dialog box for creating and using queries.

✔ **Review Results:** This is where you can see which records will be returned from the query and displayed, based on the criteria you enter (simple or advanced).

The Filter dialog box function gives you a great method to test different filters and see what data shows up. This is also a great way to check how consistently other users are entering data. If you construct a query and don't get your expected results, go through BCM's data and see if it matches what you expected. Your users might not be entering their data according to your instructions.

Simple Filter

The Simple Filter tab is a straightforward way to filter — or choose — contacts that meet specific criteria, such as leads only, leads that are active, leads assigned to a specific person, and more. Select a check box to include the criteria you desire; deselect a check box to exclude those people from the list.

The Simple Filter dialog box has different sections for different options. All of these options correspond to fields in the contact record. Whatever you enter in those fields can be filtered using these options. Similar options exist for accounts, opportunities, projects, and the other BCM data records:

✔ **Include:** You can choose business contacts or leads or both. Whatever you choose here is combined with other choices to create the complete filter. It's just simpler to do it here using check boxes than on the Advanced Filter tab that we describe in the section that follows.

✔ **Contact Status:** Include active and/or inactive records in the filter.

✔ **Payment Status:** If you're using Microsoft Office Accounting in particular, you can combine payment status (current, overdue, or others) with other criteria in your filter. Accounting updates this information for you to stay current!

✔ **Rating:** Filter records based on how you rate them.

✔ **Source of Lead:** Answers the question, "Where did you meet this contact?"

✔ **Assigned To:** Filter contacts based on which salesperson is assigned to which accounts. This list is populated by BCM with valid users of the BCM database.

✔ **Last Modified Date:** Filter recently changed contact records from ones you haven't changed within that date range. It's a good tool for finding out, for instance, which contacts haven't called in over 90 days. If you select All from the Dates drop-down list, all contacts are included, depending on the other choices you've made.

Suppose that you want to send a notice to all leads you've had some contact with over the past 30 days. You select the Leads check box in the Include section (and no other boxes) and choose Previous 30 Days from the Dates drop-down list.

Advanced Filter

The Advanced Filter tab, shown in Figure 17-2, is where you can really rev up the power of selecting which data is included in a filter's results. You can specify *criteria* (such as State=OK) and link multiple criteria using operators (such as And or Or).

You can make the advanced filter as simple or complex as you choose. Within each line, you have Boolean operators (greater than, less than, equal to, not equal to, and others) for specifying what the criteria or conditions must be in order to include or exclude that contact from the results set.

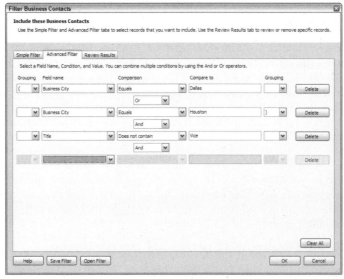

Figure 17-2:
The Advanced Filter tab of the Filter dialog box.

Follow these steps to create an advanced filter:

1. **Select one of the available fields in the Field Name drop-down list.**

   All your applicable fields are listed in the Field Name drop-down list, which makes life easy.

2. **Select one of the options in the Comparison field.**

   Knock yourself out! Indicate whether you're looking for a specific word, a field that contains a part of a word, or even a range of figures or dates. In Figure 17-2, we're looking for contacts whose business is in Dallas.

3. **In the Compare To field, fill in the specific criterion that you're looking for.**

4. **To select more than one criterion, repeat Steps 1 through 3.**

   In Figure 17-2, we added a second filter looking for contacts whose business is in Houston.

5. **Click the And/Or field and select an option, if necessary.**

   Okay, you're not going to see an And/Or field, but you're going to see a field directly under the Comparison field with the choices of And and Or. This column helps you group your criteria in order to indicate the relationship between each set of criteria.

   When using the And/Or criteria, it's important to fully understand how these options work. Using *Or* indicates that the result can be in either Florida *or* Georgia, for example. *And* indicates that the contact fulfills both criteria.

6. **Use the Grouping column, if necessary.**

   This might give you flashbacks to your high school Algebra class. The Grouping column allows you to use parentheses to group the various lines of your filter. The example in Figure 17-2 groups the two city criteria with parentheses so that these queries are carried out together. This is a particularly important step if your query contains both And and Or criteria.

Review Results

You can see the results of the criteria you specified — whether simple or advanced — on the Review Results tab. (See Figure 17-3.) As you change your criteria, this tab is busily reordering itself to display the results of your filter.

Depending on how large your database is, you might need to wait while the results are compiling on the Review Results tab.

Figure 17-3 shows the results from a filter that selected contacts for an e-mail campaign. The Number of Records Found field shows the number of records the filter found.

Here's what you can do with the results:

✔ **Search for a name:** Enter the first few characters in the Type or Select from List text box. BCM finds the first result based on those characters.

✔ **Sort the list:** The list sorts based on which column has the triangle showing ascending or descending order (arrow pointing up means *ascending;* pointing down means *descending*). Click the column header name to sort the column by that field.

✔ **Specify who to include in your filter:** Deselect the check box if you don't want to include that person in the group of recipients. Keep a check mark there if you want to include them.

To select all the contacts, click the Select All button. To deselect all the check boxes, click the Clear All button.

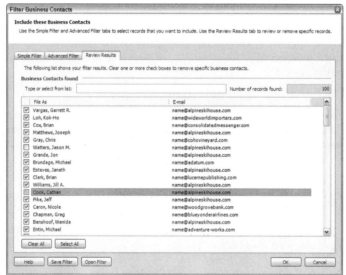

Figure 17-3:
The Review
Results tab
of the Filter
dialog box.

Saving a filter

If you're going to be doing this filter thing a lot, it's a good idea to save the filter you've constructed to reuse next time you want to find the same data. Creating a filter for a weekly report — to get a snapshot of which deals are close to closing, for instance — is a great first step in seeing the results you want. Starting with one filter, making changes, and saving it as a different filter is an easy way to use complex filters without taking a lot of time. You've already done most of the work. Why do it again?

To save a filter from the Filter dialog box, follow these steps:

1. **From the Filter dialog box, click the Save Filter button.**

   The standard Windows Save As dialog box opens. The Save as Type drop-down list specifies the extension for Business Contact Manager query files (*.bcmq).

2. **Enter the filename in the File Name text box.**

   This can be any valid filename you choose.

   The filter has to be the same data entity type in order to be used across different views, search folders, or reports. A filter for contacts doesn't open correctly if you're in an Opportunity Filter dialog box. So, it's a good idea to name your queries with the type of data they pertain to, such as the following:

   • Contacts — prospects from Spring Trade Show

   • Opportunities — deals over $100K with existing customers

   • Project Tasks — high priority tasks more than three days overdue

3. **Choose a different folder, if necessary, to store the file.**

   This .bcmq file is just like any other file in Windows.

You can send it to another user on your team who needs to do the same filter, or you can store it on a server that is accessible to everyone. This is the strategy to make sure everyone is on the same page.

Opening a filter

After you save the filter, you can use it over and over. You can use a previously saved filter that instantly modifies the Filter dialog box with its criteria when it loads.

Click the Open Filter button in the Filter dialog box. Choose a .bcmq file from your hard drive or network server and click OK. All the criteria from the first filter is now entered in the Filter dialog box, overwriting the existing criteria. Click the Review Results tab to see the data returned by that query.

Don't forget that the filters for a contact won't work if you open that file in an opportunity filter dialog box, or project, or any other type except contact filter. Each filter file is specific to one type of data.

Deleting a filter

There's really no need to delete a filter, other than the cleanliness of your hard drive and folders. Filters don't take up much space on your hard drive but can clutter your consciousness.

Go into Windows Explorer (press Windows+E on your keyboard), find the .bcmq files (click the Search button for search options), and delete the ones you don't want to keep.

Working with Search Folders

Search folders are the most versatile folders, designed to hold data you specify in a filter. They're considered *virtual folders* — displayed lists of records that match specific criteria in a filter. A search folder is a place to hold the results of a filter.

If you're doing a lot of mail merges, using search folders is a great way to create groups that you merge to. Each folder is a specific filter that creates a subset of your BCM database. When you enter the mail merge settings to do a blast, you can easily pick a search folder as the data source from which to merge names. Jump to Chapter 14 for more help on merges.

One way to think of a search folder is as a living report. By specifying the data you want in the folder using a filter and modifying the way it's displayed, you can see up-to-date data instantly, just by viewing the search folder.

Creating a search folder

You can create as many search folders as you want, and they're shown in the Navigation pane. You can also access search folders by pressing Ctrl+6 on your keyboard or from the Outlook menu bar by choosing Go➪Folder List.

You can't add, delete, rename, or customize the search folders in an offline database. You have to create these folders on the server, not the remote database.

To create a search folder, follow these steps:

1. **From the Navigation pane, right-click Search Folders and choose New Search Folder.**

   The New Search Folder dialog box, shown in Figure 17-4, opens.

Figure 17-4:
New Search
Folder
dialog box.

New Search Folder

Name: Hot Prospects from Spring Trade Show

Select "Filter" to change what items this Search Folder contains.   Filter...

Items of this type are included in this Search Folder:

Business Contacts

Help   OK   Cancel

2. **Enter the name of the search folder in the Name box.**

   This name can be descriptive; it doesn't need a filename structure. You might want to preface this name with the data type.

3. **Choose the type of data your search folder will hold from the Items of This Type Are Included in This Search Folder drop-down list.**

   This is where you choose among business contacts, accounts, opportunities, business projects, project tasks, business contact history, account history, opportunity history, and business project history. Based on your choice here, other options change because you have different data types.

4. **Click the Filter button.**

   The Filter dialog box opens. You can open a saved filter or create your own new filter.

5. **Click OK to create the search folder.**

   The search folder is created.

You can customize the view settings of these search folders exactly the same as you do any other view — check out Chapter 7.

Deleting a search folder

When you decide that you no longer need a search folder, you easily can delete it from view. Just right-click the folder and choose Delete. The folder is deleted, but not the data that is contained there. The filter file (.bcmq) that it was based upon also isn't deleted. That file stays on the hard drive.

Using Filters Every Day

In what circumstances can you use filters? What parts of BCM require that you use them?

You'll be surprised at how many places in BCM allow you to filter your data and customize your views. Here's a list of some of our favorites — yours might differ, based on your use of BCM:

- ✔ **Reports:** Whenever you view a report, click the Filter Report button to open the Filter dialog box. Creating complex filters for data and summarizing and grouping the data to create totals is a common use of filters.

- ✔ **Views:** Your data makes more sense when it's displayed in an order you relate to, sorted the way you think about it, and grouped in appropriate ways so that you can easily find what you're looking for. Being able to filter the data and customize the views gives BCM excellent flexibility and power.

- ✔ **Marketing campaigns:** Using a filter allows you to specify the recipients of a marketing campaign — which is required to generate a campaign. This approach makes doing a monthly newsletter an easy process by always having the correct group of recipients ready to go. You can also create a search folder to display the most successful campaigns.

- ✔ **Opportunity forecasting:** How many times has the boss or Big Boss asked for a forecast of what's in the pipeline, when it's going to close, and what they're going to buy? Have a filter created to choose that data or easily customize the filter based on the boss's whims of the moment.

- ✔ **Export to Excel:** Using a filter to create the data subset and then exporting a report or view to Excel gives you great flexibility in getting that data out of BCM in a format that Excel can slice and dice to your heart's content.

- ✔ **Project tasks and reporting:** If you're using the project tasks function of BCM, you can create filters for task reporting and managing your people that give you instantaneous access to who's on track or who's behind.

Chapter 18

Measuring Your Progress with BCM Reports

*A*fter you build your database, the fun part is sitting back and using it. If paper is your game, then BCM is surely the name — at least of the software that you should be using for any type of reporting. In this chapter, we discuss the various BCM reports that are available. We also include basic information on editing report templates.

In this chapter, we show you everything you always wanted to know about BCM reports but were afraid to ask. After reading this chapter, you'll be familiar with the various reports, know how to run them, and also know techniques for sharing those reports with colleagues.

Knowing the Basic BCM Reports

BCM comes with a menu of 50 basic reports right out of the box. Later in this chapter, we show you how to customize existing reports. In this section, we list the basic reports, briefly describing each. Chances are good that at least one of the basic BCM reports gives you exactly the information that you're looking for without even having to customize it.

The BCM Reports menu is divided into seven sections; you'll probably find it to be no small coincidence that these sections reflect seven of the most valuable areas of BCM.

Accounting for your accounts

Your BCM accounts drive your business, so it's only fitting that BCM comes equipped with 12 account reports. The titles of several of these reports reflect how the accounts are grouped together in the body of the report:

- ✔ **Accounts by City:** Groups your accounts by city.

- ✔ **Accounts by State/Province:** Groups your accounts by state or province.

- ✔ **Accounts by Zip/Postal Code:** Groups your accounts by zip code.

- ✔ **Accounts by Category:** Groups your accounts by category. If you didn't assign a category to some accounts, they're grouped together in the Unspecified category.

- ✔ **Accounts by Rating:** Groups your accounts by the information in the Account Rating field.

- ✔ **Accounts by Payment Status:** Groups your accounts by the information in the Payment Status field.

- ✔ **Accounts by Assigned To:** Groups your accounts by the information in the Assigned To field.

- ✔ **Accounts by Territory:** Groups your accounts by the information in the Territory field.

- ✔ **Accounts by Source of Lead:** Groups your accounts by the information in the Source field.

Not sure where to enter the information for any of these reports? Take a look at Chapter 5 for more information on accounts.

Don't worry if some of your accounts are missing the information used to group accounts together in a report. For example, you might want to run the Accounts by Rating report but are concerned that you didn't rate many of your accounts. Worry not — those accounts are grouped together as unspecified. Figure 18-1 shows unspecified information in an Accounts by Rating report.

Three account reports look a bit different than the rest of the account reports:

- ✔ **Account Activity Summary:** Shows the outstanding opportunities, how often you've contacted those accounts, and even the last time you contacted that account. Figure 18-2 shows a snippet of an Account Activity Summary report.

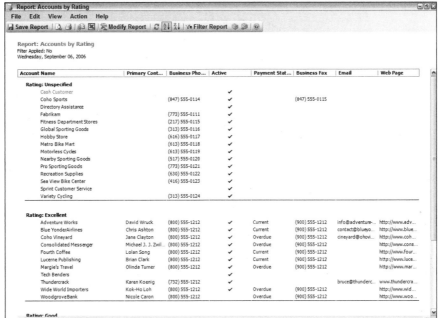

Figure 18-1:
The Accounts by Rating report with unspecified accounts.

Figure 18-2:
The Account Activity Summary report.

✔ **Quick Account List:** This page lists all your accounts. Although it's a relatively basic report, you can customize it quite a bit if you like. We show you how to customize reports in the "Giving Your Reports a Complete Facelift" section, later in this chapter.

✔ **Neglected Accounts:** Also known as the Hide This One from the Boss report, the Neglected Accounts report shows you all the accounts that you haven't touched base with in the last week or within the last month. Ouch!

Tracking your activities

If you're the boss, you might be wondering exactly what your employees are doing all day. If you're the employee, you might want to prove to your boss that you are indeed up to good things during the day. Either way, the Activity reports give proof to the pudding. These are the different activity reports:

- ✔ **Activity by Business Contact:** Shows you the completed communication history (meeting, note, phone log, task, opportunity, project, or marketing campaign) for each contact during a specified date range. This report is sorted by contact so that you can see a listing of all the time that you've spent with any given contact. Figure 18-3 shows an Activity by Business Contact report.

- ✔ **Activity by Account:** The Activity by Account report is pretty much a clone of the Activity by Business Contact report except that it lists the completed communication history for each account.

- ✔ **Activity by Opportunity:** Again, the Activity by Opportunity report parallels the Activity by Business Contact report except that it lists the completed communication history for all of your opportunities.

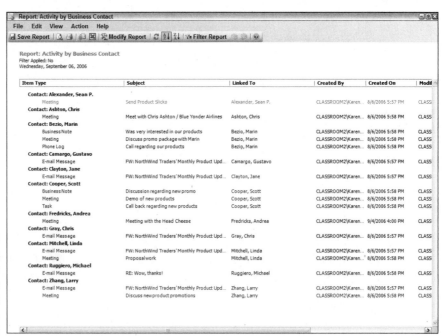

Figure 18-3:
The Activity
by Business
Contact
report.

Making contact with your business contacts

Most of the business contact reports are clones of the corresponding account report (see the "Accounting for your accounts" section, earlier in the chapter). What makes business contact reports different is that they draw their information from business contact records rather than from account records. These are the business contact reports you'll probably use the most:

- **Business Contacts by Account:** Shows all your business contacts grouped together by account.

- **Business Contacts by Anniversary:** Lists your business contacts by the month of their anniversary.

- **Business Contacts by Birthday:** Lists your business contacts by the month of their birthday.

The gentlemen in the crowd probably learned a long time ago that they are much better off not asking for the *year* in which a young lady was born. BCM helps you to avoid that delicate question — and a possible slap in the face — by allowing you to enter *any year* in the Birthday field. BCM politely ignores the year and reports strictly on the month of the birthday as shown in Figure 18-4.

Report: Business Contacts by Birthday

File   Edit   View   Action   Help

Save Report | Modify Report | Filter Report

Report: Business Contacts by Birthday
Filter Applied: No
Wednesday, September 06, 2006

Business Contact Name	Account	Business Phone	Mobile Phone	Address -...	Address - City	Address - State
Nicole Caron	WoodgroveBank	(800) 555-1212	(425) 555-1212	216 S. Monar...	Woody Creek	CO
Nicole Holliday		(800) 555-1212	(425) 555-1212			
Nigel Westbury	Adventure Works	(800) 555-1212	(425) 555-1212	1512 3rd Street	Crested Butte	CO
Olinda Turner	Margie's Travel	(800) 555-1212	(425) 555-1212	7031 S Lawre...	Roaring Fork Val...	CO
Ovidiu Burlacu	Adventure Works	(800) 555-1212	(425) 555-1212	789 3rd Street	Toronto	ON
Patrick M. M. Cook	Litware	(800) 555-1212	(425) 555-1212	818 Market St...	San Francisco	CA
Paula Barreto Barreto de Mattos	Contoso, Ltd	(800) 555-1212	(425) 555-1212	121 South Ga...	Aspen	
Rob Young	Variety Cycling					
Ryan Calafato	Adventure Works	(800) 555-1212	(425) 555-1212	789 3rd Street	Toronto	ON
Sam Abolrous	Contoso, Ltd	(954) 234-5678	(425) 555-1212			
Scott Cooper		(800) 555-1212	(425) 555-1212	340 Carriage...	Aspen	CO
Sean P. Alexander	Adventure Works	(800) 555-1212	(425) 555-1212	789 3rd Street	Toronto	ON
Sunil Koduri	Margie's Travel	(800) 555-1212	(425) 555-1212	7031 S Lawre...	Roaring Fork Val...	CO
Susan W. W. Eaton		(800) 555-1212	(425) 555-1212			
Tete Mensa-Annan		(800) 555-1212	(425) 555-1212	338 5th St.	Detroit	MI
Tim O'Brien	Nearby Sporting Goods					
Toby Malice	Thundercrack	(732) 555-1212		1 Stratocaster...	Les Paul	NJ
Toby Nixon	Trey Research	(800) 555-1212	(425) 555-1212	45 Village Sq...	Woody Creek	CO
Tommy TestPerson		(214) 555-6677	(972) 334-5532	123 Main Stre...	Dallas	TX

Birthdays in January
Alyssa Fredricks   Tallahassee   FL

Birthdays in June
Gary Kahn   Boca Raton   FL

Birthdays in July
Andrea Fredricks   Gainesville   FL

Figure 18-4:
The Business Contacts by Birthday report.

Leading up to your leads

You can find the lead reports together in a subsection of the main Reports menu. These reports give you different ways to view the new leads that are coming into your database. If you aren't tracking leads, these reports won't mean much to you; however, if you're paying a lot of money to get new leads for your database, these reports are invaluable:

✔ **Leads by Assigned To:** Groups your leads by the user of your database to whom they were assigned.

✔ **Leads by Assigned To and Rating:** Groups your leads by the user of your database to whom they were assigned and then subdivides each group by lead rating.

✔ **Leads by Rating:** Groups your leads by lead rating so you can see all your hot prospects listed together followed by your cooler prospects.

Seeing your opportunities at an opportune time

BCM provides you with a variety of opportunity reports. The opportunity reports use information that you entered into an opportunity record. If you aren't using the opportunities feature (head to Chapter 12 for the lowdown), you can't use these reports. The opportunity reports are all housed in a separate opportunity section on the Reports menu.

For most of you, the whole purpose of running a company is to make money. And you probably make money by selling your products and services. If you don't make money, the doors of your business will soon slam shut on a permanent basis. The opportunity reports provide you with a great way to measure your progress.

✔ **Opportunities by Account:** Groups your opportunities by account.

✔ **Opportunities by Business Contact:** Groups your opportunities by business contact.

✔ **Opportunities by Assigned To:** Groups your opportunities by the member of your company to whom they were assigned.

✔ **Opportunities by Source of Lead:** Groups your opportunities by the source of the lead. This report is particularly important for those of you who are spending a bunch of money on marketing efforts — and would like some feedback on how those efforts are paying off.

✔ **Opportunities by Product or Service Item:** Lists your sales opportunities by product or service. Figure 18-5 shows an Opportunities by Product or Service Item report.

You can list several items in one opportunity. Consequently, a single opportunity might be listed several times throughout the Opportunities by Product or Service Item report.

✔ **Opportunities Funnel:** Groups your opportunities by sales stage. This is probably one of the most popular reports because you can see — and focus on — those opportunities that have the best chance of closing in the very near future. You can also track your progress from week to week as your opportunities progress from the simple prospecting stage to the final, "the check's in the mail" stage. Figure 18-6 shows an Opportunities Funnel report.

✔ **Past Due Opportunities:** BCM is particularly good about preventing things from falling through the cracks. In the case of the Past Due Opportunities report, you can see which of your opportunities were scheduled to close 7, 30, or even 90 days ago — and are still outstanding.

✔ **Opportunity Forecast:** If the Past Due Opportunities report left you feeling slightly depressed, then the Opportunity Forecast report should perk you up a bit because it gives you a list of all the opportunities that are scheduled to close within the next week.

Figure 18-5:
The Opportunities by Product or Service Item report.

Report: Opportunities by Product or Service Item
File   Edit   View   Action   Help   Close
Save Report | 🖫 🖨 📄 📧 | 🔧 Modify Report | 🔁 ⬇️ ⬆️ | ▽= Filter Report

Report: Opportunities by Product or Service Item
Filter Applied: No
Wednesday, September 06, 2006

Title	Account/Contact	Stage	Close Date	Probability	Unit Price	Quantity	Amount	Closed	Source
Total for Baseball Uniform						**2.00**	**$99.98**		
Basketball									
Coho's Baseball Extravaganza	Coho Vineyard	Prospecting	2/7/2006	10.00 %	$21.99	15.00	$329.85		
Store Giveaway	Fourth Coffee	Qualification	2/24/2006	40.00 %	$21.99	250.00	$5,497.50		
Total for Basketball						**265.00**	**$5,827.35**		
Basketball Hoop & Board									
Store Giveaway	Fourth Coffee	Qualification	2/24/2006	40.00 %	$189.99	5.00	$949.95		
Total for Basketball Hoop & Board						**5.00**	**$949.95**		
Bicycle - Blue									
High Profile Consumer Challenge	Blue YonderAirlines	Prospecting	2/24/2006	15.00 %	$79.99	15.00	$1,199.85		Trade Show
Total for Bicycle - Blue						**15.00**	**$1,199.85**		
Bicycle - Red									
High Profile Consumer Challenge	Blue YonderAirlines	Prospecting	2/24/2006	15.00 %	$79.99	25.00	$1,999.75		Trade Show
Total for Bicycle - Red						**25.00**	**$1,999.75**		
Bike Helmet - Adult									
Good customer give-away	City Power & Light	Proposal/P...	2/27/2006	50.00 %	$26.99	100.00	$2,699.00		External Refe
High Profile Consumer Challenge	Blue YonderAirlines	Prospecting	2/24/2006	15.00 %	$26.99	400.00	$10,796.00		Trade Show
Total for Bike Helmet - Adult						**500.00**	**$13,495.00**		
Discount									
Writer Promo	Lucerne Publishing	Negotiatio...	2/27/2006	80.00 %	$5,000.00	0.10	$500.00		
Total for Discount						**0.10**	**$500.00**		
Exotic Bicycle									
Good customer give-away	City Power & Light	Proposal/P...	2/27/2006	50.00 %	$109.99	15.00	$1,649.85		External Refe
Total for Exotic Bicycle						**15.00**	**$1,649.85**		
Golf Club Set with Bag									
New Product review	Lucerne Publishing	Prospecting	4/4/2006	30.00 %	$1,299.99	1.00	$1,299.99		
Total for Golf Club Set with Bag						**1.00**	**$1,299.99**		

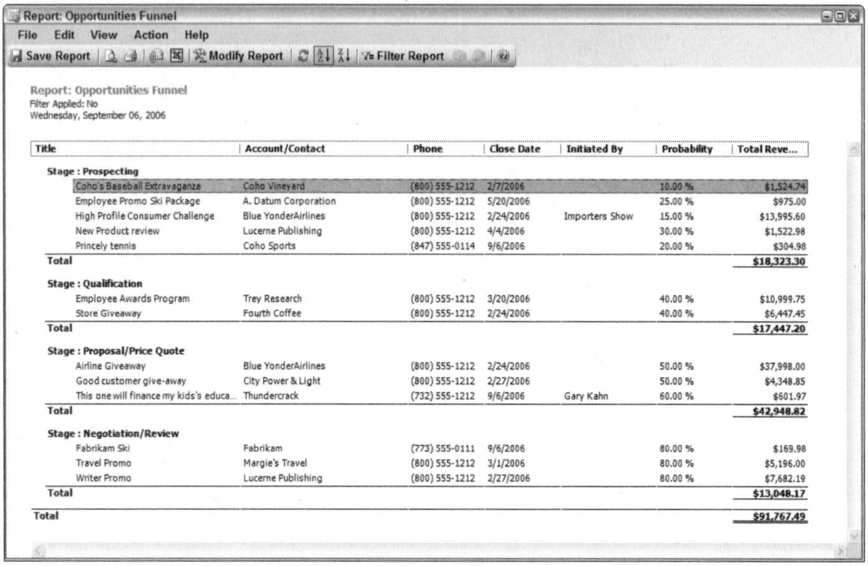

Report: Opportunities Funnel
Filter Applied: No
Wednesday, September 06, 2006

Title	Account/Contact	Phone	Close Date	Initiated By	Probability	Total Reve...
Stage : Prospecting						
Coho's Baseball Extravaganza	Coho Vineyard	(800) 555-1212	2/7/2006		10.00 %	$1,524.74
Employee Promo Ski Package	A. Datum Corporation	(800) 555-1212	5/20/2006		25.00 %	$975.00
High Profile Consumer Challenge	Blue YonderAirlines	(800) 555-1212	2/24/2006	Importers Show	15.00 %	$13,995.60
New Product review	Lucerne Publishing	(800) 555-1212	4/4/2006		30.00 %	$1,522.98
Princely tennis	Coho Sports	(847) 555-0114	9/6/2006		20.00 %	$304.98
Total						$18,323.30
Stage : Qualification						
Employee Awards Program	Trey Research	(800) 555-1212	3/20/2006		40.00 %	$10,999.75
Store Giveaway	Fourth Coffee	(800) 555-1212	2/24/2006		40.00 %	$6,447.45
Total						$17,447.20
Stage : Proposal/Price Quote						
Airline Giveaway	Blue YonderAirlines	(800) 555-1212	2/24/2006		50.00 %	$37,998.00
Good customer give-away	City Power & Light	(800) 555-1212	2/27/2006		50.00 %	$4,348.85
This one will finance my kids's educa...	Thundercrack	(732) 555-1212	9/6/2006	Gary Kahn	60.00 %	$601.97
Total						$42,948.82
Stage : Negotiation/Review						
Fabrikam Ski	Fabrikam	(773) 555-0111	9/6/2006		80.00 %	$169.98
Travel Promo	Margie's Travel	(800) 555-1212	3/1/2006		80.00 %	$5,196.00
Writer Promo	Lucerne Publishing	(800) 555-1212	2/27/2006		80.00 %	$7,682.19
Total						$13,048.17
Total						$91,767.49

Figure 18-6: BCM's Opportunities Funnel report.

Seeing your business projects flash before your eyes

Two of Outlooks strengths have always been the ability it gives you to schedule and follow up on tasks. BCM runs with that concept and takes it to a whole new level. You might think of a project as a super-sized task. Whereas a task involves one chore that needs to be done by one individual, a project involves a multitude of tasks that need to be done over a period of time, generally by several individuals. BCM offers a wide range of reports to help you keep track of your projects:

- **Business Projects by Status:** Groups your projects by those that haven't started, those that are in progress, and those that are completed. Figure 18-7 shows a Business Projects by Status report.
- **Business Projects by Due Date:** Lists your business projects by due date.
- **Business Projects by Assigned To:** Groups your business projects by the person in your organization who is heading up the project.
- **Business Projects by Type:** Groups your business projects by type.
- **Business Projects by Priority:** Groups your business projects by priority.
- **Business Projects by Account:** Groups your business projects by account.

Figure 18-7:
The
Business
Projects by
Status
report.

Figure 18-8:
The Quick
Business
Projects
List.

- ✔ **Business Projects by Business Contact:** Groups your business projects by business contact.
- ✔ **Quick Business Projects List:** Lists all your outstanding business projects. Figure 18-8 shows the Quick Business Projects List report.
- ✔ **Project Tasks per Project:** Shows the tasks that were assigned to each business project.
- ✔ **Project Tasks by Assigned To:** Lists the tasks that are assigned to business projects by the person assigned to the task.

Going to market with your marketing campaigns

It's probably fairly safe to make one major assumption about your marketing campaigns: If they don't result in new business, they aren't worth the time and money you spend on them. Perhaps you spent quite a bit of money last year on three separate marketing campaigns; perhaps you sent a direct mailer, signed up with an e-marketing company, and attended a really large trade show. This year, you might be in a situation where your marketing budget has been slashed and you want to know how to get the most marketing bang for the buck. The BCM marketing reports let you do just that:

✔ **Opportunities by Marketing Campaign:** Shows the opportunities that resulted from a marketing campaign.

✔ **Business Contact by Marketing Campaign:** Lists the business contacts that you acquired as a result of a marketing campaign.

✔ **Accounts by Marketing Campaign:** Shows accounts that you acquired as a result of a marketing campaign.

We spend Chapter 15 talking about how to set up a marketing campaign.

Running a BCM Report

Creating a BCM report is ridiculously easy — you choose a report by clicking it. Here's the drill for running any one of the out-of-the-box BCM reports:

1. **From the Outlook menu bar, choose Business Contact Manager⇨ Reports.**

   Although BCM comes with over 50 reports from the get-go, you just might feel that none of the reports is exactly what you're looking for. Not to worry — just choose the report that is closest to what you're looking for. After you run a report, you can customize the report to your liking.

2. **Select the category of the report that you want to run.**

   Here's the fun part — you get to pick which type of report. Not sure which one to pick? Flip back to the section "Knowing the Basic BCM Reports."

3. **Select the specific report.**

   In a flash, your report springs to life.

4. **(Optional) Click a column heading to re-sort your report.**

   By default, most of the BCM reports appear in alphabetical order. If you are left-handed — or just enjoy seeing your reports sorted in *Z* to *A* order — you can do so with a single click of any column heading.

5. **(Optional) Change the order of the columns by dragging them to a new location.**

   If you're not thrilled with the order in which the columns appear in the report — or if you just like to exercise a bit of control — drag a column to a new location by holding down your left button on a column head and moving to the left or right.

6. **Choose what you want to do with your report:**

   • *Print:* Choose File⇨Print.

- *Send it in an e-mail:* Choose File➪Send E-Mail with Excel Attachment. This has to be one of the neatest of the report features; BCM opens a new e-mail message with your report already attached as an Excel attachment.

- *Save it in Excel format:* Choose File➪Export to Excel.

7. **Choose File➪Close when you finish working with the report.**

Giving Your Reports a Complete Facelift

We mentioned in the previous section that chances are you begin with a basic report and decide to modify it somewhat — or even give it a complete makeover. Start by tweaking some of the fields already on your report template. You could remove one or two of the existing columns and replace them with columns that are more to your liking. You might want to make the font a wee bit larger to accommodate your 40-something eyes. The more ornery members of the crowd might not be happy with the order in which the fields appear in one of the opportunity reports. Like anything else, it's simple to modify BCM reports if you know the trick.

Modifying an existing report

Probably the first thing you want to do is decide which fields will — or won't — appear in your report. Being familiar with the structure of your existing database can prove helpful when you attempt to do this. Thus, you need to know the field names that you're working with. For example, if you want to include the name of a company, you must know that the field is called Account.

Once you make the momentous decision of which fields should appear in your report, follow these steps to get the job done:

1. **Open the report that is closest to what you're looking for.**

   With over 50 reports to choose from, there's no point in choosing a report that's not even close to what you're looking for when another report can do the trick quite nicely.

   The report window often opens in a normal window size — that is, it's not maximized to its fullest size. You might want to maximize the report window before you start to customize a report.

2. **Click the Modify Report button on the Report toolbar.**

   The Modify Report dialog box opens on the right side of your report. The Modify Report dialog box allows you to make changes to the report's fonts, headers and footers, and columns.

3. **Click the plus sign next to one of the column types to display more field choices.**

Probably the first way you'll want to modify your report is by adding or removing the columns that you see in the existing database. Each column of a BCM report is based on a field in an account, business contact, opportunity, and business project record.

Depending on the report you select, you have different columns types available to you:

- *Basic:* This is where you find fields for first and last names, title, and account, as well as for other basic fields such as birthday, anniversary, and category.

- *Address:* This option provides you with postal address fields, including city, state, and zip code.

- *Contact:* The fields in this area help you contact an account or business contact, including fax, phone, page, and e-mail address.

- *Mail:* These fields show the recipient, sender, and date of an e-mail message.

- *Tracking:* These fields show the date that an account or business contact was created or edited, as well as the person who did the creating or editing.

- *Other:* Includes duration of a phone log and the filename and location of an attached file.

- *Custom:* These are the fields that you have added to your account, business contact, opportunity, or business project records.

You can add as many custom fields as you like to your account, business contact, opportunity, and business project records. If you want to find out how, take a look at Chapter 7.

Figure 18-9 shows the columns available for a Quick Account List report.

4. **Select the check box next to any of the fields you'd like to add to your report.**

You can select as many fields as you like; the fields you select are added as new columns at the end of the report.

5. **Remove any columns that you don't want to appear in your report by deselecting the check box next to any of those fields.**

Sorry to be the bearer of bad news, but most paper holds only a finite number of columns. If you add a bunch of new columns, you'll probably want to remove a few as well.

Figure 18-9:
Adding new columns to the Quick Account List report.

6. **Rearrange the columns on your report by dragging them to the left or right.**

You'll be amazed at how easily you can drag a column — and all the information that it contains — to a new spot on your report.

7. **(Optional) Save the report.**

You have two options here:

- *Choose File⇨Save Report if you want to permanently change the existing report.*

- *Choose File⇨Save Report As if you want to save your modification as a whole new report.*

Either way, BCM saves your report for future use, with the `.bcr` extension. Could it be that the *r* stands for report? You be the judge!

8. **Choose File⇨Close to close the report.**

Filtering your reports

Another way in which you can modify your BCM reports is by changing the content of the report. You do this by creating filters to determine what data should show up in your report. Although you can create very complex queries, the process that you follow is quite simple:

1. **Open the report that is closest to what you're looking for.**

2. **Click the Filter Report button on the Report toolbar.**

   Alternatively, if you just modified a report, you can click the Filters link at the top of the Modify Report dialog box.

   The Filter dialog box opens, as shown in Figure 18-10.

   For purposes of these steps, we're using the Quick Account List report. The options you see in Figure 18-10 might be slightly different than the ones you see if you filter a different report. No problem — the concepts work exactly the same.

3. **Select the check boxes for the data that you want to appear in your report.**

   If you're one of those people who have trouble deciding what flavor you want at the local ice cream shop, you might have problems here because there are a lot of choices. However, if you believe the more the merrier, you should have a field day here.

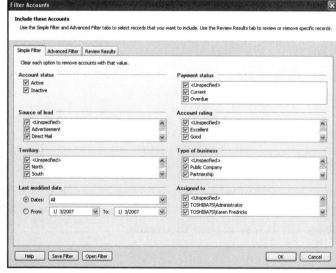

Figure 18-10:
Filtering
a Quick
Account List
report.

Each of the options represents one of the fields in the account, business contact, opportunity, or business project that you're reporting on. The choices within the option are the values of the drop-down list for that field. In our example of the Quick Account List report, we see the option of Account Status, which represents one of the account record fields, and the choices of Active or Inactive, which are the two options for that field.

There really is a lot of information to choose from when filtering a report — and not all of it is visible to the naked eye. You'll notice scroll bar indicators after many of the fields; this means that there are more field choices. If you're interested in seeing — or not seeing — information from a given field, you want to give those scroll bars a scroll.

4. (Optional) Click the Save Filter button.

The only thing worse than doing work is having to do the same work over again. After you slave over the various filter options, you might want to save your work so that you don't have to save it again later. BCM assigns your saved query the `.bcmq` extension.

5. Click OK to see the results of your filter in the report.

If you've already saved a query, you can click the Open Filter button to open an existing filter.

If a simple filter doesn't do the job for you, check out Chapter 17, where we discuss how to create more complex filters.

Performing a Minor Report Makeover

If you've read this chapter thus far, you've worked really hard at modifying and filtering a BCM report. And, hopefully, you still have enough time left to get some well-deserved R&R. This section deals entirely with the appearance of your reports. If you don't think appearance is everything, go have a chat with the lady at your local makeup counter.

Heads up on your headers and footers

A *header* is the information that appears at the top of every page of your report. A *footer* is the information that appears at the bottom of every page of your report. Both report headers and footers can be tweaked quite easily. Follow these steps to do so:

1. Open the report that is closest to what you're looking for.

2. **Click the Modify Report button on the Report toolbar.**

   The Modify Report dialog box opens. (Refer to Figure 18-9.)

3. **Click the Header and Footer link.**

   The Header and Footer options appear, as shown in Figure 18-11.

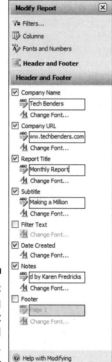

Figure 18-11:
Modifying
report
headers and
footers.

4. **Select the option you want to change and fill in the juicy details.**

   You can change several areas:

   - *Company Name:* Fill in the name of the company you want to appear at the top of each page.

   - *Company URL:* Fill in the Web address you want to appear at the top of each page.

   - *Report Title:* Change the default report name that appears at the top of each page.

   - *Subtitle:* No, you're not watching a foreign flick; if you want to give the report a subtitle, here's your chance.

- *Filter Text:* Selecting the check box here results in a header message indicating that you've applied some sort of filtering to this report.

- *Date Created:* Adds today's date to the header.

- *Notes:* Just in case you feel that you need to add yet another tidbit of information to your report's header area, here's where you can add that tidbit.

- *Footer:* Adds information to the bottom of each page of your report in addition to the page number that already appears there.

Fashioning a few fonts

Another way to tweak your reports is by changing the font type that appears throughout your report. Although not critical, these changes can improve the readability of your reports — thus making them a whole lot more useful!

Changing the fonts is a very easy thing to do. After you've changed a font or two, you can save the report so that your new and improved fonts appear the next time you run your report.

Follow these steps to "fonticize" your report:

1. **Open the report you want to tweak.**

   Not sure how to do that? See "Running a BCM Report," earlier in this chapter.

2. **Click the Modify Report button on the Report toolbar.**

   The Modify Report dialog box opens to the right of your report. (Refer to Figure 18-9.)

3. **Click the Fonts and Numbers link.**

   The Fonts and Numbers options, shown in Figure 18-12, appear.

4. **Select the part of the report you want to change.**

   You can change the font, font style (bold, italics), size, color, and underline style for each of the following areas of the report:

   - *Column Labels*

   - *Row Labels*

   - *Report Body*

   - *Sub Total*

   - *Total*

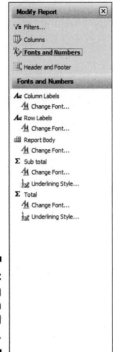

Figure 18-12:
Changing
the fonts in
a BCM
report.

5. **Make your change and click OK.**

You can repeat the process for all the elements of the report that you want to change.

6. **Choose File➪Close to close the report.**

If you've made changes to the report, BCM asks you if you want to save them for posterity. Click Yes if you want to have the report appear with the font changes the next time you run it.

Changing Report Information

The entire purpose of a BCM report is to provide you with accurate, up-to-the-minute information. Before you hit that Print button, it's always a good idea to give your report a look over to make sure that all the report information seems to be correct.

BCM's capability to edit information on-the-fly from within a report is a great way to modify incorrect information and to add missing information. Follow these steps:

1. **Move your mouse over the area of your report where you see inaccurate or missing information.**

   You'll notice that your mouse cursor looks like a hand.

2. **Double-click that report item.**

   Zoom! You're transported to the BCM record that stores the information. For example, if you're looking at a business contact report and notice that a phone number is missing, give that contact a double-click. The corresponding business contact record opens.

3. **Make your changes.**

   In this case, more is more. You might notice that in addition to missing a phone number, the city and state fields are also blank. You might as well make as many corrections as you want.

4. **Click the Save & Close button on the Ribbon.**

   Double zoom! You land with a thump back in your report.

Refreshing your report

After you change the information that appears in your report, you'll probably rush right over to gaze fondly at the new data. But wait. What happened? The new information didn't magically appear! Typically, you first blame yourself and redo the steps you followed to correct the information. But it still doesn't work! At this point in time, you're probably composing a nasty letter to Microsoft in your head complaining about the BCM reports.

BCM doesn't *refresh* the report information until you tell it to do so. This is meant to allow you to correct many items in your report without having to wait for the report to reappear on your screen.

You can get that information to appear in three different ways:

- ✔ Press the F5 key on your keyboard.
- ✔ Choose View➪Refresh Report on the Reports menu bar.
- ✔ Click the Refresh Report icon (it looks like two arrows on top of one another) on the toolbar.

Whew! Problem solved.

Creating an Excel-ent report

A time will come when you'll want to save your report. Or, as hard as it might be to believe, not everyone you'll deal with will be using BCM, so you'll have to get the report to them in a form they can use. As usual, BCM provides you with two solutions for transporting your report from Point A to Point B, both of which can be accessed from the BCM Reports menu:

- ✔ Choose File⇨Export to Excel to create a spreadsheet version of the current report.

- ✔ Choose File⇨Send E-Mail with Excel Attachment to create an e-mail message with your report already included as an attached Excel spreadsheet. Figure 18-13 shows an e-mail with a report attached.

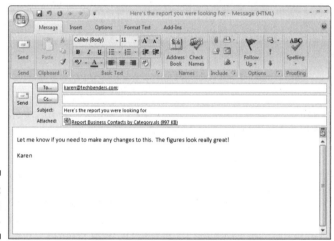

Figure 18-13:
E-mailing a
BCM report.

Chapter 19

Managing Your Projects and Teams

*P*rojects are new to Business Contact Manager 2007, and if you're the kind of person who manages other people or does work that lends itself to projects, you have a new best friend! Projects in BCM can be thought of as having three parts: the business project record that defines the project, the contacts or accounts involved in the project, and the project tasks that are linked to the project. Think of the business project as the container that holds the contacts and the tasks. A business project also contains the same communication history as other data records and keeps a chronology of what's happened with your project, for all the people involved.

Maybe you're a computer consultant and your employees help you with client work (and use BCM to track it all). Say that you have a new client who needs Microsoft Office Accounting software implemented into their business. You hold meetings with the client to decide on the implementation schedule. The first things that need to be done are to order a new server and set up wireless access points for the client's network, and then your bookkeeper needs to write some reports in Microsoft Office Accounting that match the spreadsheets they've been using.

So, imagine that you set up a business project named Implementing Microsoft Office Accounting at XYZ Corp. Then you set up project tasks for the server order, the wireless network installation, the software installation, and the reports that need to be written. You can assign each task (with a due date) to the BCM user who's doing that work. If you're using Microsoft Office Accounting, you can keep track of the time worked on each task. You can put that information directly into the Accounting system and use it to bill the client.

If your business is not project-oriented and you don't see a need for business projects and project tasks, you can use regular tasks (which are also billable, by the way). There's really no rule that you have to use the business projects feature for actual business projects — if you're training for a marathon and have a training schedule and goals, these records can be a great way to track your progress. But, we digress — that's another book.

Creating the Business Project

In this section, we create a project — the container, if you will — and name it Implementing Microsoft Office Accounting at XYZ Corp. By the way, there's no way to link one project to another, and there's no way to create dependencies from one task to another (for example, the network installation task can't start until the server installation task is finished). If this is what you want to do, you should look at Microsoft Office Project for more robust features. BCM's project tracking is more basic and easier to use!

In order to create a new business project, you have to open the Business Project window, shown in Figure 19-1, in one of the following ways:

- From the Outlook menu bar, choose Business Contact Manager⇨ Business Projects and then click the New button.

- From the BCM menu, choose Display⇨Business Projects and then click the New button.

- In the Navigation pane, click Tasks; under Business Contact Manager, click Business Projects and then click the New button.

- From the Business Contact Manager Home screen, click the Projects tab and then click the New Business Project button.

Follow these steps to enter details about a project:

1. **Enter the name of your project in the Project Name field.**

   This name can be descriptive; it's not a filename. One suggestion is to name it in a way that it will sort in a meaningful way in a list. For example, start the name with a client's name or your employee's name so that, when the project list is alphabetized, all the projects for XYZ Corp. show up together.

   A business project has two required fields: the Project Name and Link To. You must link every business project to a contact or account.

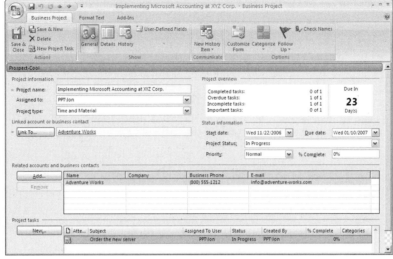

Figure 19-1:
The
Business
Project
window.

2. **Choose a BCM user from the Assigned To drop-down list.**

   This is useful if you have multiple users and you want to track what each person is doing. It isn't required.

3. **Choose a value from the Project Type drop-down list.**

   This list is a way to keep track of different types of projects. To customize the list with different values, select Edit This List from the Project Type drop-down list.

4. **Click the Link To button and choose an account or contact.**

   The Link to an Account or a Business Contact dialog box opens, as shown in Figure 19-2. This dialog box enables you to link that project to a contact or an account.

5. **Choose Accounts or Business Contacts from the Folder drop-down list.**

   Choose one of those — unfortunately, a project can link only to one, not both or multiple accounts or contacts.

6. **A list of accounts or contacts appears in the main area of the dialog box. Select a record to link that project to by clicking the record once to highlight it.**

7. **After you select your record, click the Link To button below the list, and then click OK to finalize the selection.**

   The record is added to the Linked To field next to the Link To button.

If you want to add a new contact or account at this point, click the New button, enter that data, and then click Save & Close to enter the new contact and link it to that project.

You can use the Search field (found near the upper-left side of the Link to an Account or a Business Contact dialog box) to move through a long list of contacts or accounts by typing the first few characters of the entry you're searching for. The list moves to the part of the list that matches the characters you type. You can also double-click that record to enter it into the Linked Records field.

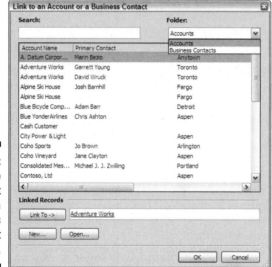

Figure 19-2:
The Link to
an Account
or a
Business
Contact
dialog box.

8. **Back in the Business Project dialog box, in the Status Information section, enter the Start Date, Due Date, Project Status, Priority, and % Complete.**

   These values are optional but valuable in tracking your progress or your team's progress in completing the project. If you want to change the values in the Project Status list, select Edit This List to change them.

9. **(Optional) Enter more related accounts or contacts.**

   This gives you a way to associate accounts or contacts with this project. Click Add and choose from the dialog box.

10. **Enter project tasks by clicking the New button.**

    The Add Project Task dialog box opens, which we discuss in more detail later in this chapter. The great advantage of clicking the New button from here is that the project task is automatically linked to this business project, saving you a few clicks, which is more time and money!

To customize the way these tasks are displayed in this grid, right-click the list of tasks and choose Customize Current View. This function gives you the same ability to customize this display as you've discovered in other areas of BCM. Refer to Chapter 7 for more details about how this works.

Alternatively, you can click the New Project Task button on the Ribbon, in the Actions group, to add a new project task instead of using this section of the dialog box.

11. **On the Ribbon, click Save & Close to save the business project record.**

   If you have another project to enter immediately, click the Save & New button instead of Save & Close, and you get a new Business Project window.

Entering more information in the project

But wait, there's more! You have more functionality in the business project record. We've been looking at only the general screen of this record. This project really is a container for all kinds of items: You can create notes and phone logs for this project, just like you do for a contact, account, or opportunity. You can use categories and follow-up options to keep these project tasks together with the rest of your life. And you can add fields to this record to keep track of more data about the project. We discuss each of these tasks in the following sections.

Entering details with a time stamp

Using a time stamp is one way of keeping track of notes about a project. See the section "Entering and viewing communication history" later in this chapter, to find out how to enter a business note and link it to the project. If you're entering a *lot* of notes, and from multiple users, the business note is a better strategy. Using details is good for fewer notes.

Follow these steps to add details to your project, along with a time stamp:

1. **From the Ribbon, in the Show group, click Details.**

   This displays the Details dialog box.

2. **Click the Time Stamp button to enter a date and time entry.**

3. **Enter comments or notes.**

4. **Click Save & Close to save your changes.**

   The next time you come back to this dialog box, click the Time Stamp button again to record your next note. Your previous note moves down.

Entering and viewing communication history

Just as you can with a contact, account, or opportunity record, you can create communication history records that are connected to the project. However, communication history records are unlike project tasks in that you can link them to as many contacts, accounts, opportunities, and projects as you choose. You can categorize each history entry as well.

Follow these steps to enter a communication history item to your project:

1. **To enter a communication history item, from the Ribbon, in the Communicate group, click New History Item. Choose the type of record you want to create from the drop-down-list.**

   You can choose these types of records: Business Note, Phone Log, Mail Message, Appointment, or File.

2. **Enter the details of the project. Click Save & Close to save the item.**

3. **To view the communication history items, from the Ribbon, in the Show group, choose History.**

   This displays a grid of all the history items. Click the View drop-down list to see the different choices of how the grid is sorted and grouped.

   Click the New button to enter a new communication history item, exactly the same as in Step 1.

   To remove an item, click once to highlight it and then click the Remove button.

Adding user-defined fields and customizing forms

You can add fields to the business project record, similar to many other data types. This is valuable for adding data fields to track additional information and customize the record to your business.

On the Ribbon, from the Options group, click the Customize Form button to bring up the Manage User-Defined Fields dialog box. Check out Chapter 7 to find out all about adding fields to records using this dialog box.

Assigning categories

As you discover in Chapter 6, categories are a powerful way to group and organize your data. You can assign one or more categories to each project.

From the Ribbon, in the Options group, click the Categorize icon. This displays the Category drop-down list. Choose a category. Or select All Categories from the list to get to the Category dialog box. If you need some help, check out Chapter 6 for more information on using this dialog box.

Follow ups

One of the handy ways to keep up with your projects is to set a reminder to follow up on it. Setting a Follow Up brings the project to your attention regularly and shows it in your To-Do List and To-Do bar.

From the Ribbon, in the Options group, click Follow Up. The Follow Up drop-down list displays. Choose your time period for following up on this project — doing so sets a Follow Up flag. Choose Add Reminder to also set an alarm to remind you to follow up. You get the same Reminder pop-up for this as any task or appointment for which you set a reminder.

Deleting a project

Be careful about deleting a project. When you delete a business project record, Business Contact Manager for Outlook deletes all its linked communication history items. Because some of these can be linked to other contacts, accounts, or opportunities, you don't want them to go away.

A better strategy might be to change the project status to inactive. You can check out Chapter 7 to find out how to customize views to exclude inactive projects.

Working with Project Tasks

After you have a business project created, you can create some project tasks. *Tasks* are the step-by-step functions that, taken together, result in completion of the project. You can have as many tasks as you want that are part of the project, and each task can be assigned to a BCM database user and tracked to completion.

Project tasks are different than regular tasks in two ways:

- ✔ **A regular task can link to a contact, account, or opportunity, but a regular task can't link to a project.** A project task links to a project only and the project links to the contacts or accounts. A project task also can't have any recurrence (every Wednesday a status report is due, for example). You would need to set a new task for that each week or use a regular task.

- ✔ **When a regular task is assigned to someone, that person can send a status report to the assignor. A project task doesn't have that functionality.** If regular status reports are important to you, you might not want to use a project, but instead group regular tasks in a category and manage your people that way.

Creating a project task

The hallmark of a project task is that it's linked to a project. The most efficient way to accomplish the link is to create the task either from inside the Business Project window (as you see in the previous section) or by right-clicking the project record when looking at the list of business projects.

However you choose to start the entry of the project task, here are the steps to accomplish it:

1. **Open the Project Task window using one of these methods:**

   - From the Ribbon inside a business project, in the Actions group, click New Project Task.

   - From the Project Tasks section inside a business project, click the New button.

   - From a business project list view, right-click the project, and choose Create➪New Project Task for Business Project.

   The Project Task window appears, as shown in Figure 19-3. When you create a new project task from within the project, it is automatically linked to that project.

   If you don't start from the project this way, you must link the task to the project by clicking the Link To button in the Business Project window.

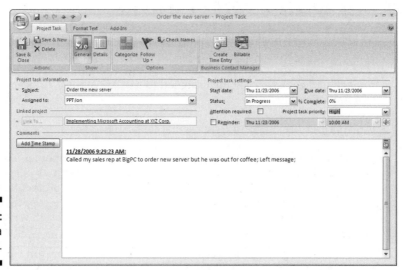

Figure 19-3:
Creating a
project task.

2. **Enter a subject in the Subject field that names the task.**

   This name is a descriptive name, not a filename. As we've recommended in other naming conventions, think about how the subject will be sorted in a list of other tasks that makes it easy to understand and group similar tasks together. Subject is a required field.

3. **(Optional) Assign this task to a BCM database user from the Assigned To drop-down list.**

   This is useful if you want to manage who is responsible for each task.

4. **Click the Link To button to link this task to a contact or account.**

   This is a required field. If you started the project task from a project, this field is already filled in for you.

5. **In the Project Task Settings section, enter the Start Date, Due Date, Status, % Complete, Project Task Priority, and Attention Required.**

   These fields are all optional, but it makes sense to use their capabilities to help you manage who's doing what and when and how close to completion these tasks and projects are.

   If you want to set a reminder for this task, select the Reminder check box and set the date and time using the drop-down lists for those fields.

6. **In the Comments section, click the Time Stamp button to enter a date and time stamp. Then enter notes about your progress or problems with the task.**

   The Comments text box is a place where you can enter notes about the task.

7. **Click Save & Close to save the task.**

   If you want to assign a category or follow-up to this task, click those icons on the Ribbon.

Completing a task

It feels great to accomplish or complete a task, doesn't it? Knowing that it's finished and off your plate gives you a boost. So, after you complete the work, make sure you mark the task as complete. From within the open Project Task window, change the % Complete field to 100% and then click Save & Close. Alternatively, you can select Completed from the Status drop-down list, and the % Complete field changes to 100%. Or, from any list of project tasks, right-click the task, choose Follow Up, and choose Mark Complete.

All lists or views that you've customized to show tasks that aren't complete are updated, and the task no longer shows up in those views.

Using the project task to bill time

If you use Microsoft Office Accounting, you can use project tasks to track your billable time and send it into Accounting without entering more data. Because you're already entering information in the task, a few more keystrokes will handle billing the customer for your work.

Here are the steps for entering billing information in the project task:

 Tracking your billable time through Office Accounting not only keeps you on track with tasks, but also it can save lots of time in turning in your time for inclusion on clients' invoices. For more information about moving these billable time tasks into Microsoft Office Accounting, check out Chapter 13.

Follow these steps to track your billable time:

1. **Inside a Project Task window, from the Ribbon, in the Show group, click Details.**

   You see the dialog box shown in Figure 19-4.

2. **Enter the Date Completed.**

   This date is the date the project task was completed.

3. **Enter the Mileage, if you're tracking that.**

4. **Enter the Total Work.**

   This is the estimated hours for this task.

5. **Enter the Actual Work.**

   This entry is the amount of time you will bill the customer for.

6. **Click Save & Close to save the details.**

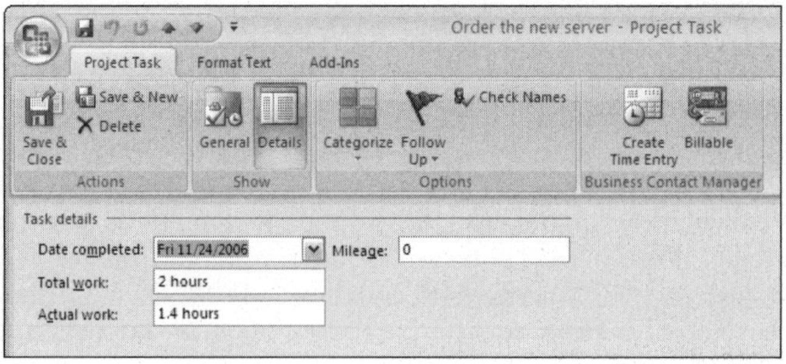

Figure 19-4:
Entering the billable time in a project task.

Order the new server · Project Task
Project Task   Format Text   Add-Ins

Task details

Date completed: Fri 11/24/2006   Mileage: 0

Total work: 2 hours

Actual work: 1.4 hours

Assigning the task

When you assign a task to someone, that project task appears on her To-Do bar. In an ideal world, the person assigned to the task updates the information in the task as she proceeds toward completion. She might change the % Complete field or the Status field. She should write some comments, adding a time stamp so you can see when she entered the comment. She can select the Attention Required check box. This means that the task is flagged in your project task list and you can open it up to review.

Choose a database user from the Assigned To field in the Project Task window. If you're the assignor, you're considered the Project Owner.

Deleting a project task

You can delete a project task different ways. The possible methods for deleting other records are the same as for a project task:

✔ With the project task opened, from the Ribbon, in the Actions group, click the Delete button.

The window closes, and the task is sent to the Deleted Items folder.

✔ From a list of project tasks, right-click the task and choose Delete.

✔ From a list of project tasks, click once to highlight the task, and then either press Ctrl+D or click the X on the Outlook menu bar.

No matter which method you use to delete a project task, the task just disappears without asking if you're sure you want to delete it. Fear not — it's put in the Business Contact Manager Deleted Items folder, and you can rescue it from there.

Here's how to undelete a task:

1. **From the Outlook menu bar, choose Go⇨Folder List.**

   The Navigation pane shows the hierarchy of folders.

2. **Click the + sign next to Business Contact Manager to open the folders. Click once on Deleted Items.**

   The Folder Contents pane shows all deleted items from BCM.

3. **Find the record you deleted. Click it and drag it back over to the same folder from whence it came.**

   If it was a project task, drag it to the Project Tasks folder under the Business Projects folder. The record is restored.

Managing the Project

As it turns out, just entering the business projects and project tasks doesn't mean they are completed all by themselves. Yes, unfortunately, that's the case. Someone has to accomplish all those tasks — sometimes it's you and sometimes it's your worker bees.

Keeping track of all those steps can be overwhelming. Fortunately, BCM gives you a variety of views to use to organize your tasks and keep up with them and the people trying to accomplish them.

Using the Business Project and Project Task views

You can see business projects in the Business Projects view. As we noted before, project tasks show up in either the Project Task view or the To-Do bar or calendar. Figure 19-5 shows the project tasks view, grouped by Assigned To. To get to this view, do either of the following:

- From the Outlook menu bar, choose Business Contact Manager⇨ Business Projects to see the list of projects.

  The list of business projects appears, organized according to the choice made in the Navigation pane under the Current View section.

- From the Outlook menu bar, choose Business Contact Manager⇨Project Tasks to see the list of project tasks.

  The list of project tasks appears, organized according to the choice made in the Navigation pane under the Current View section.

On the Navigation pane, notice some options in the Current View section. For the Business Projects view, you can choose to see a list of projects, or you can choose to see the projects grouped by Assigned To, Due Date, or Status. You can change these options and add more views of your own design. Flip to Chapter 7 to review how these views are constructed or modified.

If you want to see all your project tasks grouped by project, follow these steps:

1. **From the Outlook menu bar, choose Business Contact Manager⇨Project Tasks to see the list of project tasks.**

   The list of tasks appears, organized according to the choice you made in the Navigation pane under the Current View section.

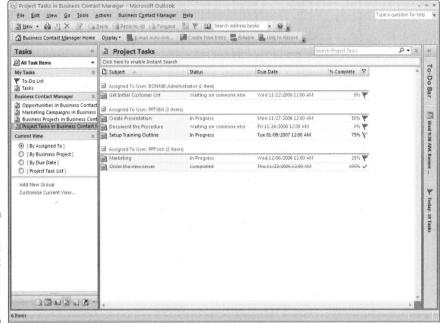

Figure 19-5:
The project
tasks list
showing
Assigned
To.

2. **If it's not already selected, choose By Business Project in the Current View section in the Navigation pane.**

   Your tasks are now grouped by business project. Chapter 7 tells you how to further customize this view and how to create a new one.

You have the same capabilities for these views as any other view in BCM:

✔ Click any column heading to sort the view by that column. Click again and sort in descending order.

   This is handy for pulling up a list of projects or tasks sorted by Due Date; you can then quickly rearrange them and sort by % Complete. It's an easy way of getting a quick snapshot of the status of your projects or tasks.

✔ Use Current Views to make *living reports* so that you see the exact data you want, grouped the way you want. Using filters in Customize Current View allows you to specify which data appears, sorted and grouped in what order. Making a change to data in any record instantly changes the records that are displayed — like a living report!

   In each view, you can use any of the settings in Customize Current View to get it just as you like it.

Using Project Overview inside the project record

Some built-in tools give you a snapshot of what's happening with a business project by looking inside the dialog box of the project record. The Project Overview section (see Figure 19-6) gives you a summary of tasks that have been completed, plus ones that are overdue, incomplete, and important. In big numbers, it shows you how many days are left until the project hits its due date. If you modify any of the data in the business project record, these numbers don't get updated until you save the project record and reopen it.

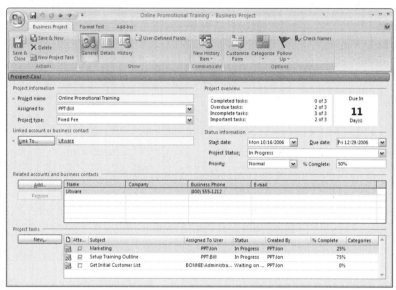

Figure 19-6: The Project Overview section inside a project record.

The Project Tasks area of the Business Project window shows the tasks that are part of this project and that the Project Overview summarizes. You can customize this mini-view just as you do the Project Tasks view.

You can manage a project from the Business Project window in the following ways:

- ✔ **See all project settings:** Right-click in the Project Tasks area and choose Customize Current View.

- ✔ **Sort the view:** Click the column headers.

- ✔ **Modify or add comments:** Double-click a task.

- ✔ **Open, print, follow up, categorize, or delete:** Right-click a task and choose from the menu.

As you're managing your project status, modifying tasks from here is a quick way of updating your activities easily.

Using the To-Do List to manage projects and tasks

One way to think of the To-Do List is as the *mother of all task lists* in BCM. Because BCM separates project tasks from regular tasks, the views we've shown you contain one only type of task, not both types. But the To-Do List contains both types and even gives you a new timeline way of viewing them, as shown in Figure 19-7.

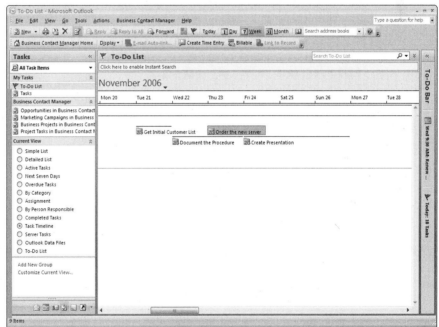

Figure 19-7: A Timeline view on the To-Do List.

As with other parts of BCM, you can find the To-Do List multiple ways:

- ✔ From the Outlook menu bar, choose Business Contact Manager⇨ Business Projects (or Project Tasks) and then click To-Do List in the My Tasks section at the top of the Navigation pane.

- ✔ From the BCM toolbar, choose Display⇨Business Projects (or Project Tasks) and then click To-Do List in the My Tasks section at the top Navigation pane.

✔ From the Outlook menu bar, choose Go⇨Tasks (or press Ctrl+4) and then click To-Do List in the My Tasks section at the top of the Navigation pane.

✔ Click Tasks at the bottom of the Navigation pane and then click To-Do List in the My Tasks section at the top of the pane.

✔ From the Business Contact Manager Home screen, click the Business Projects (or Project Tasks) tab and then click To-Do List in the My Tasks section at the top of the Navigation pane.

The options in the Navigation pane give you many ways to view the To-Do List — a simple list, overdue tasks, completed tasks, and more. As with all the views in BCM, you can customize the view, click headers in the columns to sort the data, and search through the list to find information inside the tasks. One column, the In Folder column, shows whether the task is from the tasks folder or the project tasks folder. Clicking that header sorts the list so you can see all the project tasks together and the regular tasks together.

Timeline view of tasks

Another way to view your tasks and manage them is to use a timeline view. This is almost like a Gantt chart, but it's not as robust. Microsoft Office Project produces glorious Gantt charts, but BCM isn't that powerful.

A timeline view shows a running calendar by day across the top of the view (the timeline). Entered at different days are the tasks, using the start date as the first date the subject of the task appears, and stretching the correct number of days until the due date. If there are more tasks than fit in one time slot, they're listed vertically down the display. This gives you a way to see how stacked up your workflow is at any given point in time.

Here are some facts to know about how timeline views work:

✔ Clicking the arrow to the right of the Month name at the top of the view accesses a drop-down calendar that enables you to move to that part of the timeline. Choose a date and the timeline switches to that view.

✔ On the Outlook toolbar, clicking Day, Week, or Month changes the timeline view to those increments. If you're viewing a monthly scale, hold the mouse over the task, and you see the subject of the task.

✔ Right-clicking a task allows you to open it to see the details, print it, set a follow-up flag, categorize it, delete it, or quickly mark it for attention required. This is an easy method for updating tasks in this view.

✔ Double-clicking it enables you to open it to see the details.

Chapter 20

Maintaining Your Database

· ·

In This Chapter

▶ Maintaining your BCM database for good health — its and yours!

▶ Fixing database problems

▶ Moving a database from one PC to another

· ·

*A*s you collect more and more data and it becomes more a part of the collective intelligence of your company, it's required that you, or someone like you, take charge of the proper care and maintenance of the BCM database. In the old days, computers were housed in special air-conditioned rooms with raised floors, extravagant power conditioners, and a staff that stood guard over the system 24, 7, 365. That's what it took to maintain even less powerful computers than what you can now carry under your arm!

This chapter tells you what the pros do to protect their databases against corruption, move databases from one PC to another, and take action when good databases go bad. Most people have to reenter all their data only one time before they get the Database Backup Religion. Take it from us — it's better to get in these good maintenance habits now than to rebuild your entire database later.

We use the term *backup* to mean a copy of the data in your BCM database that includes the business contacts, accounts, opportunities, projects, project tasks, and marketing campaigns. It doesn't include e-mails, tasks, and appointments that are stored in Outlook (usually in a .pst or .ost file). We use the term *restore* to mean copying data from a backup file into an empty (or non-empty) BCM database. When you restore a database, it overwrites any of the data currently there.

Managing Your BCM Database

Maintaining your database is the number one thing you can do to sleep better at night! Doctors might not agree with us, but they've never reentered data after a crash. You should do at least two of the three levels of backup on a regular basis — the additional level just gives you more protection and might not be worth the extra percentage of security they provide:

✔ **Level One:** Back up the database to the same hard drive it's on.

This is sufficient for protecting you against accidental deletion, or corruption of the database in case of a power surge or outage. However, if the hard drive that holds both the main database and the backup of it crashes, you're out of luck.

✔ **Level Two:** Back up the database to different media than the hard drive or to a hard drive on a different PC.

This protects against the hard drive failure in Level One. If you back up to a tape, or burn a CD/DVD every time you back up (which can be automated with inexpensive backup software), or back up to a server or other PC on the network (which in turn might get backed up to CD/DVD or tape), you handle 95–98 percent of the failures that can occur. USB drives (sometimes called *flash* or *thumb* or *jump* drives) are great options for backing up. The chance of two drives on two different PCs going out at the same time is low. If you use tape or CD/DVD, be sure to test the backup procedure to make sure it works correctly.

✔ **Level Three:** Back up to an offsite storage place.

This used to mean taking the tapes to an offsite storage vault. Now, you can transmit your data to an online backup service that stores it for you on their servers. What this protects against the most is fire or theft of the PCs in your office. Even if you back up religiously, you have no backup if your office burns down or someone takes off with the PCs!

Backing Up Your BCM Database

Follow these steps to back up your database:

1. **From the Outlook menu bar, choose Business Contact Manager⇨ Database Tools⇨Manage Database.**

   The Manage Database dialog box opens, as shown in Figure 20-1. This is action central for database management, where you can do a backup, a restore, check for errors, and delete the databases you don't want.

   The Backup/Restore tab shows the database name, the computer name (where the database is stored), the date and time the database was created, the database owner, and its size. This information changes depending on the database that you're logged in to at that moment.

If you're logged in to a shared database (such as the master BCM database), you can't back up because that database is shared and on another PC. You must go to that PC and have the proper permissions.

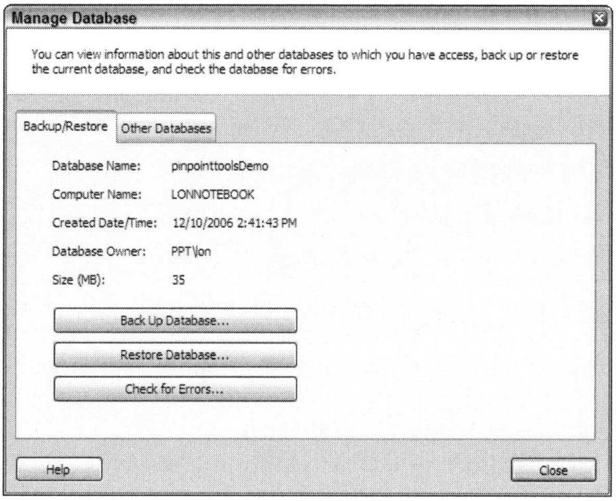

Figure 20-1:
Managing
your
database.

2. **Click the Back Up Database button.**

   The Database Backup dialog box opens, as shown in Figure 20-2.

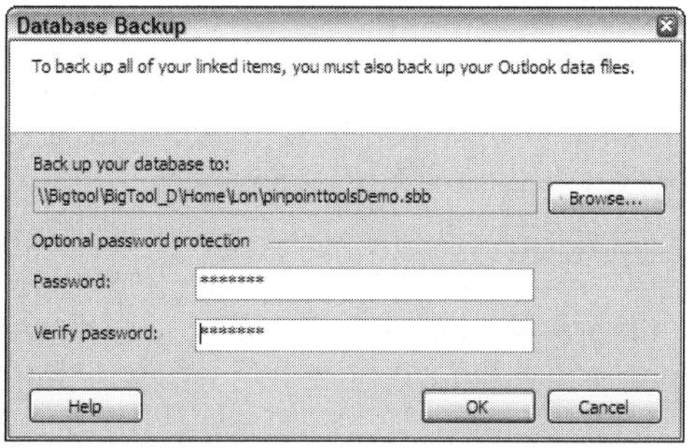

Figure 20-2:
Database
Backup
dialog box.

3. **Click the Browse button and browse to the place you're backing up your database.**

   Ideally, you're backing up to a network PC, so the backup isn't on your own hard drive.

4. **Name your backup file.**

   The database is backed up in a compressed (zipped) format with an
   .sbb extension. The filename suggested by default is the database
   name. You can change the filename to anything you desire, but we recommend leaving the .sbb extension on it so that BCM recognizes valid
   backups when you need to restore them.

5. **Click Save.**

   You return to the Database Backup dialog box. (Refer to Figure 20-2.)

6. **(Optional) Password protect the file.**

   Enter a password, and then reenter it to verify.

7. **Click OK to start the database backup.**

   You see a progress bar as the database is backed up. Depending on its
   size and whether it's backed up to the local hard drive or across the network, this could take between 1 and 15 (or more) minutes.

Sleep easy tonight, you good BCM database user, you!

Restoring the database

Restoring the database happens when you've lost your main database and
you need to get the data you backed up. There are a whole slew of reasons
why this might happen, but here are a few:

- **Your hard drive crashed and you were a good BCM database user so
  you had a backup stored on some other media than the hard drive
  that died.** You can create a new, empty BCM database on your new hard
  drive, and then *restore* the backup into the new one.

- **A more fortunate event occurred and you received a new PC.** Before
  you give up your old PC, you make a backup of the BCM database onto
  the network server (along with all your other data files, documents,
  spreadsheets, and so on). You get your new PC, create a new BCM database, and then *restore* the backup into that empty database.

- **You want to create a similar PC environment on your home PC as
  your office PC so that you can work in either place.** You can make a
  backup of your office database onto a thumb drive, let's say, bring it
  home, plug it into your home PC, and tell BCM to *restore* the office data
  and overwrite your BCM database at home.

When you restore a database, it overwrites the database it comes into, so it's
best to start with a new, blank database. See Chapter 3 if you need to create a
new database.

Follow these steps to restore your backup to another database:

1. **From the Outlook menu bar, choose Business Contact Manager⇨ Database Tools⇨Manage Database.**

   The Manage Database dialog box opens. (Refer to Figure 20-1.)

2. **Click the Restore Database button.**

   The Database Restore dialog box opens, as shown in Figure 20-3.

3. **Click the Browse button.**

4. **Browse to the location of your backup file (with a .sbb extension), choose it, and click Open. If it requires a password, enter it in the Password field.**

   If you backed up your database onto multiple floppies, CDs, USB drives, or Zip drives, put the last one in the drive and select it. The last one contains all the information about which files are which in the backup file.

5. **Click OK to start the restore process.**

   This step could take a while, depending on the speed of your network and the amount of data to be restored.

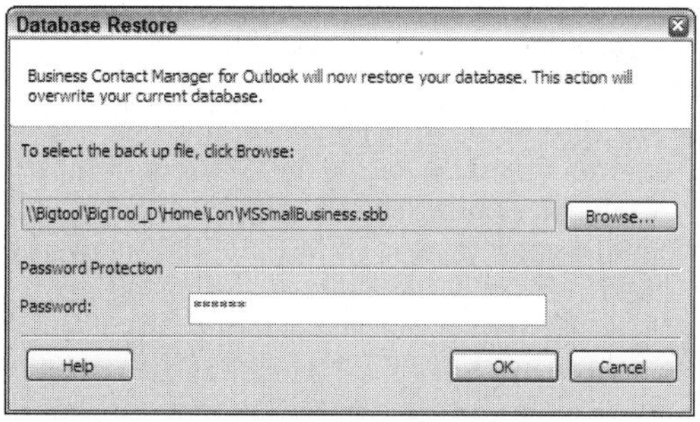

Figure 20-3:
Getting your
data back.

Database Restore

Business Contact Manager for Outlook will now restore your database. This action will overwrite your current database.

To select the back up file, click Browse:

\\Bigtool\BigTool_D\Home\Lon\MSSmallBusiness.sbb   Browse...

Password Protection

Password: ******

Help   OK   Cancel

Checking for errors

Sometimes, your database might run very slowly — finding data takes longer, moving from screen to screen takes longer, and just general sluggishness abounds. This can be because of some corruption or internal problem, or maybe you've been doing a lot of importing and deleting of records.

BCM has a Check for Errors function to go through your database and find corruption or errors. Click the Check for Errors button in the Manage Database dialog box. (Refer to Figure 20-1.) The Check for Errors dialog box opens, as shown in Figure 20-4. Click the Start button, and BCM goes through your database looking for errors. When BCM finds errors, it shows them in the Details window. You can see the progress in the progress bar at the top of the dialog box. When it's finished, click the Close button to return to your BCM screen.

Deleting a BCM database

Careful here, Quick Draw! You can really delete some valuable information if you're not cautious. No problem — you're reading this book!

There are valid times when you no longer need a database and it's time to send it to Alphabet Heaven. Maybe you made a new database and imported the leads you got at a trade show. You massaged the data, pruned the bad data, and imported those leads into your master BCM database. Now, there's no reason to keep this old database any longer — it's just taking up disk space.

If you're the kind of user who does heavy database manipulation and administration, you probably do lots of imports, transfers, and search and replace operations. The best way to save your you-know-what when good data goes bad is to have a backup and an original database ready to replace the corrupted one. So, you would be the kind of person who needs a database cleaning coach to help keep your hard drive cleaned of unneeded databases.

When time comes to delete a BCM database, there's a way to delete it, but it's not easy to find. Maybe that's on purpose, but it works.

Follow these steps to delete a database:

1. **From the Outlook menu bar, choose Business Contact Manager⇨ Database Tools⇨Manage Database.**

   The Manage Database dialog box opens.

2. Click the Other Databases tab.

The Other Databases tab of the Manage Database dialog box appears, as shown in Figure 20-5. This shows you all databases on your local PC only, not on the server or other PCs on your network.

The BCM database that you're currently logged into isn't listed because you're not allowed to delete the database you currently have open.

3. Select a database to highlight that row in the grid.

4. Click the Delete Database button.

5. Confirm that you really want to delete the database.

Think about it again — your data is going a long way away. Click Yes, and it's off to Alphabet Heaven. This really does delete the files from the hard drive. It is possible to retrieve the files from your Recycle Bin (if they're small enough) and get your database restored, but it'll probably take a computer professional to help you.

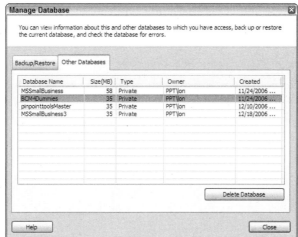

Figure 20-5:
Other
Databases
tab.

Moving a Database from One PC to Another

When you know the procedures to back up and restore, and how to create a new database, you can move a database from one PC to another. In the old days, you'd just find out in which files the data is stored and you'd copy those files from one PC and paste them into another. BCM doesn't work that way because of the way that SQL Server holds on to database files. When you try to copy the BCM database, you get an error that says another program has control of that file. So, you have to do a backup and restore procedure to get around SQL's lock on the files.

Follow these steps to move a database from one computer to another:

1. **Back up the database you want to copy to another PC.**

   Always, always, always do a backup before you attempt anything that could affect your data. See the earlier section "Backing Up Your BCM Database."

2. **Copy the backup file to the PC you want to move the database to.**

   Or, you can put the backup file on a server that is accessible by both your current PC and the new PC.

   Use standard Windows Explorer commands to copy and paste, whether you're copying from one PC to another or over the network. You can also copy the file to a flash drive or a CD, then move that to the target PC and copy it to that PC's hard drive. You get much better performance on the restore part of this process if the file is on the same hard drive as the new BCM database.

3. **On the target PC, create a new database.**

4. **After you create the new database, restore the backup file you made from the source database.**

   This copies the data into the new database, creating a copy of the original one on the old PC. See the earlier section, "Restoring the database."

Part VII
The Part of Tens

The 5th Wave · By Rich Tennant

In this part . . .

*E*very *For Dummies* book has The Part of Tens. By golly, this book is no exception to that rule. Think of this as the icing on your BCM cake. Here's where we answer two of your more burning questions:

- ✔ What are ten cool things I should know about BCM?
- ✔ Is there an easy way for me to move my data into — and from — BCM?

Chapter 21

Ten Cool Things You Can Do In Business Contact Manager

In This Chapter

▶ One-stop shopping for your contacts

▶ Integrating with other software

▶ Growing your business

*O*utlook 2007 with Business Contact Manager combines the best of both worlds: the power of contact management with the ease of Outlook. BCM allows your business to share and manage customers, sales, and project information all in one place. BCM gives you a better handle on sales opportunities and allows you to respond to customer needs more efficiently. You can manage leads, prospects, and customers; track and forecast sales opportunities; assign and follow up on project tasks; and deploy more successful marketing campaigns. And if you're already familiar with Outlook, you don't have to face a huge learning curve. All of this, of course, translates into more time doing what you love — and more money in your pockets.

In this chapter, we list a few of our favorite things about BCM.

Keep All Your Contact Information in One Place

Using BCM, you can have all your contact information at your fingertips in one central place. You can store dozens of phone numbers (business, car, home, fax) and multiple addresses (business and home) for each contact (Chapter 4). You can view and send e-mail (Chapter 14). You can track phone calls, appointments, and tasks (Chapter 9). You can see the accounting history of your customers (Chapter 13), as well as a pipeline of your prospects

(Chapter 18). You can use Outlook to keep track of your personal life while using BCM to keep track of your business life. Suffering from yellow sticky note syndrome? Then you might consider using BCM to track all your notes about contacts (Chapter 10).

Customize Your Information

BCM comes with hundreds of fields that track everything from phone numbers to specific areas of interest. However, because variety is the spice of life, you can customize BCM from here to Kalamazoo. Add drop-down lists to track your products, yes/no check boxes for easy data entry, and date fields to track important milestones (Chapter 7). And best of all, you can easily add new fields — and place them on record tabs. After you add those new fields, you can query them and use the information that they contain in your reports.

Integrate with Other Office Products

You've probably used Outlook, Word, Excel, and perhaps even Publisher for years. You know the products, you like the products, and you don't want to spend your time learning new software. BCM is designed to work seamlessly with other Microsoft Office products. Want to send a mail merge? You can use Word. Want to link an e-mail to an account record? You can link it to Outlook. Need to import an Excel spreadsheet? No problem. Want to save some of your information in Excel format? Can do. Want to share a report with someone? You can send it in Excel if your little heart desires.

Less is more — at least when it comes to software. And the less software you have, the less likely you enter the same data in two different places. Most businesses use contact management software to bring in the business and accounting software to count the cash as it rolls in. Using Business Contact Manager and Office Accounting 2007 gives you the best of both worlds (Chapter 13).

You can combine BCM with Office Accounting to get a complete picture of your company all in one place. You can see a customer's complete accounting history, including quotes, sales orders, invoices, and payments. You can synchronize the two products so that contact information that you add in Office Accounting appears magically in BCM — you don't have to do double entry. Also, you can automatically turn BCM opportunities into Office Accounting quotes, sales orders, and invoices. You can mark BCM appointments, projects, tasks, and phone logs as billable and automatically send that information to Office Accounting to create customer invoices. Add to the products and services list in one application, and the changes magically appear in the other.

Use Your Existing Data

BCM is a great tool for you to use if you have a brand-new business. However, if you have an existing business, you can use BCM as well.

If you've been using Outlook, you're already ahead of the game. You're familiar with the Outlook interface; now all you have to do is move your existing business accounts and contacts into BCM and you're ready to fly.

If you're using QuickBooks, you can continue using it right along with BCM; simply export your pertinent name lists and import them into Business Contact Manager (Chapter 3). If you decide to take the plunge and start using Office Accounting as well, it comes equipped with a wizard that can convert your data. After that data's converted, it's a snap to link Office Accounting to BCM to make lots of CA$H.

Create an Opportunity Pipeline

A well-run business — no matter what size — should have a set of sales processes that it uses to attract new business. Salespeople can then use those processes to create the sales stages that are a central part of BCM's opportunities (Chapter 12). BCM has a variety of ways to help you track a sales opportunity as it progresses through the various sales stages.

Keep Checking the Dashboard

If a picture is worth a thousand words, surely a dashboard is, as the commercial goes, priceless (Chapter 12). Sometimes, you want to run a quick check on your business without printing a report. The dashboards provide you with quick, visual ways to check all aspects of your business, from lead to marketing effort to sales funnel to the closing of the deal.

Run Reports on Your Progress

If you're the big cheese, you probably want to run a lot of reports to find out how your business — and the people who work for you — are doing. If you're the little cheese, you probably need to hand reports to the big cheese. And if someone moves the cheese, you'll both want to find out why and when the movement of the cheese occurred.

BCM lets you run reports on everything from your accounts and business contacts to your leads, opportunities, and marketing campaigns (Chapter 15). You can sort and filter to make your report just the way you want it, and you can drill a little deeper into the report to see even more detail. When you're finished with your report, you can even export your findings to Microsoft Office Excel for further analysis.

Market Your Heart Out

Snail mail, e-mail — you can market your business in a variety of ways. Traditionally, you either hire a company to take care of all your marketing, or you devote hours of your time to complete the marketing tasks yourself.

After you enter all your pertinent account and business contact information into Business Contact Manager, you can create mailing lists by filtering your customer and prospect data (Chapter 15). You can create personalized templates by using Microsoft Publisher or Word. Better yet, you can select from the hundreds of free Microsoft templates found at `http://office.microsoft.com/en-us/templates/default.aspx`. If you're doing e-marketing, you can use Microsoft E-Mail Marketing Service to help you build a better database of e-mail contacts.

Send out a mailing and BCM automatically updates the communications history for each record. You can even track campaign responses to measure the overall effectiveness of your campaign and plan improvements for your next campaigns.

When you have your marketing in place, try the pinpointtools marketing tool to get your campaign started: Check it out at `www.pinpointtools.com`. You can send several e-mails with just a few clicks of the mouse!

Keep Track of Your Projects

In the beginning, there was contact management software. And accounting software. And project management software. With the dawning of BCM, you can kiss that project management software good-bye. You can create and update your projects so you know who's doing what to whom — and when they did it (Chapter 19).

You can share project information across your company so that the right people have access to the information they need to work effectively. You can assign project tasks to others and automatically transfer task information to their individual task lists using the Project Tasks feature. Tasks appear on both the BCM To-Do bar and on the Outlook reminders for easy follow-up.

Share Your Information with Other Users

As your business grows, BCM can grow right along with you. You can easily place BCM on a server and share it with the other members of your staff (Chapter 11). And, should the need arise, you can put BCM on Microsoft Office Live for users who don't come into the office on a regular basis (Chapter 16). Users can access information on a real-time basis, meaning that everyone in your company can remain safely "in the loop" without having to lift a finger.

Chapter 22

Ten Cool Ways to Get Information into BCM

*B*y now, you've come to realize the power of BCM. You understand the importance of tracking your data and see the benefits that it can have on your financial outlook (pun intended). But now comes the hard part. Where do you begin?

Starting a database from scratch is a daunting task. However, Rome wasn't built in a day — and your database won't be either. In this chapter, we recommend several ways to speed up the data entry process.

BCM includes neat ways to import information into your database. However, a few of the items that we discuss in this chapter carry a price tag and are, of course, optional. If you'd like to purchase one of the products mentioned here, feel free to go to www.techbenders.com and click the For Dummies tab for more information.

Incorporate Microsoft Office Live

Perhaps the coolest way to get information into BCM is to let other people do it for you. By using Microsoft Office Live, you can let other people enter business contacts and accounts. You can then export all that information directly into BCM and come out looking like a hero.

Using a company calendar? Even better. You add information to your Office Live calendar and synchronize it to your Outlook calendar.

Improve Your Data Entry Outlook

If you were using Outlook before moving to BCM, you're in pretty good shape when building a database.

You can get your data into BCM in three ways:

- ✔ Drag your contacts from the Outlook Contact folder to the Business Contact Manager Accounts or Business Contacts folder.
- ✔ To import several Outlook folders, choose Business Contact Manager⇨ Database Tools⇨Import and Export and select Outlook.
- ✔ Restore an existing Outlook .pst file to your computer and drag or import the Outlook contacts to BCM.

Whatever method you use, you'll be able to be up and running in BCM in no time without having to waste your precious time adding contacts to BCM!

Import Data from Your Existing Software

Sometimes users try software for a period of time and then decide not to use it. Other times you might find yourself in a situation in which you no longer work for a company — but still have the database that you were using. Whatever the case, you can import various sources into BCM. And you're not limited to just one source. You might want to import your customers and vendors from QuickBooks and your prospects from an Access database.

BCM automatically converts your ACT! database if you're currently using ACT!. This includes your contacts, groups, products, activities, attachments, e-mails, notes, and opportunities. If you're using QuickBooks, you can import your various lists (including customers, vendors, and items) as .iif files and import them into BCM. If you have Access .mdb and .accdb files, you can also import them.

With a bit of ingenuity, you can export information from just about any existing software package. If your software doesn't offer an exporting feature, try snooping around in the reporting area. Many products include a Print to File option, which creates a .txt file that you can easily import into BCM.

Track Your Spreadsheets

You probably consider Excel to be a number-crunching piece of software. However, Excel excels at data entry as well. Because Excel is a standard fixture on many desktops, it's a common way to transport data from point A to point B. If you attend a tradeshow, chances are good that you receive a list of the attendees in spreadsheet format. The same holds true if you purchase leads or routinely download information from a Web site.

Consider doing a search through your computer for all `.xls`, `.csv`, and `.txt` files. Who knows what you might come up with? Importing those files into BCM is much quicker than adding that data one record at a time. You can read more about the Excel connection in Chapter 3.

Link to Your PDA

Mobile devices and smartphones are all the rage these days. Chapter 16 discusses linking BCM to your Windows Mobile devices. If you have one of these cool devices that's loaded with information, don't forget to hook your device to your computer and synch away.

You can also have someone beam information directly into your PDA. This trick is sort of like a PDA leap frog because the contact information leaps from your contact's PDA to your PDA with the click of a button. When the information is happily located in your PDA, you can synchronize it to BCM.

You might be wondering what your options are if you own a Palm or Blackberry device. Don't worry — you can cover your bases with Companion Link. This product will make synching a cinch, no matter which PDA make or model you have.

Synchronize with Your Laptop

Perhaps you're a road warrior who spends a lot of time hanging out in airports or hotel rooms looking for something to do. Or maybe you're a type-A couch potato (if those animals exist!) that likes to fiddle around while watching the tube. Well, here's your golden opportunity to turn downtime into profitable time by typing your contact information into BCM. This idea probably sounds boring to you, but think of the possibilities: Instead of reaching for a potato chip, you can reach for your laptop. And when you arrive back at the ranch, you can synchronize your data with the mother ship. Okay, you're synching it with the main database — we've just been watching too many *Star Trek* reruns! Chapter 16 is the place to go if you want more information on synching your laptop to your desktop.

Grab Some Tidbits from Your E-Mail

If you like add-ons, here's one you just can't live without: the eGrabber.

Basically, if you can see the information on your computer, you can highlight it, click a button, and have it magically appear in BCM using one of the eGrabber products.

You can use AddressGrabber to take signatures from incoming e-mail messages and Web response forms and automatically create a new BCM business contact. Or try ResumeGrabber to input contact information — including attached resumes — from various sites like Monster.com. You can also create a search on the Internet for a list of people and plunk that list of contacts directly into BCM using ListGrabber.

Send Out E-Marketing Swiftly

So you think you're sitting pretty, just about now? You've lots of contacts in BCM, and you're running marketing campaigns with the best of them. Chapter 15 shows you the benefits of Microsoft's List Builder for your marketing campaigns. However, you might also want to check out another product: Swiftpage.

Swiftpage is a cross between a piece of software and an online service that lets you maintain your contact list in Outlook rather than having to export your information into another product. You can use your Outlook information to send personalized e-mails to targeted parts of your database. Its servers actually transmit the e-mail so that you won't get into trouble with your ISP or system administrator. Once sent, Swiftpage can provide you with a list of bounces and opt-outs that you can import back into BCM. You also receive a list of any e-mail addresses that your e-mail was forwarded to.

Swiftpage has another cool benefit as well. You can use Swiftpage to create a survey or Web submission form. Now here comes the fun part. When someone fills out one of those forms, you can click a button and let all that contact information automatically flow into BCM. Of course, if you prefer, you can stay up late and enter that information yourself; automatic or manual entry — you be the judge!

Start Scanning

Scanning devices should be a fixture in offices everywhere — or at least if you have a mountain of business cards sitting on a desk corner somewhere. About the size of a radar detector, these scanners are designed to scan the contents of your business cards and parse the information into the pertinent fields, such as First Name, Last Name, Phone Number, Address, and State.

Here's how it works: Plug the scanner into your computer, start scanning your cards one at a time, and indicate when you're finished scanning. You're rewarded with a list of all the contacts that you just scanned; and you can import that list into BCM.

Not all business cards are created equally; the scanners do much better with black-and-white cards using simple fonts than they do with multicolored cards with lots of fancy stuff on them. You need to review the list for accuracy before importing it into BCM, but that bit of effort far outweighs the time you'd take to type the data from each of those cards individually.

Write with the Logitech Pen

Those of you who don't always have access to a computer can continue jotting down contact information on paper — and then easily transfer it into BCM.

The Logitech io digital writing system instantly translates your writing into editable electronic text, even if your left-handed scrawl makes you a contender for having the world's worst handwriting. Logitech guarantees nearly 100 percent accuracy without any sort of training.

The io pen requires a specific type of paper; the pen itself uses special ink. When you stick the pen into the docking station that comes with the product, the information you wrote down on the paper is transferred to your computer as a text file. With a little practice, the pen becomes just about foolproof.

Index

The Clinician's Practical Guide to Attention-Deficit/Hyperactivity Disorder